Operant Conditioning:

An Experimental Analysis of Behaviour

Derek Blackman

METHUEN & CO LTD
11 New Fetter Lane
London EC4P 4EE

First published 1974
by Methuen & Co Ltd,
11 New Fetter Lane,
London EC4P 4EE

©1974 Derek Blackman
Typeset in Great Britain by
Preface Limited, Salisbury, Wilts
and printed in Great Britain at
the University Printing House,
Cambridge

ISBN hardbound 0 416 13660 5
ISBN paperback 0 416 81480 8

Distributed in the USA by
HARPER & ROW PUBLISHERS, INC.
BARNES & NOBLE IMPORT DIVISION

Contents

Acknowledgements

Thanks are extended to the following for permission to reproduce copyrighted materials:—

Academic Press, London. Fig. 23 reproduced from 'Behavioural contrast and the peak shift'. by T. M. Bloomfield, in *Animal Discrimination Learning* (1969) edited by R. M. Gilbert and N. S. Sutherland, p. 218.

American Association for the Advancement of Science. Fig. 30 reproduced from 'Assessment of drug effects on emotional behavior' by J. V. Brady, in *Science* (Vol. 123, 1956, p. 1034).

American Psychological Association. Figs. 20 and 21 reproduced from 'Effect of discrimination training on auditory generalisation' by H. M. Jenkins and R. H. Harrison, in *Journal of Experimental Psychology* (Vol. 59, 1960, p. 247 and p. 248).

Appleton-Century-Crofts, Inc., New York. Fig. 2 reproduced from *Behavior Principles* (1968) by C. B. Ferster and M. C. Perrott, p. 208. Figs. 3, 18 and 26 reproduced from *The Behavior of Organisms* (1938) by B. F. Skinner, p. 68, p. 83 and p. 154. Fig. 31 from 'Schedules as fundamental determinants of behavior' by W. H. Morse and R. T. Kelleher, in *The Theory of Reinforcement Schedules* (1970) edited by W. N. Schoenfeld, P. 143.

The Dorsey Press, Homewood, Illinois. Fig. 19 reproduced from 'Conditioned reinforcement, choice, and the psychological distance to reward' by E. Fantino, in *Conditioned Reinforcement* (1969) edited by D. P. Hendry, P. 165.

Federation of American Societies for Experimental Biology. Fig. 35 reproduced from 'Escape behavior and punished behavior' by R. T. Kelleher and W. H. Morse, in *Federation Proceedings* (Vol. 23, 1964, p. 812).

Society for the Experimental Analysis of Behavior, Inc. (all from *Journal of the Experimental Analysis of Behavior*). Fig. 17 reproduced from 'Conditioned suppression or facilitation as a function of the behavioral baseline' by D. E. Blackman (Vol. 11, 1968, p. 55); Fig. 22 from 'A peak shift on a line-tilt continuum' by T. M. Bloomfield (Vol. 10, 1967, p. 365); Figs. 24 and 25 from 'A method for obtaining psychophysical thresholds from the pigeon' by D. S. Blough (Vol. 1, 1958, p. 33 and p. 41); Figs. 27 and 28 from 'Effects of punishment intensity during variable-interval reinforcement' by N. H. Azrin (Vol. 3, 1960, p. 134 and p. 138); Fig. 34 from 'Fixed-interval schedules of electric shock presentation: extinction and recovery of performance under different shock intensities and fixed-interval durations' by J. W. McKearney (Vol. 12, 1969, p. 310); and Figs. 37 and 38 from 'The effectiveness of fading in programming a simultaneous form discrimination for retarded children' by M. Sidman and L. T. Stoddard (Vol. 10, 1967, p. 6).

Scott, Foresman and Co., Glenview, Illinois. Fig. 10 reproduced from *A Primer of Operant Conditioning* (1968) by G. S. Reynolds, p. 77.

Springer-Verlag, Heidelberg. Fig. 36 reproduced from 'Determinants of the specificity of behavioural effects of drugs' by R. T. Kelleher and W. H. Morse, in *Ergebnisse der Physiologie* (Bd. 60, 1968), p. 31.

Preface

What is *voluntary* behaviour? Although we may claim that we are free to act in whatever way we decide, how free are we really to make up our own minds? Can a scientific study of behaviour ever come to grips with the vagaries of such free will and individual choice? These are the fundamental questions which this book addresses. However, they are approached on the basis of experimental evidence rather than in terms of philosophical theorising. The prototypical experiment on operant conditioning is probably known to most people – a rat pressing a lever in order to obtain food. This simple situation provides a beginning for an experimental analysis of voluntary behaviour, for after all the rat is free to decide for himself whether or not to press the lever, and to emit this pattern of behaviour whenever the whim takes him. Nevertheless, in certain conditions we may be very confident indeed as to the precise outcome of the rat's whims: we may predict the occurrence of his voluntary behaviour with considerable accuracy, even when he is faced with various rules for the earning of his food so that his sequences of behaviour become fairly complicated. This book is an attempt to put such simple experiments into their widest psychological context. The role of operant conditioning within experimental psychology as a whole is elaborated, and thereby a systematic interpretation of *human* behaviour is introduced which offers insights into both normal and abnormal behaviour.

On the whole, I have interacted with few colleagues when writing this manuscript, although this is not to say that my interpretations have not been influenced by others. My main thanks must therefore go to those who have proved so adept in the skills which I particularly lack. My wife, Rosemary, has typed much of the manuscript, but has contributed much more by her patient organisational abilities; I am exceedingly grateful to her for her encouragement. Miss Margaret Wanless and Mrs. C. Milsom are also to be thanked for translating my idiosyncratic handwriting into impeccable typescript. I am grateful to Sam Grainger for his photographic work on many of the diagrams. The sources of those Figures which have been reproduced from books or reports by others are acknowledged elsewhere, but I should like to thank their original authors for their permissions. Finally, all those who have supported me are thanked, especially those with whom I worked in the Animal Laboratory of the Psychology Department at Nottingham University. I should particularly like to mention from among these Glyn Thomas, now at Stirling University, and N. W. Bond, who is now at Macquarie University in Australia.

Derek Blackman, *1973*

CHAPTER 1
Science and behaviour

One of the most obvious qualities of animate creatures is that they behave; they *do* things that change their relationships with the objects about them, whether these other objects are themselves animate or inanimate. Such activity, this *doing*, provides a subject of study for psychologists and for this book. In the pages that follow, an attempt is made to consider some aspects of behaviour according to specifiable scientific principles. This preliminary chapter provides a brief history of how these principles have evolved in the study of behaviour.

Perhaps the most basic characteristic of science in general is that it organizes and develops our knowledge of the world in which we live. This is achieved by asking questions of nature, by investigating observable phenomena. At one level, such attempts to organize our knowledge may entail no more than an agreed description of the subject being scrutinized. Some may recall zoology lessons at school for apparently endless descriptions and classifications of all manner of animals. In a behavioural science, too, descriptions such as these are of the utmost importance. They are also often fascinating, as evidenced by the popularity of naturalists' films showing the behaviour of animals in their natural environments.

Behaviour, then, is the activity of animate creatures, and psychology the study of this activity. However, even the first step, describing behaviour objectively, may soon encounter difficulties. Some of these are obvious enough, not least the problems of measuring behaviour in some reliable way. But confusions may result even from the simple notion that activity provides the basis for distinguishing what we regard as animate creatures from inanimate objects. For example, one creature which is accorded the rank of animal by zoologists suffers the indignity of being likened to a plant in its popular name — the sea anemone. This apparent inconsistency may result from the fact that its repertoire of behaviour is exceedingly limited; it does few things which will interest a human observer. Its sedentary existence seems uninspired, and it might be argued that its sharing of a name with the beautiful, but admittedly inanimate, woodland anemone is as much as this creature deserves. Yet zoologists could affirm that the sea anemone deserves the more exalted rank in man's affections, because, after all, it is an animal. On the other hand, some plants, at least in terms of botanists' classifications, have traditionally exerted a degree of fascination for man, because they seem to behave like animals in some respects. Perhaps the best known example of such a plant is Venus's Flytrap, to which is sometimes attributed the sinister motive of hatching a plot to ensnare its unsuspecting prey because of the relatively sudden movements of the plant which trap an insect.

Although we spend so much of our time in the company of other behaving creatures, it seems that we rarely stop to think about the defining characteristics of behaviour. If it is accepted that one of the primary tasks of psychology is to describe behaviour, which events qualify for the use of that word? Does the sea anemone behave? Does Venus's Flytrap? At first sight, the activities of the latter seem to offer the more likely events for an appropriate use of the term. However, we may wish to revise our opinion when confronted with the authoritative statements of zoologists and botanists, which are, of course, based on criteria other than what the sea anemone and Venus's Flytrap *do*. We may now prefer to use the term behaviour to describe the apparently aimless flutterings of the sea anemone's peripheral parts, but describe the more striking movements of the plant as behaviour only in a metaphorical sense: perhaps we were misled by the apparent purposefulness of the Flytrap, because when we are told that we are observing a plant our view changes. Our criterion for judging an event as behaviour, then, seems to depend not merely on its complexity: the reasons for the occurrence of these events are also taken into account. Here perhaps lies the fascination shown by Victorians for automata. The monkey sitting on the mantelshelf may move his hand to his mouth, puff at the cigarette held in it, and then move his head to one side and close his eyes for a period before beginning the cycle again; in the Victorian drawing-room this has many of the characteristics of 'real' behaviour and apparently reflects satisfaction and purpose. However, this is not 'real' behaviour, for it is merely the result of a clockwork mechanism within the automaton.

Clearly we have taken the decision to reserve the appropriate use of the word behaviour to living animals (including man). Plants, automata, machines, may appear to 'behave', but use of this word is merely to indicate an analogy between their activities and the behaviour of animals. The difference between them lies in the reasons for the actions in all these cases. In a sense, this decision reflects the influence of our culture and of science upon us. We live in an age that emphasizes man's responsibility for his own actions, but in one that has also been dominated by the progress of science. In the recent past man has organized his knowledge of the world about him ever more effectively, and has thereby produced an accompanying increase in the speed with which new knowledge has developed. This has particularly been the case with the so-called physical sciences, such as chemistry. Our knowledge of inanimate objects studied by such physical sciences is now so great that we are able to change our world radically to our own advantage, if we can prevent ourselves from using our understanding to our own profound disadvantage. The methods of the physical sciences are now also being applied more and more effectively in studies of living creatures, as evidenced by the increasing impact of such disciplines as biochemistry and physiology. This rapid increase in our understanding and control of the world has depended to a large extent on the abandonment of previous explanations for the metaphorical 'behaviour' of physical events.

There was a time when all phenomena in the world about man were explained by him in terms of spirits or forces 'inside' these observable occurrences. Such a view is termed animism. The internal spirits were not open to the direct inspection of mere humans, but by assuming that they existed it became possible to 'explain' all the phenomena that were seen to occur in the physical world. For example, it might be considered an adequate explanation for the fact that a stone rolled down a hill to assert that it was *motivated* to do this by a propensity to approach the centre of the earth; this motivational force, *vis viva*, impelled the stone to move. Stones and waterfalls, trees and clouds, the wind and the sea: the actions of all these were once interpreted by appeal to internal spirits which motivated them to behave in the ways that were observed. Nowadays we recognize that such an explanation is not the most useful in our attempts to organize our knowledge. In order to make the stone roll, or to stop it, we attend not to its internal motivations, but rather to our knowledge of observable events which have previously led to such occurrences. This knowledge is summarized in our description of the world in terms of scientific laws, the power of which makes it seem unnecessary to seek an explanation of an animistic kind. Similarly, with the organized knowledge of science we do not need to explain the 'behaviour' of the monkey automaton in terms of its internal motivating spirits; nor does an appeal to such unobservable forces in the Venus's Flytrap help us to explain its 'behaviour' more satisfactorily.

In spite of this scientific movement away from animism in our considered explanations of physical events, in our everyday language we continue to use expressions that imply that we still believe in animistic explanations. Our language frequently continues to attribute animistic feelings to inanimate objects: the sea rages, the sky is gloomy or cheerful, the weather mischievous. In using such language we undoubtedly enrich our vocabulary and add emotive quality to our lives. Perhaps this is the reason why, for example, many people feel great sadness when a majestic tree is felled. The point is made even more noticeable by the fact that poetry is often perfused with animistic language.

The use of quasi-animistic language in everyday conversation is certainly no bad thing on the whole. However, there is some danger that animistic concepts may even now colour our appreciation of the physical world more than we ordinarily recognize. A possible example of this is to be found in one of the most fundamental concepts which we use, that of causality. In a well-known series of experiments, Michotte (1954) studied this concept by using the simple apparatus shown in Figure 1. Two thick lines were drawn on a cardboard disc, which could be

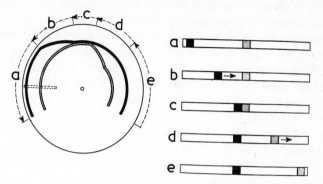

Figure 1   The disc rotated in Michotte's experiments (left), and the sequence of events seen through the slit by an observer. After Michotte (1954).

rotated about its centre in a vertical plane. Between the subject and the disc was mounted a large shield, in which was cut a horizontal slit. The subjects could see small portions of the two lines through this slit. By rotating the disc, Michotte made these two squares of line appear to move along the slit, these movements being governed, of course, by the curves of the lines themselves. On the left of Figure 1, one of the patterns used by Michotte is shown, and the letters round the periphery show the five separable stages induced by rotating the disc counter-clockwise. The right section of Figure 1 translates these five stages into what can be seen through the slit in the shield. At first (a) the black and the grey squares are both at rest; then (b) the black square appears to move along the slit towards the grey. For a brief period (c) the two squares are touching but not moving. Then (d) the grey square moves off away from the black, and eventually (e) comes to rest.

Michotte investigated a number of variations on this basic procedure, but these are not important here. The major finding of the series of experiments was that the subjects reported that the black square caused the grey to move. This observation may be expressed in various ways: black makes grey move, black pushes grey, grey is forced to move, or grey has to move in these circumstances. Another common description is that the grey square moves because of a transfer of a force of motion from black to grey. Expressions like these are common as attempts to convey the concept of causality in other contexts too. Michotte's procedure, however, really amounts to an illusion, because, of course, the movements of the black and grey squares are determined merely by the curves of the black and grey lines on the rotating disc. Yet, a simple report of what is actually seen (as throughout the five parts of the sequence outlined above) seems to the observers to be inadequate as a description of what they think they see. This may be because the verbal expressions used to convey causality almost all contain the ghosts of animism; they are verbal remnants of the time when animism was taken to be a literal explanation for observable phenomena. We are so accustomed to using these animistic remnants in everyday language that we feel deprived of 'explanatory' power if we are forced to remove them and report merely what is observable rather than inferable. A factual language which is studiously non-animistic often seems to be stripped of explanatory power; we feel that we mean more than this, but we are unable to say what this extra is.

It would seem, then, that science does not use animistic explanations for physical events, although some aspects of animistic thought have been retained in our everyday language. Non-animistic reasons are now also sought for events in the physical systems of living plants and organisms. Reliance on animistic explanations may even be said to be pre-scientific. We have also seen that we reserve the appropriate use of the word behaviour to the activities of animals, and that psychology is the scientific study of such activities. The question now arises: should psychology rely on animistic explanations of behaviour? On the basis of the preceding discussion, some might wish to be brave and answer in the negative, arguing that psychology should follow the path of the established sciences. However, the question is not an easy one to answer. The very etymology of the question emphasizes the potential difficulties and confusions here: is animism appropriate for animal behaviour? In one sense, we have perhaps already answered the question with a muted affirmative in this chapter by distinguishing the activities of the sea anemone and Venus's Flytrap in a counter-intuitive way, based not on the complexity of the activities, but on the nature of the organisms. May this not be essentially animistic? The truth of the matter is that most of us do use animistic explanations quite seriously in order to explain our own behaviour. Our activities are said to reflect the motivating influences of an inner spirit which is not open to direct observation by others; our behaviour is therefore explained by reference to this inner self. The inner man wants and the outer man acts.

In considering the difficulties of explaining human behaviour, it is unusually instructive to consider the historical development of man's attempts to explain the behaviour of infra-human species. Many owners of pets would today think it execrable if one were to suggest that their dogs' and cats' behaviour might be 'scientifically' explained without ultimate reference to their internal motivating spirits. But as long ago as the seventeenth century, the philosopher René Descartes was offering just such a possibility – that the behaviour of animals should be explained mechanistically, without recourse to their inner selves. Descartes may have been led to such an opinion in part by an acquaintance with automata similar in concept to the Victorian monkey mentioned earlier. At that time, the Royal Gardens at Versailles, as elsewhere, were ornamented by a number of mechanical figures in the form of animals or people. These were operated hydraulically, their mechanisms being activated by pressure on platforms concealed in the footpaths of the gardens. Thus, a romantic stroll might be unexpectedly interrupted by sudden bodily movements or sounds on the part of the garden furniture, sometimes of a singularly unromantic nature. Such an experience must have been disarming, but nevertheless fascinating. Descartes argued that it was possible to regard humans and animals as mechanical systems analogous to, but more complex than, these hydraulic models. Their movements, he considered, are not the result of water being pumped into the limbs, but nevertheless may be produced by an essentially similar system which transfers some as yet undiscovered substance to the muscles. Descartes suggested, for example, that inadvertently placing a hand in a flame would result in the heat exciting a nerve to the brain, which then automatically pumped animal spirits to or from the arm muscles; these caused the muscles to expand or contract, and thereby removed the hand from the flame. Notice that Descartes's invocation of animal spirits in this context is not the same as the doctrine referred to as animism above, for he did not argue that these spirits initiated action; they merely reacted in a mechanical way to other events. Although Descartes attempted to explain certain patterns of involuntary behaviour in humans in this way, it was most certainly not his purpose to explain all human behaviour mechanistically. Indeed, one of the most important and pervasive aspects of his philosophy was his unshakable belief that man is more than a mere physical system; man also had a rational soul which chose to initiate voluntary, non-automatic patterns of behaviour. This soul was thought to be immortal and intangible, not subject to mechanistic explanations, and therefore animistic in the general sense. It resided within the mechanical system of the body, whose behaviour it could initiate and direct through the pineal gland. Of particular interest in the present context, however, was Descartes's preparedness *not* to attribute such a soul to animals, thereby suggesting that animals were merely very complicated machines whose behaviour was therefore to be explained in purely mechanistic terms. Such an account deprives animals of all volitions as such, their behaviour being simply the reactions of their bodies to their environment. This in no way denigrates the complexity of some patterns of animal behaviour. On the contrary, Descartes was quite prepared to admit that animals may do some things better than humans; however, such complex behaviour is nevertheless to be regarded as 'nature working in them according to the disposition of their organs' (*Discourse on Method*; 5), that is to say, mechanistically.

Descartes' distinction between the fundamental natures of animal and man is probably not unattractive to man himself. However, confidence in this division was severely tested in the nineteenth century by Darwin's publications on the evolutionary process. The general impact of this theory was enormous, and needs no emphasis here. However, it is important to notice that any scheme which stresses the continuities between species, including man, inevitably makes it more difficult to maintain fundamental distinctions between man and animals in the way suggested by Descartes. Darwin himself published a book in 1873 entitled *Expressions of the Emotions in Man and Animals*, in which he produced a great number of comparisons between the behaviour of man and of animals within an evolutionary context. For example, he suggested that the curling of our lips when we sneer is a relic of the baring of canine teeth in rage shown by carnivorous animals. In extending the evolutionary argument to behaviour Darwin may be said to have initiated an approach to the study of behaviour which is now enjoying something of a vogue, to judge by the current popularity of the writings of Desmond Morris (e.g. *The Naked Ape*, 1967) and Robert Ardrey (e.g. *The Social Contract*, 1970).

Faced with Darwin's publications, subsequent writers adopted one of two possible reactions (both of which may still be detected in the present reactions to the publications of Morris and Ardrey). One might decry the attempt to debase man's nature, an attitude motivating Bishop Wilberforce's famous taunt that T. H. Huxley should declare whether it was through his grandmother or his grandfather that Huxley claimed his descent from an ape. To adopt this strategy makes it easily possible to maintain a Cartesian view of man and animals, by denying vigorously that man can be regarded as no more than a complex machine. However, in the context of behaviour, it is interesting to discover that the alternative position was advocated by some. It is well understood, the argument went, that man is endowed with great intelligence and many moral virtues; therefore, if evolutionary theory is accepted, these characteristics will have evolved through the species in the same way as did man's physical characteristics. It subsequently follows that some species of animals may be pretty intelligent too, and, what is more, moral virtues might be detectable in them. Such an idea was taken up by many gentlemen of the era, and in the true tradition of Victorian amateurism, the hunt for animal virtues was joined. Examples of reasoning, of self-sacrifice, of self-control and of public-spiritedness were sought in the humblest of creatures, often with apparent success. Much of this work was reviewed and summarized by Romanes in a book entitled *Animal Intelligence* (1882), a treatise which it would be difficult to better for entertainment value and for its reassuring view of nature. However, most of the evidence reported did not rest on the detached objectivity which is demanded by science. It was difficult to distinguish what in fact had been observed from the interpretations of behaviour. Untrained observers tended to seek the greatest possible virtue from the simplest patterns of behaviour. In short, much of the evidence for animal virtues was no more than anecdotal, and most interpretations of animal behaviour was blatantly anthropomorphic. Inevitably, a reaction, summarized by Lloyd Morgan, eventually set in to this profligacy. He argued that we should interpret animal behaviour as parsimoniously as possible: 'In no case may we interpret an action as the outcome of the exercise of a higher psychical faculty, if it can be interpreted as the outcome of the exercise of one which stands lower in the psychological scale.' (1894).

The current interpretation of animal behaviour would seem to endorse Lloyd Morgan's strictures. Scientific reports of animal behaviour abound, but, in these at least, psychical functions are rarely mentioned. One might rephrase this comment by saying that a science of animal behaviour has developed which is careful to avoid animistic explanations. Behaviour is described precisely, in terms of when and where it was observed. Explanations for behaviour patterns may be offered in terms of their supposed evolution within a species (because of evolutionary pressures similar to those selecting taxonomic form) or their development within an individual (by means of learning processes to which that individual has been exposed). The wants and desires of the inner animal are conspicuous by their absence in these reports, being replaced by less abstract descriptions of the behaviour actually observed or occasionally by references to physiological investigations. This is not to deny that colloquially it is usually simpler to use relatively animistic terms to explain the behaviour of animals. It will always be simpler and more elegant to describe what my inner dog likes, knows, or prefers than to describe the behaviour of my outer dog meticulously in terms of how he behaves in certain circumstances. In terms of the number of words required, the first description is the more parsimonious. But in the context of the organization of knowledge, this first description is not more parsimonious than the non-animistic paraphrase, because it involves additional concepts. So our language about animal behaviour is exactly similar in principle to our language about physical events. It is more frequently animistic, but the claim could be made that the richness of this vocabulary can be replaced by a less colourful but more precise description of observable events when necessary.

When it comes to explaining human behaviour, most of us are happy to retain Descartes' formulation of our basic nature. As noted earlier, we are usually fearlessly animistic, accounting for the behaviour of our outer selves predominantly in terms of its motivation by our inner selves. It is not necessary at this stage to explore the lengths to which we will go to do this. However, it may be useful to illustrate this process briefly by discussing some common explanations for a pattern of human behaviour which is only too common — smoking cigarettes. This habit is chosen here because it also periodically provides the subject for public discussion about its causes. In passing, one might comment that there is often remarkably little attention to any organized knowledge about the phenomenon itself. In other words, one of the first prerequisites for a scientific study of the phenomenon appears to be frequently ignored, the objective *description* of where and when it happens, of who smokes and in what circumstances. However, this is not the point at issue here, as this example has been introduced merely in order to consider some common explanations for the behaviour.

Why does a person smoke? Some explanations are no more than a rephrasing of the observable phenomenon, smoking itself. For example, to say that one smokes because one is hooked or one has the habit is rarely to say anything more than the fact that one does smoke. That one has the habit is established by the observation that one smokes; if one stopped smoking the habit would presumably have been broken or have disappeared. Even an apparently innocuous explanation like this may have a spurious power, for it may encourage the belief that by breaking the habit one will stop smoking. Attention may thereby be directed away from the problem itself, the smoking behaviour.

Another sort of explanation does apparently add to the phenomenon more effectively than the first; one smokes because one enjoys smoking, one likes cigarettes, one wants to smoke or one chooses to smoke. Explanations like these, it might be claimed, are the most obviously animistic. It is quite apparent that the observable behaviour of the outer man is explained by reference to the motivations of the inner man. Again, however, such explanations may often turn out to be no more than a rephrasing of the observed phenomenon; that one likes cigarettes is established largely by the fact that one smokes. People who do not like smoking rarely smoke. Rather strangely, however, it is not unusual to encounter people who smoke but say that they want not to! This suggests that as an explanation, appeal to the inner self governing behaviour is sometimes not even effective. How can we cope with a proposal that one does what one wants not to do? One possibility is to retreat even further inside the person and say that deep down there is an (unconscious?) desire to smoke that is stronger than the superficial conscious desire not to smoke; but such an explanation is certainly not parsimonious, and in the final analysis it might be suggested that in this case we are inventing unconscious motives merely to salvage the inadequacy of our first attempt to explain the behaviour in question.

A slight rephrasing of the second sort of explanation emphasizes even more our preparedness to invent essentially animistic reasons for our behaviour. It is often said that smoking increases pleasure or decreases unease, and such events are said to explain smoking. One problem here is that the supposed *cause* of the smoking behaviour does not occur until *after* the smoking has begun. Philosophers have for long been arguing about the nature of causation, but it is generally acknowledged that for one event to be regarded as a cause of another, it must precede it in time. Imagine using the apparatus of Michotte discussed earlier, and observing the following sequence of events: (a) the black and grey squares are separate and stationary; (b) the grey square moves away from the black and stops; (c) the black square moves to where the grey square had originally been. Nobody using the concept of causality in the usual sense would venture the suggestion that the movement of the grey square was caused by the movement of the black. Most people would begin to look for possible explanations of how the first event (movement of the grey square) caused the second event (movement of the black). So, if causes precede their effects, how can an increase in pleasure cause smoking behaviour, and therefore be an explanation for that behaviour? A simple retort might be that one part of the explanation has been omitted: one smokes because it increases pleasure and one wants to increase pleasure. Such an addition is clearly an explanation which incorporates the animism of the second class of explanation offered above. However, it is this combination of causes which is perhaps the most widely used explanation of human behaviour. One could almost proffer a rule for the formulation of such 'explanations': in order to explain a pattern of behaviour, describe something which follows that behaviour, and propose that this outcome is desired by the inner person. The reader is left to the easy task of elaborating a few explanations of this type.

The next explanation for smoking to be considered here is the claim which is often expressed by smokers that it 'calms their nerves'. Such an explanation apparently appeals to events which may be studied in a completely non-animistic way. The physical phenomena in our nervous systems are in fact studied in this way by the science of physiology, and any explanation of behaviour in such terms might appear strong. However, we are often too ready to explain our behaviour by inventing physiological phenomena without making any attempt to identify these. The appeal to the calming of one's nerves by smoking is a good example of this opportunism. After all, our nerves are tangible, physical entities within our bodies, and so this explanation is open to scientific test. The point is, however, that explanations such as this one are offered, and usually accepted as plausible, in the complete absence of such a test. In fact, those who argue in this way might well be surprised at the effect of the *stimulant* nicotine on the nerves if their explanation were to be subjected to such a test. Accounts of human behaviour are replete with stratagems of this sort, many of them being based on the mythical properties of unobserved nerves: one is said to be *nervous*, one's *nerves* are on edge or taut, one suffers a *nervous* breakdown. Such phrases are interesting as *descriptions* of certain patterns of behaviour, and they communicate meaningful impressions of these within our society. As *explanations* of behaviour, which these phrases only too quickly become, they are misleading, to say the least. They succeed in directing attention away from the phenomenon which is to be explained by asking us to substitute for that which is observable (behaviour) that which is *not* observed ('nerves'). Finally, such explanations may even then not avoid ultimate appeals to an animistic inner person or even an 'inner nerve' in order to produce a cause which precedes the phenomenon to be explained. Thus smoking cannot be readily caused by the effect it has on nerves, real, or imagined; it is therefore necessary to add that the inner person *wishes* to calm them.

It is not intended that the above comments be an authoritative or complete analysis of the kinds of explanation used in discussing human behaviour. Clearly, some possible causal accounts have been taken out of context and caricatured somewhat. An adequate analysis would inevitably have to be both long and involved, and would include philosophical evaluation of the nature of self, of free-will, of purpose, and so on. A recent book, *Explanation in the Behavioural Sciences* (Borger and Cioffi, 1970), provides interesting discussions of some of the controversies in this area. The present intention is merely to suggest how glibly we sometimes invent explanations for human behaviour. In particular, we rarely seek causes for behaviour in terms of events which have just happened to the behaver; instead, we substitute the wants, desires, and feelings of an inner self to motivate the outer body. This is obviously reminiscent of animistic accounts of physical phenomena, and may have the same limitations inherent in that philosophy. Usually, it is simply a paraphrase of observable events in terms of unobservable motivating spirits; but at the same time, it directs attention away from the observable events, and thereby from those observable (and often manipulable) occurrences which precede them. This is not, however, to say that the explanations discussed above are worthless. On the contrary, such accounts of behaviour often provide explanations which are satisfactory from the everyday point of view. For example, it is both acceptable and useful if I explain that I was driving too fast because I wanted to get home early. This statement adequately provides information additional to the bald statement that I crashed the car. And, after all, it has already been seen that we use animistic language to describe inanimate events in an interesting and evocative way; our language about both physical events and behaviour would indeed be dull if we dispensed with animistic concepts. However, animistic accounts of physical events may be readily translated into this form when required, and it is in this way that our scientific understanding and control of those events have developed. It is less clear whether such translations may be accomplished with accounts of behaviour, because we are more prepared to accept animistic explanations as satisfactory in this context. In doing this, we also gain support from Descartes's dualistic view of human nature, which is so entrenched in our outlook that one modern philosopher, Gilbert Ryle, has dubbed it 'the official doctrine' (1949).

This book is an attempt to discuss some aspects of behaviour without direct appeal to this 'official doctrine'. Some patterns of behaviour will be described in terms of the conditions in which they occur, those conditions being specified in physical terms rather than as internal motivations. In doing this, an orientation expressed by J. B. Watson (1924) is being considered: 'Why don't we make what we can *observe* the real field of psychology? Let us limit ourselves to things that can be observed, and formulate laws concerning only those things.' Such a view of psychology is known as *behaviourism*. It has been one important influence on psychology in the past fifty years, although there have been, and remain, many who have reacted to this view with extreme distaste. They object that it leaves out much of the richness of life; this prompts behaviourists to ask whether this result is fundamentally different from the impoverishment of everyday descriptions when non-animistic accounts are used to describe physical events. We now have both animistic and non-animistic language in that domain, each serving its own ends; could we have both in the context of behaviour? It is hoped that this book may help the reader to consider and evaluate this possibility.

Before the exercise begins, however, it should be made clear that the evaluation will not here be prompted by philosophical discussion. Instead, experiments on behaviour will be presented and discussed. The findings of these experiments do not depend upon a particular point of view within psychology, such as Watson's contentious suggestion that behaviourism is the 'real field of psychology'. On the contrary, many problems will be considered which are important to all of us, whatever our philosophical orientation. For example, how may teaching be best achieved?; how may we treat people who behave in unusual ways (the mentally ill)?; is punishment an effective procedure for eliminating behaviour?; what effects do drugs have on behaviour?; what is anxiety? These questions and others will be considered. It is true that they will be considered within the framework of a behaviouristic outlook, but the experimental findings themselves must be accommodated within any theoretical system of psychology.

Finally, a brief indication of the book's plan may be useful. It begins by examining very simple patterns of behaviour in very simple situations; predominantly, this is the behaviour of animals rather than of humans. It is hoped that the reasons for this initial emphasis will become clear. By discussing animal behaviour, it is hoped to establish the less emotive accounts of behaviour in a context where they lose least, and where they may be more acceptable to a sceptical reader. The simplicity of the early experiments discussed makes it possible to abstract and develop general principles about the effects of an animal's environment on its behaviour. The review of work with animals incorporates experiments of increasing complexity, and it is hoped that possible analogies to certain patterns of *human* behaviour may begin to emerge more forcefully. The final part of the book takes up these analogies specifically, discusses their implications, and reviews some of the experiments which have been carried out with human subjects within this approach to psychology. In short, the book attempts to abstract and develop general principles about the interrelationships between behaviour and the environment in which it occurs.

CHAPTER 2
'Superstition'

We have seen that one of the early tasks of a science is to describe what happens in an objective way. Any complete description will include the circumstances in which an event occurs. For example, a male robin will attack another at a certain time of the year, if the second robin intrudes on the territory to which the first has established a claim. The description of attack behaviour in the robin is incomplete without these limiting details, for robins may not attack other birds at that time of year and may not attack other robins at other times. This observation is not very remarkable, for many readers may themselves have noticed these phenomena; however, it is introduced with confidence here on the basis not of chance observations but of the comprehensive account of robins' behaviour produced by David Lack. His book *The Life of the Robin* (1943) is accepted as authoritative largely because it incorporates the results of *systematic* observations of this species, and this is also an important part of scientific endeavour. It is not sufficient merely to observe something happen once, as scientific descriptions usually imply generality in the form of an unexpressed claim that the reader would also see precisely these phenomena in exactly these circumstances.

Lack's learned, but entirely endearing, account of the robin also includes another important feature of many scientific programmes. At one stage he decided not merely to rely on the chance arrival of an intruder, but instead he placed a stuffed robin within the territory of an established male. Thus, Lack artificially induced attack behaviour, and it became possible to study this phenomenon more exhaustively and systematically. Such a procedure introduces an element of control into the situation, and it is at this stage that a study might be described as experimental in nature. It is important to recognize that the simplest experiments are really no more than controlled observations. However, by attempting gradually to control more and more aspects of the situation which is being observed, it may become possible to specify more exactly which aspects of the situation are crucial for the phenomenon of interest to occur. In the case of the robin's attack behaviour, such a procedure has shown that it is the redness of the intruder's breast that triggers off the attack. This has been established by observing that the robin will not attack a dummy which has no patch of red (or, indeed, a male robin whose red breast feathers have been experimentally painted grey), but that he will attack anything which has a patch of red on it — even a red feather duster. So we are led to understand more adequately what causes the attack behaviour of the robin in the real world by abstracting and controlling certain features in order to investigate their relevance to the phenomenon. Artificial investigations may therefore help us to understand real phenomena.

The first experimental situation which will be considered in detail shares the general properties discussed above. It uses an artificial, but controllable, procedure to study the effects of certain events on behaviour; thereby, we hope to abstract general principles which may be relevant to behaviour in the 'real' world. The experimental situation is certainly simple. An artificial world is provided for a laboratory rat in the form of an unexciting four-sided cage, in which the animal is placed for a limited period of each day. Such an austere environment provides no great challenge for the rat, once he has established that he cannot escape from the situation; it is, frankly, dull. However, there is one unusual feature about the procedure: at regular intervals, a small pellet of food is delivered to a hopper in one wall of the cage. Since the rat has not eaten for some time, it is likely that this feature of the environment may be of significance to the rat. The experimental question we pose by the use of this artificial procedure is simple — what does the rat do?

This experiment has been carried out on a number of occasions by first-year psychology students in the writer's laboratory, and the results are best described and explained by tracing the procedure through from its beginning. The rat is first deprived of food for a few hours, and is then placed in the cage for the first time. Since this may be the first occasion on which the rat has been out of his home cage and away from his fellows, he finds himself in what must be an intimidating situation — a strange environment, with no other rat behind which to hide, and, worse, occasional banging noises from the wall (these emanating from the mechanism which delivers the pellets of food to the hopper). The invariable reaction of laboratory rats to this situation is inactivity, as if they presume that the situation might change if they ignore it; they appear to be too frightened to move. However, as time passes (and the situation remains the same), the rat may begin to venture the occasional, hesitant movement. This has, of course, no dramatic effect on his world, and so, these movements may begin to become bolder until eventually the rat begins to move about the cage, warily exploring it. At this stage, it is usual to notice that the rat begins to wash himself rather frequently, a pattern of behaviour that is sometimes taken to be a sign of 'nerves' on the part of rats (without, of course, any attempt to measure the activity of the rat's nervous system by those who explain his behaviour in this way!). Eventually, the rat inevitably discovers the alcove in one wall, in which there is by now a small pile of food pellets. Since he has not eaten for some time, it is probable that the rat will begin to eat some of these pellets. Therefore he is likely to have his nose in the hopper at the very time that a further pellet of food happens to be delivered by the mechanism, and it may be that the noise of this mechanism will temporarily interrupt his eating, perhaps reinstating the 'nervous' washing. However, before long, the rat has usually eaten all the pellets of food. At this stage, post-prandial washing behaviour is often observed; and as time passes in this activity, there is an increasing likelihood of a further pellet of food being automatically delivered to the hopper. The sudden noise of this may well startle the animal once again. Eventually, however, the rat may again push his nose into the hopper, and when finding one pellet, he may promptly eat it. He may also spend some time sniffing around in the hopper, perhaps because there was only one food pellet on this occasion as opposed to the many there before. Finding no more pellets, the rat may then again indulge in a short bout of washing. After a period of time, the next pellet of food is delivered automatically, and so on.

The above description has been made rather flippant in an attempt to inject some life into a procedure that it cannot be pretended is unduly exciting, but it would be a useful exercise for the reader to reconstruct for himself the exact nature of what is *observable* and to extract the less observable, explanatory internal processes from the account. Further exposure to this situation, however, often produces an interesting effect on the rat's behaviour, which it is important to describe as objectively as possible. It very often happens that rats in this situation begin to spend more and more time grooming and washing themselves, until in the end they may be seen to do nothing but wash, except when a pellet of food is delivered to the hopper, when they will approach and immediately eat it — and then return to washing. The precise nature of this behaviour may vary from rat to rat: some may wash only their faces, some only their bodies; others may start washing their faces immediately after they have eaten a pellet of food, and then progress down their bodies until the next pellet is delivered; yet others may consistently go to one particular corner of the cage, carrying out their grooming behaviour in that place only; finally, some rats may not wash themselves at all, but instead repeat some other stereotyped sequence of behaviour between eating pellets of food.

This experimental procedure is in fact based on a report by Skinner (1948a) in which a very similar procedure was used, but with pigeons as the experimental subjects. In this case, the food was held in a tray which was swung into a position where the pigeons could eat from it for five seconds in every twenty. Skinner's results were essentially similar to those discussed above, in that most of his pigeons developed stereotyped patterns of behaviour between the five-second periods of access to food. Thus, one of the birds was seen to turn round and round in the box, always in an anti-clockwise direction. Another repeatedly thrust its beak into one of the top corners of the box. A third pigeon spent all its time tossing its head up and down, while two further birds were reported to develop a pendulum-like movement of their heads, swinging them back and forth.

As experiments, the above procedures are simple in the

extreme; the reader might reasonably marvel that the writer should see fit to ask first-year undergraduates to spend some of their time in such a way. And yet, these simple investigations contain many of the problems discussed in the preceding chapter. It is always of the utmost interest to discuss with the students exactly what is happening in this situation. Perhaps the most common account offered is that the animal has come to believe that behaving in this stereotyped manner produces food; it therefore behaves in this way in order to get the food, because it is hungry. Almost all explanations include some reference to the apparent purposefulness of the animals in these situations. Accounts like these are useful, in that they convey to a listener, who may not have seen the experiment for himself, a very strong indication of what the behaviour looked like; in other words, as everyday communications they are both successful and acceptable. Yet, in terms of the principles discussed in the previous chapter, it might be a fair question to ask to what extent such an account offers a satisfactory *explanation* for the behavioural processes observed. One might criticize the account as obtaining much of its explanatory power by recourse to unobservable and essentially animistic processes which are in fact merely paraphrases of the observable behaviour. Belief, purpose, desire, hunger: all these concepts are of processes which can never in fact be observable by the student in the experiment, for they all refer to the inner rat and they are all invented to explain the observable phenomena of the outer rat's behaviour. Clearly, it is a rather chastening experience for the students to be asked to describe only those things which they can see, and to develop an explanatory account of these phenomena by reference to observable events only. Thus, they cannot see the rat's hunger: instead, they are able to see objectively that the rat has not enjoyed access to food for a specified period before each experimental session. They cannot see that the rat wants the food, only that he reliably eats it whenever it becomes available. The students are unable to see the purpose of the rat or the development of his mistaken beliefs; what can be seen are the stereotyped patterns of behaviour occurring predictably in an environment in which the only unusual characteristic is the periodic presentation of the food which the rat eats. It is also true that these patterns of behaviour were not originally so obvious when the animals were first placed in this environment, but that the frequency increased during the experiment, this higher frequency then being maintained. On the basis of this description, one might develop an hypothesis which is open to some sort of objective test; for example, it would seem likely that the most striking aspects of the environment (the delivery of food) is in some way crucial for the above phenomena to occur. This could be easily tested by repeating the experiment as closely as possible, with the one exception that food should now no longer be delivered to the animal in the cage. One way to carry out this second experiment would be to use some fresh animals in exactly the same way: they would be deprived of food for the same period before the experimental sessions, placed in the same environment, if possible be exposed to the same banging noises from the pellet dispenser, which this time should be empty and therefore deliver nothing when it operates. Such an experiment would thereby make only one change in the experimental procedures, and all other features would be incorporated. In this way, we should hope to isolate the contribution that food makes to the development of the stereotyped behaviour. If this second experiment is carried out, it is in fact found that stereotyped behaviour does *not* develop. At first, the animals' behaviour cannot be distinguished from that of the subjects in the previous experiment; they do little when first placed in the cage, then they begin to explore circumspectly. However, as the experiment progresses, there is no sign of a stereotyped pattern of behaviour emerging unless it be the rather general and negative behaviour of sleeping. These animals do not develop unusual patterns of behaviour which are easily identifiable by their repetitiveness or apparent purposefulness. Such a finding supports the view that the delivery of food was of crucial importance in the first experiment. It appears that this variable is in some way responsible for the unusual patterns of behaviour which became characteristic of that experiment. This idea is further supported by the finding that the repetitive behaviour typical of the animals in the first experiment will itself gradually decrease in frequency and disappear if those animals are transferred to the conditions in which food is no longer delivered. It would appear that the development and maintenance of the stereotyped patterns of behaviour typical of the first experiment are in some way *dependent* on the delivery of food, and to that extent are a *function* of the repeated occurrence of that event.

We have now embarked upon an experimental analysis of this simple behavioural phenomenon; we are attempting to discover what observable and manipulable variables might be important in producing and maintaining the behaviour. In effect, this means that we are now developing an explanation of the phenomenon, but one that directs attention towards the role of specifiable events in the world of things rather than to vague forces inside the animal. Thus, we are saying that the behaviour develops in this way *because* food is delivered at regular intervals. Such an analysis may be extended into the minutiae of the environmental procedures which will produce the effect being studied. It has been shown, for example, that stereotyped behaviour is more likely to develop if food is delivered to the animals at certain regular intervals. But there is no need here to give an exhaustive account of such studies. Instead, it may be useful to turn our attention to another set of questions about this behavioural phenomenon. For example, does food always have the effect of developing stereotyped patterns of behaviour when it is delivered at the frequency used in our first experiment? The answer to this is clearly in the negative. Stereotyped patterns of behaviour are very unlikely to develop if the animal is placed in the experimental situation without having first been deprived of food for a while. This will probably not amaze the reader, who might well prefer to say that the animal has to be *hungry* for the behavioural phenomenon to develop; if he is not hungry, he will not want the food and so his behaviour will not become stereotyped. Here again, the explanatory hunger is not directly observable, being inferred from the very behavioural events it is intended to explain. It is not mere sophistry to suggest that an alternative *explanation* may be formulated in more objective terms. This may be achieved simply by specifying the amount of time for which the experimental animal has been deprived of food, a measurable period that may be readily manipulated in an experimental programme. Thus, certain periods of prior food deprivation may be optimal for the development of stereotyped patterns of behaviour in the situation in which food is regularly delivered; this is an empirical matter, open to direct investigation. Also, there are other environmental events which will develop and maintain stereotyped behaviour if delivered at regular intervals. For example, water has this effect (given appropriate antecedent conditions, such as temporary deprivation of liquids before the experimental sessions), so have solutions of sucrose (sometimes, even if the animal has been deprived of neither food nor water). Short periods of heat radiation may develop the effect, but again, only in certain specifiable conditions.

Consequently, a number of environmental events may be functionally associated with behaviour in this situation. Given appropriate antecedent and current conditions, their regular delivery may be related to the development and maintenance of stereotyped forms of behaviour. Because of the occurrence of these events, certain patterns of behaviour become more frequent, or more probable — to such an extent that the animal may appear to do nothing else. These events are generally termed reinforcers. A *reinforcer* may be defined as any event which will increase or maintain the frequency of a pattern of behaviour with which it is associated. This will be discussed more explicitly in later chapters, but it is important to notice for the moment that no attempt is made in this definition to explain *why* reinforcers have their effect. Also notice that it must always be an empirical or factual matter as to whether a particular event is a reinforcer or not, and that this is recognized to depend on the circumstances in which the event occurs. So, food is a reinforcer only if it increases or maintains the frequency of a pattern of behaviour with which it is associated. Whether this is the case depends on preceding events (whether the animal has been deprived of food, and for how long) and on how it happens to occur (for example, how frequently it occurs). But there *are* events that, in appropriate circumstances, can be described as reinforcers; that is to say, some events do increase or maintain the frequency of behaviour occurring at the time they themselves do.

To return specifically to our simple experiment using rats. It is a factual matter that the stereotyped washing behaviour is functionally related to the delivery of food, for if food is not delivered, washing does not develop as a predominant feature of the animals' behaviour. Moreover, if the delivery of food is discontinued after the washing behaviour has developed, then that pattern of behaviour will become progressively less frequent. Therefore, in this experiment, food satisfies the requirements of a reinforcer.

Further testable hypotheses may be formulated as to how the washing behaviour was developed and maintained in the experiment. It will be recalled that washing is a pattern of behaviour which tends to occur fairly often in most rats in these circumstances; when the rat first begins to move about the cage, he is likely to intersperse this behaviour with 'nervous' washing. When he begins to eat the pellets of food, he is again likely to finish each small meal by post-prandial washing. It therefore follows that there is a fairly high probability early in the experiment that the arrival of the reinforcer (food) may be closely associated in time with some pattern of washing behaviour. This will increase the frequency of washing behaviour, thereby increasing the probability that subsequent reinforcers will coincide with the grooming. This process continues until eventually the rat is washing himself to such an extent that it is almost certain that the delivery of next food-pellet must coincide with such a pattern of behaviour, and so on. This explanation is not complete, since a number of other principles are involved which will be discussed later, but it does at this stage offer an account solely in terms of observable events, and it suggests a number of further hypotheses or questions which might be subjected to experimental test.

It is very striking that Skinner's pigeons developed stereotyped patterns of behaviour which are almost exaggerated caricatures of 'normal' pigeon behaviour. It would seem that, early in the experiment, there was a relatively high probability of a period of access to food being closely associated with some movement of the head (a characteristic feature of much pigeon behaviour) and so the effects of the reinforcers on behaviour developed in the form of continuous head tossing or swinging. The process whereby one of the pigeons developed turning behaviour may also be readily reconstructed, and one can see that it is by no means surprising that this bird should turn always in the same direction.

The above analysis suggests that it is behaviour whose frequency is already quite high which is most likely to be further increased in frequency and maintained by reinforcers presented regularly; thus, rats develop exaggerated rat-like behaviour in these experiments, and pigeons caricature their own sudden head movements by increasing their frequency. Such a view may be supported by some more recent experiments. For example, Herrnstein and Morse (reported in Herrnstein, 1966) trained a food-deprived pigeon to peck at a disc in order to obtain brief access to food (a process to be more fully described and explained a little later). When this pecking behaviour was established (i.e., occurred frequently), the periods of access to food were programmed to occur regularly, regardless of what the pigeon did. In fact, although it was no longer necessary for the bird to peck the disc, this behaviour was maintained at a relatively high frequency over a further 21 experimental sessions. To emphasise the findings of this experiment by the use of animistic language; the pigeon failed to recognise that it was no longer necessary to peck because the access to food was no longer dependent on such behaviour. More objectively, the pecking behaviour was maintained by its *chance* relationships with food presentation, a reinforcer. Essentially similar results have been reported by Neuringer (1970), who, on only three occasions, gave food-deprived pigeons access to food immediately after they had pecked a disc. Again, this behaviour was maintained over a considerable period of time by subsequently providing access to food regardless of how the bird behaved. This time, however, the food was presented at irregular intervals. One bird pecked the disc 22,817 times during 48 experimental sessions. These experiments show that, if a pattern of behaviour is developed by a training procedure so that it occurs at a high frequency, *chance* relationships between the behaviour and a reinforcer will maintain that specific pattern over long periods of time.

The point may be further emphasized by reference to an experiment in which humans acted as subjects (Bruner and Revusky, 1961). These subjects were rewarded for pressing a button; however, the reward was obtained only by button-presses which were made at least a specified period of time after the previous press on that button, so the situation was essentially a simple timing or delay task, although the subjects were not told this. In addition to the effective button, there were a number of other buttons on the subjects' test panel, but these were entirely ineffective, being unrelated to the timing task. Now, most humans have a high probability of button-pushing behaviour in any case, perhaps because this pattern of behaviour often produces such interesting consequences — ringing a doorbell, turning off the bell of an alarm clock, switching on or off a light, obtaining cigarettes or the return of one's money from a vending machine, and so on, all of which events might be described as reinforcers in some circumstances but not in others. In Bruner and Revusky's experiment, their subjects began playing with these ineffective buttons. Before long, many of them had evolved complex sequences of presses to the various buttons, interspersed between the presses on the effective button. Clearly, the longer the sequence of 'ineffective' button presses, the more likely it was that enough time would have elapsed since the last press on the effective button — and so the greater the probability that the next press on that button would obtain the reward. In this way, the timing task was converted by the subjects into a sequence problem, which they worked hard to master. Since the reward (reinforcer) occurred after an appropriate press on the effective button regardless of whatever else may have happened, all these complex sequences were really equivalent to the washing behaviour of the rat in our first experiment. So these human subjects developed stereotyped sequences of behaviour in exactly the same way, merely because they came to the experiment with a high disposition to press buttons, just as the rat comes with a high disposition to wash himself.

This last experiment is a clear example of how patterns of behaviour may increase in frequency because of their chance relationships with a reinforcer. It also provides a point of contact with another body of research which is thought by some to be closely related to the phenomena discussed thus far, namely human superstitions. In fact, Skinner entitled the report outlined earlier 'Superstition' in the pigeon, and himself suggested analogies between his pigeons' behaviour and some patterns of human behaviour. One possible analogy is provided by the stereotyped patterns of behaviour which many people perform when shaking dice, especially when much may hang on that particular throw. If the dice is unbiassed, blowing on it, shaking it six times rather than five, incanting rhymes, or telling it how to fall should have no effect. It is possible to imagine that such behaviour may by chance have been followed by a happy outcome, and that the rise to a higher frequency of occurrence leads to inevitable, but chance, relationships between that behaviour and that outcome. These accidents maintain the frequency of the behaviour. A further example may be the use of some proprietary concoctions to alleviate the misery of a head cold. Since such inconveniences tend to be relatively short-lived in any case, there is a reasonably high chance that taking the preparation may be followed by a lessening of the symptoms even if it is itself ineffective, and so the behaviour of taking the mixture in those circumstances may increase and be maintained.

Skinner has developed the analogy further in his book *Science and Human Behavior* (1953), where he states (p. 85) that 'if there is only an accidental connexion between the response and the appearance of a reinforcer, the behavior is called "superstitious" '. However, there are a number of problems in making a confident transition from stereotyped patterns of rat or pigeon behaviour to the complex rituals characteristic of many human superstitions. Many of these are determined to a large extent by the society or culture in which the superstition occurs. To consider an innocuous example, a high proportion of people in this country touch wood for luck. It is difficult to believe that this is a direct result of each individual's having developed and maintained wood-touching merely as a result of chance relationships between such behaviour and subsequent good fortune. It is more probable that the example of other people is important, although, of course, this still leaves open the possibility that the superstition *originally* developed in the way that Skinner has outlined for pigeons. It has been argued that Skinner's account of superstition may not apply to humans because of these important social factors. However, it is not clear whether such an objection can be sustained as fundamental. We have seen that the independent presentation of food is more likely to select and develop species-characteristic behaviours, such as washing in rats or head movements in pigeons; presumably, these patterns of behaviour occur fairly frequently to start with as a result of the evolutionary development of these species. Social pressures and example at a human level may be merely one other way of maximising the chances that a particular pattern of behaviour is developed widely but 'accidentally'.

The complexities and richness of human superstitions have been recently reviewed in a readable book by G. Jahoda (*The Psychology of Superstition*, 1970), in which one chapter is devoted to an account and a critique of Skinner's views. These are criticised because it is claimed that they fail to distinguish the form of behaviour induced by accidental relationships with the environment (superstitious behaviour) from the *belief* that a causal connection is involved. To support this view, Jahoda claims that there is a confusion inherent in one of Skinner's comments about his experiment: 'The bird behaves *as if* there were a causal relation between its behaviour and the presentation of food, although such a relation is lacking' (Skinner, 1948a, emphases added). Jahoda suggests that this is 'absurdly anthropocentric', and that it conveys by innuendo a suggestion that belief in a causal connection is involved. However, it is doubtful whether Skinner's comment is open to either of these objections, for it is he who is at present perhaps most closely associated with the behaviouristic outlook briefly discussed in the first chapter of this book. On the basis of his many other writings, it might therefore be fairer to accept his comment at its face value: the bird comes to behave in the same way *as* it would *if* there were a direct causal connection between the behaviour and the delivery of the reinforcer. In this way, one emphasises again the relationship between behaviour and the environment rather than internal unobservables, for it is an experimental matter to establish how far these two types of behaviour are functionally equivalent.

However, it is not the present intention either to support or refute the analogy between Skinner's experiment with pigeons and human superstitions. It would seem that there are some patterns of human behaviour which may be readily interpreted in these terms, but equally that there are other superstitions for which such an attempt would be more difficult. In a sense, the concept of superstition is largely irrelevant to the aims of this chapter, but it is one which could not legitimately be ignored, because it was Skinner who both carried out the first experiment which has been the major subject of the chapter and at the same time argued the analogy to human behaviour. Whatever the advantages or limitations of such an analogy, the basic findings of Skinner's experiment should not be overlooked. Couched in general terms, these are that the regular occurrence of certain events in specified circumstances may increase and maintain the frequency of patterns of behaviour with which they initially coincided by chance. It may be argued that it is an experimental matter to determine the circumstances which are most favourable to the development of this phenomenon, and the events whose occurrence are most effective in this way.

CHAPTER 3

Reinforcement

The technical term 'reinforcer' was introduced during the discussion of 'superstitious' behaviour in animals. 'Reinforcement' is the process which results when reinforcers are delivered. The two terms will be used repeatedly throughout the remainder of this book; indeed, this work as a whole might be described as an essay on reinforcers and reinforcement. For this reason, it is crucial that the meanings of these terms are precisely established.

In the previous chapter, various environmental events, such as delivery of food, water, heat, etc., were described as reinforcers. This was done on the basis that these events appeared to increase or maintain the frequency of patterns of behaviour with which they were associated. In the case of 'superstitious' behaviour, these associations occurred by chance: no deliberate attempt was made to associate the reinforcers with a particular pattern of behaviour. It was suggested that the natural characteristics of the animals tended to make some behaviours more likely to be associated coincidentally with the reinforcer than others. It was emphasised that it is an empirical or factual matter to determine whether a particular event is actually a reinforcer or not. Striking evidence was discussed in the last chapter that the food was a reinforcer, in that the animals' behaviour was greatly affected by its chance relationships with the food; certain patterns of behaviour greatly increased in frequency, until eventually the behaviour came to appear purposeful. If such a control over behaviour can come to be exerted accidentally, the effects of a reinforcer will be much more forceful when the experimenter explicitly arranges that it can only be associated with a particular pattern of behaviour. This may be achieved most easily by making the reinforcer dependent upon the occurrence of a specified pattern of behaviour, so that the environmental event is made to occur when, and only when, the animal behaves in that way.

In deciding which pattern of behaviour is to be associated with a reinforcer, the experimenter is essentially establishing a teaching situation. Let us consider how such a procedure will develop, again basing the description on simple experiments carried out by first-year students. When they are able to report clearly what pattern of 'superstitious' behaviour has in fact developed in the case of their animals, they are asked to discontinue the regular presentations of food, and to dispense pellets only if the rat goes to a particular part of the cage. The result of such a procedural change is a fairly dramatic change in the rat's behaviour. If his 'superstition' is washing, he will at first wash more furiously than ever, but, of course, the washing will never again be associated with food. Gradually, and not surprisingly, the washing begins to become less persistent. This shows that the food was indeed a reinforcer in the previous part of the experiment, and that discontinuing an association between a reinforcer and a pattern of behaviour will result in the reversion of that behaviour to its previous frequency. (This is technically known as an *extinction* procedure).

In allowing the grooming behaviour to drop in frequency, more time becomes available for the rat to do other things — and, again not surprisingly, he does. This new activity (or behaviour whose frequency had for some time been low as a result of the maintained 'superstition') may take the form of moving about rather more in the cage, and it is inevitable that before long he will be in the part of the cage which the experimenter has previously decided is the 'right' part for the food to be delivered. So, as soon as the rat goes there, the dispenser is made to deliver food, and the characteristic noise is heard. The rat will immediately approach the hopper, and eat the pellet of food — for this is how he has behaved for some time whenever that event occurs. It is very likely that this eating will be followed once more by washing, for, again, this is what has happened for some time. However, this time, the grooming may be quite short-lived, and the rat will begin to explore again, soon finding himself in the appropriate corner of the cage for food to be delivered again. Within a very short period of time, the rat's behaviour changes completely from its previous 'superstition'. Now, all his time is spent in eating and going to the appropriate corner, which, of course, *immediately* leads to a pellet of food being delivered. The frequency of food delivery will also have increased noticeably since, although this event now depends upon behaviour which the experimenter decides is appropriate, it is now produced whenever he behaves in this way.

Many students find the results outlined above surprising. Before the event, they expect the rat's behaviour to adapt to the new conditions, but it is the speed of this transition which is unexpected. The slowest part of the experiment is the first, when the experimenter is still waiting for the superstitious behaviour to decrease in frequency; but once this happens, the increase in the frequency of 'appropriate' behaviour can be fairly dramatic. The situation can also be fascinating because there is a sense in which the animal learns what the new requirements are, and so the experimenter is able to see this learning occur quickly in an animal which may not normally be regarded as a fast learner. In addition, to the extent that the experimenter himself controls the procedure, he even claims to have *taught* the rat, for after all he specified what was to happen before the event.

In this changed situation, the fact that food is a reinforcer is even more clearly established. A reinforcer is said to increase and maintain the frequency of behaviour with which it is associated; by now specifying a form of behaviour upon which the reinforcer is to be dependent, its effect is demonstrated more unequivocally. In fact, whether or not an event is a reinforcer is usually investigated by using dependencies such as this rather than the less controlled experimental procedures discussed in the previous chapter. So the defining characteristic of a reinforcer is usually said to be the fact that the frequency of a pattern of behaviour is increased and maintained when the event is made dependent upon it.

Of course, the question still remains as to *why* the rat approaches the specified corner of the cage. As ever, many descriptions or explanations are possible, but, by this stage of the argument, it should be clear that the explanation favoured here is expressed in terms of the relationship between behaviour and observable environmental events. Thus, the frequency of approach to that part of the cage is a function of the demonstrable fact that a reinforcer is dependent upon, and therefore associated with, that behaviour. The behaviour develops because it is reinforced.

It must be admitted at this point that the argument may easily appear to become circular. The frequency of a particular pattern of behaviour is increased by its association with a reinforcer; a reinforcer is defined as an event which increases the frequency of behaviour with which it is associated. However, the most important, indeed the crucial, point here is that 'explanations' such as this do direct our attention towards specifiable and measurable aspects of the environment. Thus, the behavioural phenomena are not described by reference to internal events. To say, for example, that the rat approaches the corner of the cage *in order to* obtain food may be no more than a paraphrase of the relationship between the behaviour and the food: the important thing is that food does occur in that situation, and that it is factually described as a reinforcer. So, an increase in the frequency of a given pattern of behaviour may be produced by associating a reinforcer with it; a decrease in frequency results from removing any associations between it and a reinforcer; and in both these cases, the reinforcer is an environmental event. It is this generalisation, based upon the experiments discussed thus far, which provides an approach to the study of *any* behaviour, whatever the circumstances.

To turn for a moment to less constrained 'experimental' situations. I lecture to students in psychology, and so have to stand in front of numbers of people who have varying degrees of commitment. In such circumstances, certain patterns of behaviour on the part of the members of my audience are likely to provide events for me which may act as reinforcers. For example, if my audience looks at me intently (but not too intently), smiles occasionally, takes occasional notes, and so on, then patterns of behaviour which I exhibit may increase in frequency, or be maintained at a high frequency. These reactions from the audience thereby qualify as events in my environment which, in those circumstances, act as reinforcers. That this is the case is emphasised by the fact that if these environmental events cease to occur, and instead the members of my audience sit woodenly, or talk, or yawn, or doodle, then it is probable that my behaviour will not be maintained in its previous form. It is not necessary, however, to assume that I must be *aware* of such events in my environment for them to be effective as reinforcers. Indeed, I am invariably too pre-occupied 'consciously' to look for such events about me, and yet they may still be effective. It happens that I move about a good deal when I am lecturing (sometimes this is regarded as a sign of 'nerves'); this behavioural repertoire has before now been exploited by my audiences. For example, classes have occasionally agreed among themselves to look a little more alert when I am in a particular spot in the room. By doing this discreetly, they have succeeded in making me spend a large proportion of my time there even though I have not recognised the plot and have been unable to verbalise the situation (and have therefore suffered the ignominy of being told about the 'experiment' afterwards). Another effective ruse is to plant a stooge somewhere in the audience, preferably an attractive girl. She may be told by her colleagues to nod her head occasionally, to smile every so often, and to look alert generally — but only when I happen to look at her. The game here is to measure how frequently I look at this girl rather than at an equally attractive class-mate elsewhere in the audience who is not reinforcing my behaviour. This experiment has been reported as effective in situations in which I have had no insight into the way my behaviour is being manipulated!

Such experiments show the ways in which behaviour may be increased in frequency, and maintained, by systematically making certain consequences dependent upon it. One's behaviour might be described as a function of such events. Such forces, presumably, may be at work in a less contrived way in the everyday world. Argyle (1967), for example, has shown how the ways in which we look at each other differ in various environmental and social situations. He regards such mutual glances as an example of social skill, and has suggested that such skills are very important features of any social interaction. Yet, these skills are usually not carried out 'on purpose', in that they are brought into play 'unconsciously' (notice how the pattern of mutual glances changes, for example, if one or both participants are made 'aware' of these complex interactions). It is possible to look at these 'unconscious' patterns of behaviour as reinforcing events for other people. They are also, of course, functionally dependent upon such behaviour in other people, and so the interaction is extremely complex.

So far in this chapter, we have discussed patterns of behaviour which existed before any experimental manipulation was introduced. For example, although the rat was in one sense 'taught' to go to one corner of his cage, he did it on the first occasion 'of his own accord'. In other words, we waited for him to do it once, and then, by making a reinforcer dependent upon such behaviour, quickly increased its frequency. Similarly, my students could only make a reinforcer dependent upon my being in a particular part of the room if I went there initially for some unspecified reason. However, the procedure whereby a reinforcer is made dependent upon a pattern of behaviour may also be used most effectively to develop patterns of behaviour which would never otherwise occur at all. Essentially, the 'trainer' builds up a new pattern of behaviour by making reinforcers dependent upon behaviour which gradually approximates to the desired final act. Suppose that we now wish to train our rat to stand on his hind legs in the corner of the cage, a pattern of behaviour which has never previously occurred. This may be shaped up by delivering the reinforcer according to an increasingly strict criterion. At first, a reinforcer is delivered whenever the rat goes to the appropriate corner. Then, when this behaviour is established, the criterion is changed so that the reinforcer is dependent on the rat going to the corner, but holding his head fairly high (perhaps slightly higher than he usually does). As soon as this occurs, the reinforcer is delivered. Then the criterion for reinforcement is adjusted again: the head must now be held a little higher. And so the process continues; now the head higher still, now one fore-paw raised off the floor (an event which is quite likely, since the head is now being thrust into the air), now both fore-paws in the air, and so on until eventually the rat is standing in the required way.

This procedure whereby 'new' behaviour is generated is known as 'successive approximation'. Again, it is strikingly efficient, in terms of the time required to develop such a trick. However, it is a skill on the part of the experimenter (or trainer) to shape the desired behaviour with maximum efficiency. The skill is in adjusting one's sights progressively but not too quickly, and, above all, in being consistent. Inadvertently associating a reinforcer with patterns of behaviour which are not desired can set the process back considerably. So again, this procedure emphasises the power of certain events (reinforcers) to mould and shape behaviour. It also emphasises a further characteristic of reinforcers which has not yet been emphasised, namely that they have their maximum effect on patterns of behaviour with which they are *closely* associated in time. Their effectiveness is greatly reduced if there is a slight delay between the reinforcer and the pattern of behaviour it is desired to develop. This is merely because such a delay ensures that, at the precise moment of delivery, the animal is probably doing something else, and so this *other* behaviour will be strengthened because it is the more closely associated with the reinforcer. This is often particularly noticeable in a successive approximation procedure, when one is attempting to make progressive changes in criteria for the delivery of a reinforcer, and thereby induce progressive changes in behaviour.

The problem of providing *immediate* reinforcement becomes more severe in less controlled situations. Skinner discusses this in a paper entitled 'How to teach animals' (1951), in which he explains how the method of successive approximation may be used to develop tricks in household pets. One simple trick discussed is for a dog to nose a door-handle on the other side of the room, and it is clear that it is difficult to use food as a reinforcer because of the problem of making its delivery *immediately* associated with successive approximations to this behaviour. Skinner suggests that the best way to overcome this difficulty is to incorporate a signal that a reinforcer has been 'earned'. Thus a sharp rap on a table is an environmental event which may be effectively associated with behaviour wherever the dog is in the room. If this noise is first paired with the delivery of snippets of food, so that the animal always come to you for a morsel of food immediately after the signal, this noise will become, according to Skinner, a 'conditioned' reinforcer. The noise acquires the capacity to act as a reinforcer perhaps by reason of its pairings with food (we shall discuss this later). The noise of the food dispenser in the earlier experiments acts in the same way, so that the rat is effectively being reinforced by this noise, the efficiency of the procedure resulting from the fact that the noise can be sounded immediately a pattern of behaviour is deemed to be acceptable for reinforcement. However, the food is still the primary reinforcer in this situation, for if this is withheld the behaviour is not maintained.

The experiments outlined in this chapter have again been extremely simple, and it will be seen that they may be likened to the training of tricks as much as to the development of a science of behaviour. However, they illustrate again the fundamental point that it is useful to consider behaviour in the context of the environment in which it occurs. This is expressed here in terms of the control which may be exerted over behaviour by systematically arranging the relationships between reinforcers and behaviour. This point will be developed further in the following chapters.

CHAPTER 4
Operant conditioning

The simple experiments outlined so far show that behaviour may be regarded as a function of certain environmental events. Thus, these reinforcing events provide the conditions for such behavioural patterns to occur at their particular frequencies. It is but a short step to suggest that the environment *conditions* the behaviour, and these experiments can indeed be regarded as examples of conditioning. In some ways, however, it is unfortunate that the word conditioning carries for most people connotations which go beyond the simple assertion that the environment provides the conditions for behaviour to occur. A view which is currently more familiar implies that the frequency of a pattern of behaviour should always increase above its previous level for the appropriate use of the word. In such a case, conditioning implies a transition or change in behaviour, and so the word has become bracketed with the concept of learning, which undoubtedly does incorporate the idea of a change in behavioural repertoire. As a result, it is often now implied that conditioning and learning are essentially the same, and so we have psychology textbooks which address themselves to problems of 'conditioning and learning'. It may seem that the two concepts differ only in degreee of complexity: humans learn, but rats are conditioned. Alternatively, they may differ in the degree of control exerted: conditioning is an experimental model of learning, so that we learn in the real world, but are conditioned in the laboratory. Another distinction sometimes made implies a value judgement: it is claimed that we learned to do things which are useful or acceptable, but are conditioned to behave in more regrettable ways. It may seem unnecessarily obstinate to swim against the tide of opinion equating conditioning with changes in behaviour, but nevertheless it might be useful to suggest here that patterns of behaviour which occur at a stable frequency may often themselves be as much examples of conditioning as are transitional states. This point will assume more force in the next chapter.

In all the examples discussed so far, behaviour has been seen to interact with the environment in which it occurs. In all these cases, relationships are established (initially either by chance or by design) between the behaviour and environmental events which immediately follow it. This kind of behaviour has been designated *operant behaviour*, a phrase which is attributable to, and closely associated with, B. F. Skinner. Perhaps the best way to describe operant behaviour is by exclusion. There are certain patterns of behaviour which appear to be simple reactions to obvious environmental events which precede them. For example, the pupil of one's eye changes in size as a direct result of the intensity of light falling upon it; this is 'automatic', and, without special training, one is unable to avoid this reaction. To this extent, it is a pattern of behaviour which is exactly the same in all people. Similarly, if dilute concentrations of acid are placed on the tongue (as with lemon juice), one begins to salivate quite automatically or reflexively. The acid is an environmental event which we call a *stimulus*. It precedes the behavioural event which reliably follows it, which may therefore be called a reaction to or *response* to that stimulus. There are many such stimulus-response relationships which can be studied both in animals and man, and they seem to provide the clearest examples of creatures behaving as machines in the sense suggested by Descartes, that is, according to their natures. However, it is not easy to characterise the behaviour in the superstition experiments discussed earlier in terms of a stimulus eliciting a response in this way. The behaviour does not appear to be a response at all in this sense, although it is certainly the result of previous coincidental relationships between it and a reinforcer. There is no stimulus which reliably precedes the behaviour. This kind of behaviour is defined as operant in nature by Skinner. Operant behaviours are which in everyday speech we often find it natural to talk ut as resulting from purposes, desires and so on. They seem to emanate in some way from within the behaver rather than being prodded out of him by an eliciting stimulus. In Skinner's terms, they are *emitted* rather than elicited.

The combination of the words *operant* and *conditioning* have come to characterise an area of research in psychology which owes much to the pioneering theoretical and experimental work of Skinner. This research is essentially the systematic development of the principles which have already been introduced to the reader in the earlier parts of this book. Operant conditioning is an experimental analysis of the ways in which the behaviour which is emitted rather than elicited by external stimuli may nevertheless be a function of environmental events. Much of this approach to psychology has been achieved by the exhaustive study of the ways in which the emitted behaviour of animals in experimental situations comes under the control of different arrangements of reinforcers.

The typical operant conditioning experiment specifies the form of behaviour which is to be associated with a reinforcer, rather than allowing the reinforcer to have coincidental relationships with any pattern of behaviour. To this extent, the experiments are similar to those discussed in the previous chapter. However, instead of developing interesting tricks, a pattern of behaviour is sought which it is possible to record easily and which the subject may emit as frequently as he 'wishes'. This has resulted in the detailed study of rather arbitrary patterns of behaviour which happen to be convenient both to experimenter and subject. In the case of rats and monkeys, this is to be found in the form of a press on a lever; with pigeons, a peck on a disc. So an experiment may investigate the effects of reinforcers which are dependent on a rat's lever-presses, these effects being expressed in terms of the *frequency* with which the lever is pressed. Of course, one is not suggesting that wild rats in their 'real' world go about pressing levers. However, it is argued that these patterns of behaviour may be taken as a model for other patterns of more 'normal' activity. The lever-press and the peck at a disc are operants, because this behaviour cannot be readily identified as being elicited by a preceding stimulus in the way that acid precedes salivation. Lever-pressing and key-pecking are initially emitted in the experimental situation at a fairly low (but nevertheless detectable) rate. They may therefore be suitable for an intensive study, in the hope of isolating descriptive laws for operant behaviour in general.

These arbitrary patterns of behaviour have been chosen for two other practical reasons. First, they are without doubt patterns of behaviour which a rat or pigeon is capable of performing very frequently, hardly ever, or at any intermediate frequency. As we shall see, in appropriate circumstances such an act may be performed as often as one hundred times per minute over a period of several hours, or as rarely as once every two or three minutes (or even, of course, not at all), depending on the circumstances. We have seen earlier that reinforcers affect the frequency of patterns of operant behaviour with which they are associated, and these arbitrary bits of behaviour have the great advantage of providing considerable scope for such frequencies to change. The second reason for choosing them is no less important, although it may not at first seem so fundamental to the reader. A press on a lever, or a peck on a disc, is a behavioural event which it is easy for an experimenter to detect and to monitor automatically. Both acts can be made to close a small switch, which may complete an electrical circuit. With appropriate devices, one can count the number of occurrences of the behavioural act with little effort, but with complete reliability. This makes it possible to expose the subjects to the experimental conditions for long periods of time, perhaps even continuously, so that there is full scope for the effects of reinforcers to develop. But, just as important, the automatic monitoring of the behaviour makes it possible to establish a standard criterion as to whether the act has occurred or not. The closure of the electrical switch associated with the lever, for example, is achieved by moving the lever through a pre-arranged and constant distance. This has considerable advantages, because it would be difficult for any experimenter to decide for himself whether one lever-press was identical to the previous example, or whether it resulted in sufficient movement of the lever to qualify as the act. Automatic apparatus has no difficulty in this respect: as soon as the switch is closed, the behaviour is counted, and if the switch is not closed (perhaps because of a partial lever-press), the behaviour is disregarded. A final advantage with automatic apparatus is that a reinforcer may be made to occur *immediately* the behavioural criterion is reached, by triggering its delivery from the electrical switch associated with the lever or disc.

A typical arrangement for an operant conditioning experiment with rats takes the form of a small test chamber with a lever protruding from one wall. Near the lever is mounted a small hopper or well, to which pellets of food may be delivered. For a rat which has been deprived of food for a while, delivery of such pellets will act as a reinforcer, and this can be made immediately dependent upon a lever-press. Such immediacy of reinforcement assures the maximum effectiveness for the study. The pellets of food used in experiments with rats usually weigh about 45 mg. and are made from standard rat food. Rats are able to eat at least 150 of these pellets without becoming satiated. With pigeons, food reinforcers take the form of limited periods of access to a hopper full of food, which is presented through an aperture in the wall of the test cage, perhaps for three or five seconds.

The nature of the reinforcer studied in operant conditioning experiments is also somewhat arbitrary, usually being food or water for suitably deprived subjects. Again, this reflects a decision to use a reinforcer whose effects are likely to be maximal, and one for which the appropriate antecedent conditions may be easily specified and varied. However, the experimenter would argue that in using such a reinforcer he is studying the effects of just one example of such events. In fact, the test situation itself is such that it is ideal for examining whether certain other events qualify as reinforcers.

The test cages for operant conditioning experiments normally contain a number of additional features. For example, one or two small loudspeakers may be mounted next to the cage, and also various lights, which may be illuminated at appropriate times. In the case of pigeon experiments in particular, the lights are often placed behind the transparent disc at which the bird pecks, so that this disc may be illuminated in various colours (or even with patterns) as required by the experimental programme. Finally, in some experiments it is necessary to be able to deliver controlled aversive events to the subject — for example, in order to measure the effects of punishment procedures on operant behaviour, a topic which is discussed later. In such a case, the test cage sometimes incorporates a floor made from grids which may be briefly electrified. Obviously, the test cage will vary according to the requirements of the experiment, but the above description should give a general indication. It might also be noted before leaving the 'working' end of the experimental arrangements that the whole test cage is usually placed within another chamber, which is well-ventilated but which nevertheless attenuates sounds. This is so that the test animal is not disturbed in any way by uncontrolled extraneous sounds.

The experimental arrangements themselves are usually auto-mated, and this makes it possible to investigate complex interrelationships between operant behaviour and environmental events. As these complexities increase, there is a growing tendency for the experiments to be placed under the direct control of a small digital computer; however, conventional electro-mechanical programming apparatus is more typical. Timers and switches may be programmed in any way desired in order to establish the experimental relationships under investiga-tion. As a brief indication of how this is done, a timer may be interposed between the closure of the electrical switch associated with a rat's lever and the delivery of food; in this way, we could investigate the detrimental effects of a delay between a pattern of behaviour (the lever-press) and the delivery of a reinforcer which were mentioned in the previous chapter. Operant condi-tioning laboratories also usually include a number of recording devices, such as counters for accumulating the number of lever-presses in given periods of time and devices which record the passage of time. A device known as a cumulative recorder is frequently used so routinely for the presentation of results that we should discuss its functioning in detail.

A cumulative recorder is designed to produce graphs automatic-ally of the experimental animal's performance in the test cage. A roll of paper is fed out from the recorder at a constant speed and has a pen resting on it. Each time the animal presses its lever or pecks its key, the pen is stepped a predetermined distance at right angles across the paper. So on the graph which is plotted, time is expressed along the length of the paper and operant acts accumulate across its width (see Fig. 2). The more frequently the animal performs the act being studied, the more acts will occur per unit of time, and therefore the steeper will be the line drawn across the paper. The record is usually displayed in such a way that each step produced by the operant behaviour moves the pen upwards in the vertical direction, and one records the passage of

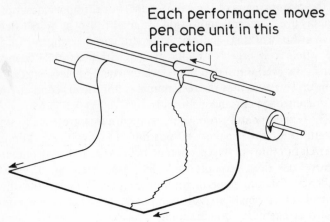

Each performance moves
pen one unit in this
direction

Figure 2   Schematic diagram of a cumulative recorder. From Ferster and Perrott (1968).

time from left to right. The pen may be reset to its resting position at any time, but will in any case reset automatically if it makes a complete excursion across the paper. The final point to be noticed is that the pen may be flicked to produce a small diagonal mark on the cumulative record; this may be used to indicate the occurrence of other events, usually the delivery of reinforcers.

The most important reason why operant conditioning experiments are often reported with extensive cumulative records is because each record is an uncontaminated account of an individual animal's behaviour over relatively long periods of time. We shall see that such records reveal a remarkable degree of consistency, and it is also probably the pride of the experimenters at producing such orderly behavioural data which has led to this form of presentation becoming almost an essential part of any report in this area of research.

Some simple cumulative records are shown in Fig. 3, which is reproduced from an early experiment by Skinner (see Skinner, 1938). These records illustrate the way in which five food-deprived rats begin to press a lever when each lever-press is immediately followed by food for the first time. Each press stepped the pen, but no marks were made to denote reinforcement, since each press was followed by a reinforcer in any case.

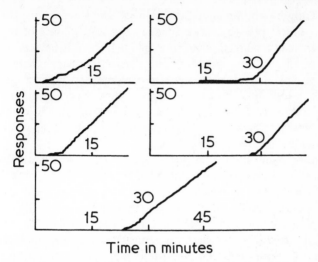

Figure 3   Cumulative records showing the acquisition of lever-pressing (responses) behaviour by rats. From Skinner (1938).

These records provide support for the findings discussed in the previous chapter when reinforcement was made independent upon a particular act (approaching one corner of the cage). In Skinner's experiment, the rats had been previously trained to approach and eat food as soon as it was delivered; at the beginning of the experimental sessions whose records are shown, the delivery of food was made dependent upon a lever press for the first time. The records show that there was a variable period of time before the first lever press was emitted, but thereafter there was a fairly abrupt transition to a consistent rate of lever pressing, as shown by the sudden change from a horizontal record to a sloped line. Some rats pressed more frequently than others after this transition, thereby plotting steeper lines on the record; this may have resulted from a difference in the speed with which the rats ate the food. One animal did not show the abrupt transition to a consistent rate of pressing until after the second or third reinforcer. Skinner made a number of interesting points about these records, perhaps the most important being his suggestion that these animals did not show the gradual change in behaviour as a result of reinforcement which has so often been regarded as typical of any learning process (the so-called 'learning curve'). Only by combining all the animals, and by reporting the number of lever presses overall in each successive minute of the experiment can a gradual acquisition of the learned behaviour be suggested. Clearly this would be an abstraction which hardly applied to any individual animals from whose performance the aggregate curve was drawn up. So in this experiment, any learning curve would merely be an artefact of the different periods between the start of the experiment and the time when each individual rat first pressed the lever.

A further point should be made about Fig. 3, which is here reproduced as it was originally presented by Skinner. The vertical axis of this diagram is labelled in terms of 'responses'. Earlier, some care was taken to point out that an act of operant behaviour could not readily be characterised as a response to any identifiable stimulus; these acts were emitted rather than elicited. However, it must now be admitted that units of operant behaviour have nevertheless come to be known as 'responses'. Thus, one lever press or one key peck is usually known as an operant response, although it is in response to nothing. This paradox is unfortunate, but is now an entrenched usage which we shall be unable to avoid in discussing operant conditioning. It would perhaps have been better if units of operant behaviour had been known as 'acts' or even 'bits'; indeed, an argument might readily be developed that Skinner's contribution to psychology has been repeatedly misunderstood because of his use of the word response. In operant conditioning experiments, a 'response' is merely a unit of behaviour, and not a reaction elicited by a stimulus.

The above should not be taken to imply that environmental events other than reinforcers are unimportant in operant conditioning experiments; on the contrary, they are of the utmost importance. To take a simple example, if we were to mount in the experimental animal's *home* cage an ineffective lever, one on which a press had no consequence, the animal would certainly not press it consistently just because pressing the similar lever in the test cage was followed by food. In other words, the test cage provides a situation which sets the occasion for such behaviour to be reinforced. The importance of setting the occasion appropriately is illustrated in a different way in Fig. 4. This is a cumulative record of a rat's operant lever pressing behaviour in a test cage. It may be seen immediately that this animal sometimes

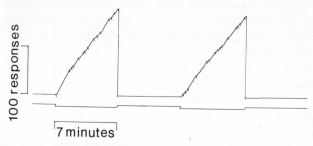

Figure 4 Cumulative record of lever pressing by a rat in the presence and the absence of a noise stimulus. Small diagonal marks denote reinforcement, and the noise was present when the lower line is displaced downwards.

emits such responses at a consistent rate, but that at other times he emits none at all, thereby allowing the perfectly horizontal sections of this record to be drawn. This behaviour also reflects the importance of environmental events other than reinforcers in operant conditioning experiments, for in this case seven-minute periods of noise (from the speaker in the test cage) were mixed at random with similar periods during which no noise was present. The noise periods are shown in Fig. 4 on the additional line below the cumulative record itself; when this line is displaced and held downwards, the noise was on. The cumulative recorder was reset automatically at the end of every seven-minute period. Clearly, the animal's operant behaviour (lever pressing) occurred almost exclusively in the presence of noise, its frequency being almost zero in the other periods. This is because lever presses were followed by a reinforcer (food) only when the noise was present. The delivery of a reinforcer is shown by the small diagonal marks on the record, and it is clear that not every lever press in the presence of the noise was followed by a reinforcer in this experiment. The reasons for such a procedure will become clearer later. When there was no noise, the rat could still press the lever as often as 'he liked', but such behaviour was never followed by a reinforcer. The record shows that the animal eventually discriminated these two conditions, by behaving appropriately at any given moment. So in this case, the noise sets the occasion for sustained responding. Any feature of the environment which acts in this way is known as a *discriminative stimulus*. The use of such a stimulus in the experiment illustrated in Fig. 4 makes it possible for the experimenter effectively to turn on and off the lever-pressing behaviour of the rat at will by presenting or taking away the noise — this in spite of the fact that the lever is available to the animal throughout the entire experimental session, and may therefore be pressed at any time.

If an animal is reinforced for pressing a lever, and is then transferred to a situation in which lever presses are no longer followed by a reinforcer, the operant behaviour shows a progressive decrease in its rate of emission, until eventually it returns to its original frequency. This is called an *extinction* procedure. In Fig. 4, the rat's lever pressing has extinguished in this way when no noise was present, for reinforcements were never delivered in this condition of the experiment.

The term *conditioning* is often associated with the name of Pavlov, a Russian physiologist who did a great deal to establish a science of behaviour at the beginning of this century. It may therefore be appropriate at this stage to consider briefly the relationships between operant conditioning and Pavlov's experiments, which are now often described as *classical conditioning*, for they are often confused by the layman. In embarking upon such a comparison, it must be stressed immediately that we are entering an exceedingly controversial and complex field, for psychologists have for long been arguing about this problem, sometimes from a theoretical point of view, and sometimes on the basis of experimental findings.

The typical experiment in classical conditioning is that in which Pavlov conditioned dogs to salivate to the sound of a bell (see Pavlov, 1927). This was achieved quite simply by ringing the bell before food was given. When food is placed in the mouth, it acts as an eliciting stimulus for salivation. The experimental procedure resulted in the dogs' salivating to a new stimulus, before the arrival of the stimulus which had previously been the only one to produce that response (although it should be noted that salivation continued to be produced by the food throughout the experiment). It is important to recognise that food was delivered to the dogs in this experiment regardless of whether or not the animal had salivated at the sound of the bell, so the conditioned salivation to this stimulus was in no sense instrumental in obtaining the food. A generalised description of Pavlov's experiment is therefore as follows:— independently of behaviour, one stimulus (known as the unconditional stimulus — US) is reliably preceded by another (the conditional stimulus — CS); as a result, the response previously elicited by the US (known as the unconditioned response — UR) apparently becomes elicited by the CS (and then becomes known as the conditioned response — CR).

Pavlov's procedure differs in two prominent ways from the operant conditioning experiments described earlier; it has no dependency programmed between behaviour and the environment, and it studies patterns of behaviour which are initially elicited by an easily identifiable stimulus, whereas operant behaviour is emitted in the absence of such a stimulus. Both these differences have provided topics for much discussion, and they will therefore be briefly considered here.

Classical conditioning experiments operate entirely independently of behaviour, at least from a procedural point of view. A succession of stimuli is presented in the form of a pre-arranged sequence which is uninterrupted by any behaviour. In operant conditioning experiments, on the other hand, what happens to the animal depends critically on what he *does*; if he presses the lever, food is delivered, but if he does not behave in this way, no reinforcer is forthcoming. So the experimental events cannot be predicted in advance in the same way as in classical conditioning. It is often said that operant behaviour is instrumental in producing certain consequences, an allusion to the term *instrumental conditioning*, which is wider than, but includes, operant conditioning. The very word instrumental emphasises the dependencies between behaviour and environment in such experiments. However, it was seen earlier in this book that these dependencies are not absolutely necessary for a pattern of operant behaviour to be increased and maintained in frequency by a reinforcer, for in the experiments on 'superstition' in animals, relationships between behaviour and reinforcers were intially coincidental, and no dependency was explicitly programmed. Yet such experiments are invariably discussed in the context of operant, not classical, conditioning. There is a confusion here, for operant conditioners have developed a rather jargonistic phrase 'contingencies of reinforcement' which has been used very freely (there is, for example, a book by that name — Skinner, 1969a); however, the phrase is often, in fact usually, interpreted to imply a *dependency* between behaviour and a reinforcer. It is important to isolate the precise relationships between behaviour and environment which are important in the analysis of behaviour, and in fact the most direct meaning of contingency (i.e., touching together) seems quite appropriate, for even though a dependency may be programmed by the experimenter, the 'touching' of behaviour and environmental events may be sufficient for the effects of a reinforcer to develop. So a dependency may merely ensure that the contacts between behaviour and environment do not vary, and that the behaviour to be modified is determined by the experimenter rather than by chance. 'Superstition' (with no dependency) is just as much an example of operant conditioning as the response-dependent studies outlined in this chapter.

The above discussion emphasises, of course, that there is a certain procedural similarity between experiments on 'superstition' and classical conditioning experiments, for in both cases specified stimuli (the reinforcer and the US) occur independently of behaviour. However, in the latter experiments, an additional stimulus (the CS) also occurs independently of behaviour, though in a consistent relationship to the US. This suggests that classical conditioning is essentially the pairing of one stimulus with another, but that operant conditioning involves the pairing of one stimulus with behaviour. Such a distinction between the two procedures has indeed sometimes been offered, but it may tend to hide a rather important point. In the *classical* conditioning experiment, the relationship between the US and *behaviour* may be a substantial contributory factor in the results, for as soon as salivation, for example, begins to occur to the bell, then the relationships between that behaviour and food are such for the behaviour to be 'superstitiously' developed and maintained — in which case, some classical conditioning experiments might to a large extent be poorly controlled observations of superstitiously maintained 'instrumental' conditioning.

The second apparent difference between classical and operant conditioning experiments centres on the different types of behaviour involved in the two procedures. In the case of classical conditioning, one begins with an unconditional response which is reliably elicited by a stimulus programmed in the experiment. In operant conditioning, on the other hand, one either has to wait for the 'response' to occur by chance in order to follow it by a reinforcer, or one has to coax an entirely new 'response' from the animal by means of successive approximation techniques (which themselves depend at the outset on some spontaneously occurring pattern of behaviour which one can develop). The distinction between these two types of behaviour has been discussed at a theoretical level, and the terms *elicit* and *emit* have in fact been taken from Skinner's comparisons (e.g., Skinner, 1938). However, the discussions have gone beyond this, and it has been suggested that the reactions which can be conditioned by means of Pavlov's procedures are the behaviour of the autonomic nervous system. This is, in general terms, the part of our physiological system which successfully keeps us alive without our having to pay attention to what we are doing, so to speak. The autonomic nervous system is responsible for regulating our bodily functions, for the distribution of supplies of nutrients throughout the body, for the digestive processes, for the working of the heart, for our glandular reactions, and so on. These reactions of our body occur automatically, and adjust delicately to different internal or external conditions, thereby maintaining our internal environment in a sensitive state of equilibrium. Operant behaviour, on the other hand, is usually behaviour which acts on our external environment, such as 'deliberate' movements of our skeletal system. If it were established, as was thought until quite recently, that classical conditioning procedures modify only the activities of the autonomic nervous system and instrumental conditioning modifies only the movements of the skeletal system, and that these effects were mutually exclusive, then the interesting suggestion might be made that classical conditioning is associated with Descartes' animal nature, but that instrumental, or operant, conditioning modifies the acts said to be prompted by our rational souls.

Although this last suggestion may be appealing, it cannot be confidently sustained in the light of recent work. It implies that the behaviour of the autonomic nervous system is unaffected by instrumental conditioning procedures. Thus, for example, if one waits for 'spontaneous' salivation (which does sometimes occur) instead of eliciting it by an obvious stimulus, one should be unable to increase this 'response' merely by associating it with a proven reinforcer. If this were true, the earlier suggestion that 'superstition' might be a contaminating influence in classical conditioning experiments could hardly be maintained. However it is not the case, for Carmona and N. Miller (1967) carried out exactly the experiment outlined above, associating water with spontaneous increases in salivation by dogs deprived of water. The result was an appreciable increase in the amount of salivation. The suggestion inherent in this work has recently been the subject of an intensive research programme by Miller and his associates (see Miller, 1969). In the previous experiment, the possibility could not be ruled out that the apparent instrumental conditioning of salivation was a side-effect of reinforcer-dependent changes in skeletal activity which themselves affected salivation; in this case, the experiment would not be crucial, for the results would be contaminated. In order to overcome such possible objections, Miller designed experiments which involve a degree of control which may limit their immediate impact for the general reader. Nevertheless, his findings have enormous implications, especially for psychosomatic medicine. Miller used rats in his experiments, and in order to ensure that no skeletal activity might interfere with his results, he administered curare to them. This substance has the effect of completely paralysing the skeletal musculature, without depriving the animal of its 'consciousness'. To keep these rats alive, Miller had to respirate them artificially. Clearly such a preparation presents very great difficulties when it comes to selecting an appropriate reinforcer, for the animal is unable to swallow or move in any way. This problem was overcome by giving the rats very brief and very slight shocks directly to a part of the brain where this had previously been shown to be a reinforcer for rats (by making such shocks dependent on lever presses, for example, it has been found that lever pressing is maintained for very long periods of time at very high frequencies: e.g., Olds, 1956). This stimulation could therefore act as a reinforcer in the technical sense for the immobilised rats, since no skeletal movement is necessary for it to have its effect. Miller therefore made its delivery dependent on various unelicited changes in the activity of the rats' autonomic nervous systems. In some experiments, he additionally used a technique of successive approximation in an attempt to shape up large differences in such activity. As a result, Miller and his associates have been able to condition either increases or decreases in heart rate, according to which direction of change was associated with the dependent reinforcer. They have also demonstrated reinforcement-dependent effects on intestinal motility, on blood pressure, and even on the rate of urine formation by the kidney.

These technically demanding experiments demonstrate, it is claimed, that autonomic nervous system functioning may be affected by conditioning procedures which make reinforcers dependent on changes in such behaviour. So it is difficult to adhere to a distinction between classical and operant conditioning procedures in terms of the different behavioural systems which they have in the past been assumed to affect.

In an introduction of this nature, it is not necessary to consider these complex problems in more detail, and so we cannot give a definitive answer to questions concerning the relationships between typical operant and classical conditioning experiments. At the very least, the above discussion indicates the dangers of assuming that all conditioning experiments are basically similar. Therefore, operant conditioning techniques should not be regarded as a simple variation on the early work carried out by Pavlov. The experiments reviewed in this book are within the *operant* conditioning tradition, in which the frequency of skeletal acts is studied in situations in which reinforcers are usually made dependent in some way on those acts.

CHAPTER 5

Four basic schedules of reinforcement

In many ways, the most interesting results in operant conditioning experiments appear when the reinforcers no longer follow all,
but only some of, the emitted acts whose frequency is being
studied. In Fig. 4 (p. 47) for example, it may be seen that lever
pressing behaviour occurred at a fairly high frequency whenever
the discriminative stimulus (the noise) was present, even though
very few of these responses were followed by a reinforcer, as
denoted by the diagonal marks on the cumulative record. During
the three seven-minute periods of noise shown on that record,
only 43 pellets of food were delivered in all, although the rat
emitted many more responses. The behaviour produced in
circumstances like these is said to be maintained by a schedule of
intermittent reinforcement, and many different arrangements for
delivering a reinforcer intermittently have been investigated in
operant conditioning experiments. Indeed, in some observers'
eyes, studying the effects of different schedules for their own
sake has become the hallmark of an operant conditioner. This is
unfortunate, for it is not only the behavioural effects of these
procedures which are important, but also the use which may be
made of the various patterns of behaviour which the different
schedules control. In this chapter, the effects of some of the

more basic schedules of reinforcement will be discussed and
described.

At one time it was conventional to suggest that there are
basically two types of intermittent schedule. In the first, the
reinforcement follows a lever press as a function of how many
times that act has been performed. For example, the experimenter may decide to programme his apparatus so that only
every tenth response is followed by a reinforcer. In making this
decision, he is effectively specifying a ratio between responses
and reinforcements, and for this reason, such arrangements are
known as *ratio schedules.* If this ratio is specified as invariant (as
here), the schedule is further described as fixed. Thus the
schedule described above would be defined as a *fixed ratio*
of ten, usually abbreviated as FR10. So with FR20, every
twentieth lever press is immediately followed by a reinforcer. In
Fig. 5, the cumulative records obtained from one rat exposed to
such a schedule are shown. These records show the performance

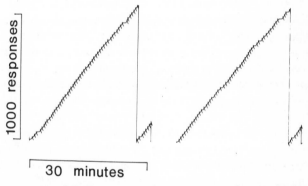

Figure 5   Cumulative records of a rat's fixed ratio behaviour
(FR20).

of this animal in two successive experimental sessions. Each
session ended after the 62nd reinforcement (an apparently
strange decision which was justifiable in terms of the details of
the experiment, which will not be discussed here). The first
comment to be made concerns the similarity of these two
records. This shows the degree to which the rat's lever pressing
behaviour had become predictable as a function of his previous
exposure to this schedule of reinforcement. This is an important

point, and will be implied in the discussion throughout this chapter. It may be generalised by the assertion that a given schedule of reinforcement develops characteristic control over an animal's operant behaviour. In the case of Fig. 5, this control is shown to be consistent, in that the animal's lever-pressing behaviour does not differ substantially from one session to the next. Each of these records is also characteristic of the effects of fixed ratio schedules with specifications such as this. They show that the rat presses the lever at a rather high frequency until a reinforcement is delivered (shown by the diagonal marks); thereafter there is invariably a pause in responding (denoted by the horizontal sections of the record), followed by a relatively sudden transition to the high rate of responding again. In this case, the overall rate of responding is approximately 40 per minute, but of course, if one disregards the time spent after each reinforcement when no responses are emitted at all, the 'running' rate of responding is considerably higher, approximating 80 per minute in fact.

Such behaviour is typical of that generated by fixed ratio schedules using many different species as subject. So it is possible to describe the patterns of behaviour generated by these schedules in terms of a post-reinforcement pause in responding, followed by a sudden transition to a sustained 'run' of responses until the next reinforcement is delivered. It has been reported (Felton and Lyon, 1964) that the duration of the post-reinforcement pause in responding is a function of the size of the ratio requirement. With pigeons acting as subjects, this pause was of the order of four or five seconds on average when the fixed ratio was 50; when the schedule was changed to FR150, however, the average pause was as long as a minute or so. With intermediate ratio requirements, intermediate pause lengths were observed. However, with all these schedules, the 'running' rate of responding was approximately constant (about 150 key presses per minute). These data show that the post-reinforcement pauses shown in Fig. 5 cannot be regarded as merely the time taken for the rat to eat the food which has just been delivered; indeed, on other schedules of reinforcement, rats do not allow the ingestion of their food-pellets to interfere with their lever pressing at all. So, the pauses in responding after a reinforcement must be regarded as a function of the fixed ratio schedule requirements. They have also been shown to be a function of the prior deprivation conditions to which the subjects are exposed (Sidman and Stebbins, 1954).

It should be explained that animals are not normally transferred to a high fixed ratio requirement direct from a situation in which each operant response is followed by reinforcement (FR1 — also known as continuous reinforcement, or CRF). A procedure which is reminiscent of successive approximation is usually employed, whereby the ratio requirement is increased progressively as a function of the animal's performance. If this is done carefully, remarkably high fixed ratios may sustain operant behaviour. In one of his papers, Skinner (1957a) shows cumulative records of a pigeon's performance on an FR900 schedule of reinforcement; clearly, such an enormous ratio requirement would have to be built up progressively, for the behaviour of any animal placed on such a schedule directly after continuous reinforcement would inevitably extinguish through lack of reinforcers.

In the case of animals with which a fixed ratio is successfully established, the effects of discontinuing reinforcement completely are interesting, taking the form of periods of rapid responding interspersed with pauses which become longer and longer (Ferster and Skinner, 1957).

We shall return later to a discussion of why these characteristic patterns of behaviour develop when animals are trained on fixed ratio schedules. However, before leaving this schedule, it might be useful to note that FR requirements may find an analogy in human behaviour in the method of payment in industry known as piecework. Here, men or women receive their pay as a function of the amount of work they do. We must be careful in making this analogy too readily, for these people are usually paid at a pre-arranged time on the basis of how much work has been done, whereas the rat in Fig. 5 received his 'payment' solely at the completion of each block of 20 responses. However, the analogy may encourage us to consider whether the frenetic work patterns which employers may hope to be typical of piecework industries (equivalent to the rat's run of responses?) may be preceded by a low level of work (the post-reinforcement pause?) as a direct result of their method of payment. Another superficial example of an FR schedule in human behaviour may be found in writing 'lines' as a punishment in school, where the consequences depend upon a specified amount of work being emitted. Casual observation suggests that such punishment sessions may begin with prolonged pauses (often accompanied by depression or anger on the part of the detainee), followed by a sustained emission of words at a fairly high frequency. One additional finding from animal work may also be important. Appel (1963a) has reported that his experimental subjects exposed to a fixed ratio schedule would reliably press a second lever in order to switch off the schedule of reinforcement completely! Although his animals were deprived of food, they learned to deprive themselves of the opportunity to work for a food reinforcer on a fixed-ratio schedule; on such occasions, the response on the second lever turned off the discriminative stimulus associated with the schedule for a period of time, so that responses of the first lever had no programmed consequence. Although the reasons for this phenomenon have not yet been fully identified, the finding is suggestive indeed in the context of human performances which appear similar to fixed ratio schedules.

In a second type of ratio schedule, the requirement is specified in terms of an average rather than as a fixed quantity. These are defined as *variable ratio* schedules, abbreviated as VR. For example, if an animal is exposed to VR20, this means that the overall ratio of responses to reinforcements will be 20 : 1. Sometimes, however, the animal will be required to emit perhaps only 2 or 3 responses between one reinforcement and the next, while at other times perhaps as many as 40 or 50 responses will intervene between successive reinforcements. The operant behaviour generated by such schedules of reinforcement is typified by sustained high rates of response emission. An example of such behaviour is shown in Fig. 6, which is the cumulative record of a rat exposed to VR60. In this case, the vertical scale is quite small, and the delivery of reinforcers (food) is shown by small marks in the usual way. The pen was reset automatically at the end of every eight minutes. In this case, the record is condensed into a more compact form than seen before in this book. This is achieved by cutting out the white space between one segment of the record and the next, which results from the vertical reset movement of the pen. The second segment of record is then shifted left into this space, thereby 'collapsing' the segments onto each other. In this way, 32 minutes of record (in this case) may be condensed into a fairly narrow diagram, but each segment remains completely uncontaminated by any experimental inter-

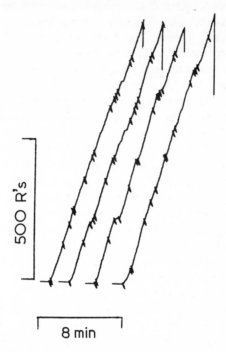

Figure 6   Cumulative record of variable ratio behaviour (VR60).

vention. Such a procedure is common in presenting cumulative records, because of its obvious economy of space, which makes it possible to put more information into a diagram. Now that these procedural modifications have been explained, the patterns of behaviour generated by this VR60 schedule may be discussed. Clearly, the rate of response emission is high; over 3,600 lever presses are recorded in these 32 minutes, the mean overall response rate being in fact a little less than 120 per minute. By the nature of this schedule, this ensured that reinforcement delivery occurred a little less than twice per minute on average, but the records clearly show how irregularly spaced these events were. Notice that there are no appreciable post-reinforcement pauses in responding, in contrast to the effects of FR schedules discussed earlier.

Again, such general patterns of behaviour have been found to be typical of the effects of variable ratio schedules. These schedules usually generate and maintain consistent high rates of responding. One obvious point that should be made is that any animal which responds in such a way on a VR schedule is behaving in an eminently rational way, for the number of reinforcements obtained depends merely on the number of responses emitted. Pigeons are so 'sensible' in this respect that they may emit as many as 15 pecks per second on such a schedule! (Reynolds, 1968).

As with fixed ratio schedules, variable ratio requirements of any size are usually built up slowly by the experimenter. An animal may be trained to emit responses on a continuous reinforcement schedule, then transferred to a VR4 perhaps; when his behaviour is being sustained at a reasonably high frequency by this schedule, the requirement may be increased to 8, and so on. Using such a procedure, very high ratios may be reached, even higher than with fixed ratio schedules. Indeed, it has been reported that an animal will work so hard on a large variable ratio schedule that he may operate at a net loss in terms of energy expended balanced again the food obtained (e.g., Skinner, 1957a).

When animals which have been trained on VR schedules of reinforcement are transferred to an extinction condition in which reinforcements are withheld, the patterns of behaviour are essentially similar to those noted for fixed ratio extinction procedures – periods of sustained high rates of responding now become progressively shorter, but they alternate with increasing periods of no responding at all.

There is one situation in the real world of humans which may bear an uncomfortable similarity to these variable ratio schedules and their effects on behaviour, namely the fruit machine or 'one-armed bandit' which is found so frequently in our society. The very use of the word bandit implies a belief that the machines are more likely to profit in the long run than are its users; and the machines would scarcely survive if such were not the case. Yet they are used enthusiastically by people, many of whom would not gamble in other ways. Many punters have developed stunning techniques for operating the machines quickly. The variable ratio schedules programming these fruit-machines are certainly effective in sustaining high rates of responding in a situation of net loss to an individual, and this analogy has been made many times. However, once more we should not be too ready to claim that the variable ratio behaviour of the rat or pigeon is similar in every way to this pattern of human behaviour, for the latter has the additional complication that successive gamblers use the machines, each one hoping that he will be luckier than his predecessor. Nevertheless, the similarity is sobering, and the author has noticed that not many of his operant conditioning colleagues seem to be tempted by fruit machines.

The two general schedules of intermittent reinforcement discussed so far both share the feature that the frequency or number of reinforcements depends on the frequency or number of responses. Such ratio schedules have usually been distinguished from arrangements whereby the availability of a reinforcer is determined by time rather than by the amount of preceding behaviour. With *interval* schedules of reinforcement, a maximum frequency of reinforcement is specified. Such schedules are defined in terms of fixed or variable intervals.

A *fixed interval* (FI) schedule specifies that a fixed period of time must elapse from the delivery of one reinforcer to the availability of the next. The delivery of a particular reinforcer is still dependent upon the emission of the operant response chosen for study, but with an FI 10 minute schedule, for example, the response which is followed by a reinforcer will be the first response to occur after ten minutes have elapsed since the previous reinforced response. The animal may emit no other responses at all between these two reinforced operants, or may emit several hundred, without affecting in any way the minimum time which must elapse between them. The behaviour typically resulting from such a schedule is shown in Fig. 7, which is an extract from a cumulative record produced by a rat on an FI 3 minutes schedule of food reinforcement; the delivery of reinforcement is shown by the small diagonal marks. Clearly, the overall rate of responding is very much lower in this Figure than in either of the preceding cumulative records. Moreover, the behaviour between reinforcements often shows a gradual and systematic change which was not seen with either of the ratio schedules. After a reinforcement, there is typically a pause, as with fixed *ratio* schedules; however, this is followed not by the sudden transition to high rates of responding seen with FR, but by a slow and rather delicately progressive increase in response rate. Eventually, a fairly moderate rate of responding is sustained

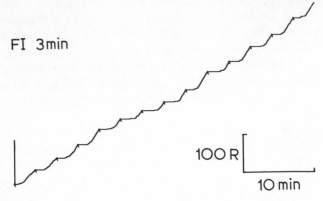

Figure 7   Cumulative record of a rat's behaviour maintained by a fixed interval 3 minute schedule, showing typical 'scallops' between reinforcements. By permission of G. V. Thomas.

until the next reinforcement is obtained. In the case of the rat in Fig. 7, the overall rate of responding is approximately 10 per minute, but clearly this information is far less meaningful than the response rate data given for the variable ratio schedule. Overall response rates are not very good descriptions of typical FI behaviour, because the rate of responding changes systematically during each interval between reinforcements. Once again, this performance must be described as suited to the circumstances, for the rat does not 'bother' to press the lever just after a reinforcement has been obtained, because the occurrence of that event means that no other reinforcement may be obtained for some time; but as time passes his operant behaviour increases in frequency, until the final sustained rate of responding ensures that the next reinforcement is secured almost as soon as it is made available by the schedule (this availability is not signalled to the animal in any way).

Cumulative records such as those shown in Fig. 7 are frequently referred to as 'scalloped', in order to emphasise the systematic changes in response rate between one reinforcement and the next. Such scalloped records are often referred to as the typical results of fixed interval schedules, but in a number of experiments, continued training with such a schedule has resulted in the scallop giving way to a rather more abrupt transition from a response rate of zero to the moderate rate of responding just

FI 3 min

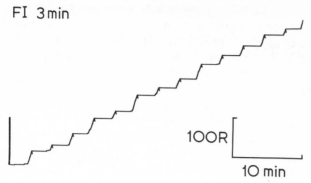

Figure 8   'Break and run' behaviour on an FI 3 min. schedule.
By permission of G. V. Thomas.

before reinforcement (e.g. Schneider, 1969). The reasons determining whether the scallop should be superceded by this 'break
and run' pattern of behaviour in some experiments have not been
adequately defined at present, but the latter pattern has been
observed in the writer's laboratory by G. V. Thomas. Figure 8
shows such a 'break and run' behaviour on an FI 3 minute
schedule; this record was obtained from the same rat as was Fig.
7, but from a later experimental session. Such behaviour appears
in some senses reminiscent of the typical fixed ratio records,
except, of course, that the running response rate is very much
lower. Data such as these suggest that the scalloped pattern of
responding is not necessarily typical of fixed interval behaviour,
as is sometimes suggested. However, they in no sense affect the
observation that animals adjust their behaviour sensitively to the
temporal requirements of fixed interval schedules. In all cases,
their behaviour takes the form of an appreciable pause after a
reinforcement and a moderate rate of responding at the time the
next reinforcement becomes available.
    Again, the patterns of behaviour described above for fixed
interval schedules may be taken as typical of the behavioural
effects of such schedules with a wide variety of intervals, and
with a wide variety of species as experimental subjects. The
method for establishing the final patterns of behaviour varies; in
some experiments, animals are transferred directly from the
continuous reinforcement schedule with which the operant
behaviour is initially established to the final FI value, but in

others the interval is progressively increased to that terminal value. If reinforcement is discontinued for animals which have been extensively exposed to FI schedules, the pattern of extinction in responding is characteristic. The first interval is, of course, normal except that the final rate of responding continues beyond the time at which the reinforcement would have occurred if the schedule had still been in operation. Eventually, this responding ends abruptly; after a pause, the previously typical transition to a sustained rate of responding is again shown, the previous 'running' rate of responding continues for a while, and then ends abruptly once more. As extinction progresses, the pauses become longer, and the periods of responding shorter, in a way rather similar to that described for the ratio schedules of reinforcements.

Analogues of FI schedules may exist in our everyday world; watching for a kettle of water to boil may be such an analogue, for the frequency with which one glances at the kettle may be similar to the patterns of behaviour discussed as typical of animals' fixed interval performance.

Just as the ratio between responses and reinforcements may be variable or fixed, so there are fixed and variable varieties of interval schedules. With a _variable interval_ (VI) schedule of reinforcement, an average minimum delay is specified between the delivery of one reinforcement and the time at which the next becomes available to an operant response. For example, with a VI 30 second schedule, food will sometimes become available for pressing the lever only 5 seconds after the previous reinforcement was delivered, but this interval may at other times be as long as 90 seconds. It is the mean interval which defines this schedule. When exposed to a VI schedule, animals again adapt their behaviour in an effective way, as shown in Fig. 9. This shows the 'collapsed' cumulative record of a food-deprived rat exposed to a VI 30 second schedule of food reinforcement. The animal emits his lever presses at a consistent, but rather low rate — in this case, about 20 per minute throughout the 50-minute session. However, this is again an entirely 'rational' way in which to behave. There is little reason to press the lever more frequently than this, because the availability of the reinforcements is determined by the passing of time. On the other hand, by emitting his responses at a consistent rate, the animal ensures that each reinforcement is collected by a lever-press within a short time of its becoming

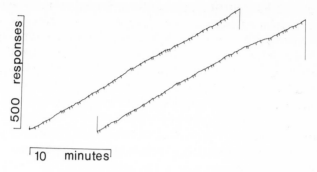

Figure 9   Cumulative record of a rat's behaviour on a variable interval schedule (VI 30 sec.).

available. So the characteristic pattern of VI behaviour takes the form of steady but moderate rates of operant responding, producing reinforcements occasionally as determined by the intervals of the schedule. Again, this is typical of various VI schedules with many different species. The rate at which an animal responds has been shown to depend on a number of specifiable variables, among which may be mentioned the level of deprivation, and the mean interval length (Clark, 1958).

(The rat whose responding was shown in Fig. 4 in order to illustrate the effects of a discriminative stimulus was in fact exposed to a VI schedule when the noise was present.)

Animals are transferred to variable interval schedules after continuous reinforcement in the same way as outlined for FI schedules, that is to say either directly or by means of progressive increases in the mean interval length. When animals are transferred from VI schedules to extinction, they may initially show a slight *increase* in response rate, but this gradually and progressively subsides as time passes with no reinforcements being made available.

Variable interval behaviour is easily described, but is by no means less interesting than the other patterns of behaviour discussed in this chapter. The marked consistency in the emission of operant responses in time is both impressive and useful (as we shall see later). It is easy to see analogies in our everyday lives, for practically any pattern of looking at other things occurs in similarly scheduled ways; we scan our world to detect events which occur independently of our behaviour. An interesting situation in which this occurs systematically is provided by the scanning of a radar screen for aircraft. It seems that the frequency of glancing at such a screen depends, among other things, on the frequency with which an object is detected on the screen, in the same way that a rat's lever pressing behaviour depends on the frequency of reinforcement on a VI schedule. In the case of the radar, the occurrence of a 'blip' is independent of the observer (as is the availability of the rat's reinforcer), and occurs at irregular times (i.e., at variable intervals). Holland (1957) has investigated these similarities; one implication of such work is that intruders will be detected more speedily if 'false alarms' are put onto the screen. This increases, within limits, the rate of scanning, but, of course, great care must be taken; if the proportion of detections which prove to be false is known to the observer, and rises to too high a level, complications will set in!

This completes a preliminary review of the four schedules which are usually regarded as basic in the study of intermittent reinforcement and its effects. We have seen that reinforcers may be programmed to follow operant responses according to fixed or variable rules. These rules may be expressed in terms of a system external to the experimental subjects (time), or dependent on the number of responses emitted. It is for this reason that interval and ratio schedules have been traditionally distinguished. However, the apparent difference between them may be more formal than substantive, as will be explained in the next chapter. For the moment, however, Fig. 10 provides a convenient summary of the principle effects discussed here. On the left of the vertical line in this diagram (which is taken from Reynolds, 1968) are shown stylised cumulative records of the behavioural patterns characteristically maintained by the four basic schedules. Each of these is an effective form of organisation in the circumstances, with the slight exception of the post-reinforcement pause on FR schedules, which in fact delays the arrival of the subsequent reinforcement. To the right of the vertical line, the typical patterns of responding are depicted which result from discontinuing the delivery of reinforcers after animals have been exposed to these schedules (extinction).

It is of the utmost importance that the ways in which a reinforcer are made to occur can produce such great differences on the operant behaviour with which they are related. It is also important that intermittencies in reinforcement may exert such

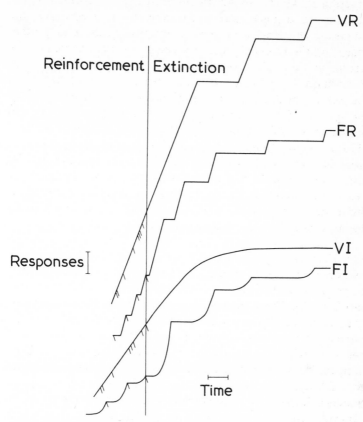

Figure 10   Stylised cumulative records illustrating typical patterns of behaviour maintained by four schedules of intermittent reinforcement. Typical extinction patterns are also shown. From Reynolds (1968).

powerful control over behaviour. It might also be mentioned that any schedule of intermittent reinforcement dramatically prolongs the extinction process in comparison to the effects of withholding reinforcement after an animal has been reinforced after each operant response. All these points have important implications for the experimental analysis of human behaviour, for although these schedules are experimental abstractions, they may have general analogies in the real world. The environmental events associated with our behaviour may not follow each occasion we behave in that way; yet, almost paradoxically, these intermittent relationships between our behaviour and those events may produce the more dramatic effects on behaviour.

A final important point should be made. There is a tendency for us to attribute greater 'motivation' to a pattern of behaviour which either occurs very frequently or extinguishes slowly. Thus, an animal may press a lever for food more frequently the more hungry he is. The results outlined in this chapter show that the relationships between the environment and behaviour may be another critical factor in determining the frequency at which an operant act will occur. In all the figures in this chapter, the experimental animals whose records are shown came to the experimental situation with similar deprivation histories (similar amounts of hunger); and yet, as we have seen, the rates at which their operant acts were emitted vary enormously.

CHAPTER 6

Schedules of reinforcement (cont.)

In this chapter, some further schedules of reinforcement will be discussed. However, the main burden of the argument is not so much on recounting endless differences between the various scheduling arrangements that are possible as on attempting to organise schedules according to the principles by which they exert their characteristic control over operant behaviour.

In addition to the four basic schedules which were discussed in the previous chapter, there is another whose effects have been investigated to such an extent that it has now become almost as basic. In this case, the availability of reinforcement for an operant response is determined by a combination of temporal and response factors. The schedule delivers a reinforcer immediately after an operant response, but only if at least a specified interval has elapsed since any preceding *response*. In this way, a *differential reinforcement of low rates* of responding is achieved, the schedule being abbreviated as DRL. So a DRL15 second schedule specifies that a reinforcement will follow any response which is preceded by a minimum period of 15 seconds without a response; any premature response merely resets the 15 second delay requirement. A typical performance of a food-deprived rat on such a schedule of food reinforcement is shown in Fig. 11. This is in the form of a cumulative record of lever presses, the delivery of reinforcements being denoted by small marks in the usual way. In this case, the mean response rate is approximately

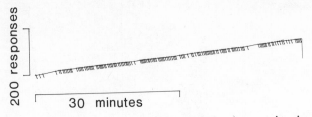

Figure 11   Cumulative record of a rat's behaviour maintained by a DRL 15 sec schedule.

3.8 per minute, and about 69% of all lever presses satisfy the time requirement for a reinforcer to be delivered. Once more, it must be conceded that such a pattern of responding is highly appropriate to the schedule maintaining it, and it is not surprising that such behaviour has been described as 'timing' (e.g., by Sidman, 1955). The record reproduced in Fig. 11 shows a consistently low rate of responding throughout the experimental session, which, in a sense, reflects the animal's repeated attempts to time 15 seconds. The record also reveals that the rat occasionally encounters poor patches, where his rate of responding must be fractionally too high and where, as a result, reinforcements are not delivered for some time. Sequential effects such as these have been noted repeatedly, and have been widely investigated with DRL schedules (see Harzem, 1969). In Fig. 11, one of the periods in which the delay requirements are repeatedly underestimated occurs early in the session, another well-documented phenomenon which has been described as a 'warm-up' effect.

When response rates are as low as those typically generated by DRL schedules, the cumulative record is not the most effective way of reporting the degree of organisation in the animals' behaviour. Of more interest is a detailed analysis of the successive time-estimations, that is of the time elapsing between successive responses. This is achieved by what is known as an inter-response time (IRT) analysis. This classifies each response into an appropriate 'bin' in terms of how long has passed since the previous response. For example, with 3 second bins, each response is recorded in terms of whether it occurred between 0 and 3 seconds after its predecessor, between 3 and 6 seconds after, between 6 and 9 seconds after, and so on. The number of

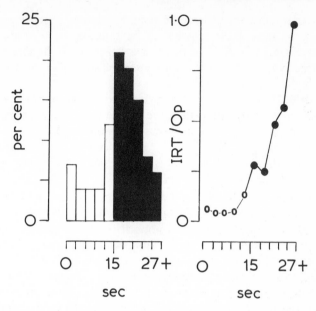

Figure 12   Distribution of inter-response times on a DRL 15 sec schedule. Left: frequency distribution; right: corresponding IRT/0p function.

responses classified into each bin is then totalled, and a frequency distribution depicted in the form of a histogram. Such an IRT distribution is shown on the left in Fig. 12, this Figure being a more detailed analysis of the behaviour displayed in the form of the cumulative record in Fig. 11. In the histogram, the number of responses in each successive 3-second bin is expressed as a percentage of the total number of responses emitted in the whole session. The final bin includes any response emitted more than 27 seconds after its preceding response, but, as can be seen, very few pauses were as long as this. The bins associated with reinforcement have their totals expressed in black columns to differentiate them. You can see that 7% of all responses occurred within 3 seconds of the previous response; few occurred between 3 and 6 seconds, between 6 and 9 seconds, and between 9 and 12 seconds after the preceding response. 12% of all responses were emitted between 12 and 15 seconds after the preceding response (and were therefore emitted only marginally too early to be followed by reinforcement). As many as 21% of all inter-response times were between 15 and 18 seconds, that is were just long enough to allow their response to be followed by a reinforcement. Slightly fewer responses were recorded in the next 3-second bin, and the number progressively decreases from then on.

Clearly, IRT analyses such as that shown on the left of Fig. 12 convey more information than the simple cumulative record. In this case, the distribution shows even more forcefully how effectively this rat had adjusted his behaviour to the requirements of the DRL15 second schedule; more responses were recorded as occurring between 15 and 18 seconds after their predecessors than in any other 3-second period. Such a finding is typical, as is the rather more surprising fact that more responses occurred within 3 seconds of a previous response than in any of the three succeeding bins of the same duration. A relatively high frequency of short IRTs has often been reported, often to a more striking extent than in the present case (e.g., Sidman, 1955); on the other hand, it is not an invariant feature of DRL performance (see, for example, Kelleher et al., 1959), and the reasons for its occurrence are not yet fully understood (see Harzem, 1969).

On the right of Fig. 12, the distribution of inter-response times is expressed in a slightly different way. This is based on a suggestion originally made by Anger (1956), and takes into account the fact that the animal has fewer opportunities to place a response in the bins most removed in time from the preceding response. For example, the first bin occurs after every response, but only if the rat does not emit a response in that three second period does the beginning of the next bin occur. Since 7% of the responses in Fig. 12 occurred in the first bin, the second bin occurred appreciably less often, a feature which has an increasingly biasing effect on the simple frequency distribution as time elapses further. Anger's statistic is known as IRT/Op (inter-response times per opportunity) and takes this into account by expressing the number of responses in each bin as a function of the number of times that bin occurred. This is described by a conditional probability, 0 meaning that no responses were emitted in a particular bin, 0.5 meaning that 50% of the occurrences of the bin ended with a response, and 1.0 meaning that a response was emitted in a bin on every occasion on which that bin occurred (and therefore that there could be no subsequent bin). Clearly, the last bin of the frequency distribution (into which are placed all responses which occurred later than 27 seconds after the preceding response) will, of necessity, produce an IRT/Op of 1.0. In the case of Fig. 12, the IRT/Op distribution accentuates the difference in conditional probabilities between premature and appropriate responses on the DRL schedule; hence, although the frequency distribution shows that only 8% of the total responses occurred in the penultimate bin, the IRT/Op statistic shows that there was a probability of 0.57 that a response would be emitted in that bin if it occurred (i.e., 57% of the occurrences of this bin ended with a response).

The DRL schedule may be further refined by setting a maximum delay between a reinforced response and the preceding response, as well as the minimum time requirement. This is known as adding a *limited hold* (LH), which is also specified in seconds. So, with a DRL15 LH3 second schedule, only responses which are preceded by a pause not less than 15 seconds but not greater than 18 seconds will be followed by a reinforcement. It is usual to add the LH requirement only after the DRL schedule has developed a certain amount of behavioural control. The effects of adding a 3 second limited hold to a DRL15 second schedule are depicted in Fig. 13, which shows the IRT distribution (left) and the IRT/Op graph (right) for such a schedule, these data being supplied, in fact, by the same animal for whom the simple DRL data were reported. Although the cumulative records obtained from this phase of the experiment do not appear substantially different from those generated by the simple DRL schedule (and are therefore not shown), these more detailed analyses reveal an even more controlled pattern of behaviour. Now, 46% of all responses are emitted between 15 and 18 seconds after the preceding response; 32% of all responses are emitted in the 3-second bin immediately before the reinforced bin, so no less than 78% of all responses are emitted within 3 seconds either side of the time when a reinforcement was made available for a response. The IRT/Op graph emphasises the sudden change in the conditional probability of a response at this time.

A comparison of Figs. 12 and 13 suggests that the addition of the limited hold to the DRL 15 sec schedule has had the effect of sharpening the efficiency of the time-estimations shown by this

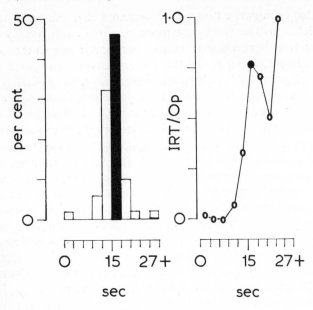

Figure 13   Distribution of inter-response times on a DRL 15 sec LH 3 sec schedule. Left: frequency distribution; right: corresponding IRT/Op function.

rat. In particular, the 'tail' of rather long inter-response times (which were previously, but are no longer, followed by reinforcement) has been considerably shortened. This is the general effect of a limited hold, but it should be stressed that the comparison between Figs. 12 and 13 must be made with caution, for no direct evidence has been offered here to support the view that this sharpening effect is not simply due to the further training on these schedules which intervened between the two sets of data. It is obvious that the DRL LH schedule has developed a striking skill on the part of the rat, and clearly such a skill provides the opportunity for an even more detailed analysis than is possible here (see Weiss, 1970). The single important point to be stressed here is simply that an animal's behaviour can show a most remarkable degree of organisation when the schedule establishes such a stringent criterion for reinforcement. One may, in effect, condition a rat to press a lever at various rates by manipulating the requirements of a DRL schedule with a limited hold. We shall return to this point.

It has been noticed on several occasions that animals exposed to DRL schedules (with or without a limited hold) spend much of the time between lever presses behaving in some other way. For example, Laties et al. (1965) found that a rat exposed to a DRL 22 second schedule of reinforcement spent almost all its time nibbling its tail, 'moving its mouth over the surface from one end to the other while holding the tail in its front paws'. This behaviour was found to be closely related to the lever-pressing, to such an extent that Laties and his associates decided that the nibbling was in fact mediating the lever pressing. Although such mediating, or collateral, behaviour has not always been observable in animals exposed to a DRL schedule, there has recently been much experimental interest in the rôle of such behaviour, and in why it develops. Sometimes it takes the form of a complicated chain of behaviour; for example, in one experiment (rat 1 in Blackman, 1968a) a subject repeated the following sequence between lever presses: he crossed the experimental chamber to face the wall opposite the lever, reared up until his two front feet were touching the ceiling of the chamber, walked his front feet across the ceiling towards the lever until this led to his toppling over backwards, picked himself up, moved over to the lever, and finally pressed it. Of course, such a sequence of behaviour took some time to carry out; in fact, it took approximately 15 seconds, which was the requirement of the DRL schedule to which the animal was exposed, and so performing this chain of behaviour led to a high probability that the lever press which terminated it would be followed by reinforcement. This, in turn, led to an increased probability that the whole sequence would be repeated. Since this pattern of behaviour was not specified by the schedule, it could be described as 'superstitious', resulting from the chance occurrence of reinforcements for the lever presses after such a chain. The similarity between such behaviour and that reported earlier with human subjects by Bruner and Revusky (1961) needs no emphasis (their subjects being exposed, in fact, to a DRL schedule on the single effective button).

When the chains of behaviour between lever presses consist of identifiable components, as above, it is tempting to suggest that the complicated concept of 'timing' need not be invoked as a description of DRL performance: this animal had replaced the timing task by that of carrying out a sequence of behaviour, each part being triggered off by the completion of the preceding part. Such a view was supported in the above case by the effects of subsequent injections of drugs to this animal; when he was given a sedative drug which made him unsteady, he fell over earlier in the sequence, but still followed this act by immediately approaching the lever, which he therefore pressed too early for a reinforcement to be delivered. However, the mediating or collateral behaviour often takes the form of a simpler repetitive act; in the experiment in which the above animal acted as subject, another three subjects all developed this kind of behaviour. One of these groomed himself energetically between lever presses, and again the 'superstitious' nature of such behaviour may be readily appreciated. However, such repetitive acts introduce a further complexity to the analysis of DRL behaviour: how does the animal 'know' when to press the lever? Such a sequence does not culminate so obviously in a lever press as the previous chain of behaviour, for the animal is simply repeating a simple act several times between lever presses: if we are to suggest that this is not carried out merely for the required *time*, we should have to argue that the rat presses the lever after a *number* of these acts, or in other words, that he is counting. However, the concept of counting seems even more complex than that of timing, so in this case the identification of patterns of collateral behaviour does not advance our *explanation* of DRL behaviour to a simpler account.

The most important point to emerge from this discussion is that one should not consider lever pressing in operant conditioning experiments in isolation from other patterns of behaviour which may occur in the test cage. It is naive to suppose that an animal does not behave in any way between the lever presses which we record, for behaviour is a continuous stream, of which we measure only part. Unrecorded patterns of behaviour may assume considerable importance by reason of chance relationships which may occur between them and the reinforced responses which may follow them.

Low consistent rates of responding have been observed with many different animals exposed to DRL schedules, both with and without limited hold requirements. However, it seems that the key pecking behaviour of pigeons does not adapt so readily to these schedules (e.g., Reynolds and Catania, 1961). The effects of prior food-deprivation on DRL responding have been investigated (e.g. Conrad et al., 1958), but, on the whole, established patterns of behaviour are quite resistant to disruption by changes in motivation. When animals are transferred from a DRL schedule to an extinction procedure, by discontinuing the delivery of reinforcements, their rates of responding decline progressively, although there is some evidence that the responses tend to occur in strings in which they are separated by the inter-response times which had previously been appropriate to the schedule (Hurwitz, 1957).

It is possible to *add* a DRL requirement to the basic schedules discussed in the previous chapter. This has been done, for example, by Skinner (1938) and by Anger (1956). The results of such a procedure will here be discussed by reference to an experiment reported by the present writer (Blackman, 1967), in which a DRL5 LH3 second requirement was added to a variable interval schedule (VI 30 sec). Here reinforcement became available to a lever-press on average every 30 sec., but only a response which was emitted between five and eight seconds since the previous response could obtain it. In the case of one animal (rat 2), this led to a drop in overall response rate from 40 per minute to approximately 9 per minute, although the frequency of reinforcements was hardly affected. The reasons for this fall in response rate are shown clearly in Fig. 14 by means of inter-response time analyses. Here, each response was categorised into 1-second bins in terms of the period elapsing between it and the preceding response. Histogram A shows that, before the DRL requirement was added, most responses occurred between 1 and 3 seconds after their predecessor. This histogram is depicted in black to denote that a response following any IRT might be followed by a reinforcement on the VI schedule at this stage of the experiment. Note that there were a few IRTs of 5 to 8 seconds, but not many. Histogram B shows the effect of adding the DRL5 LH3 second requirement: its obvious effect was to shift the histogram to the right, so that now about 60% of all IRTs were between 5 and 8 seconds (shown in black). Clearly, the DRL requirement has exerted control over the VI behaviour by selectively reinforcing responses which followed such IRTs, thereby increasing the proportion of such IRTs at the cost of those values which had earlier predominated.

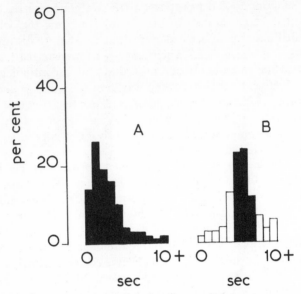

Figure 14   Frequency distributions of inter-response times. Left: VI 30 sec; right: same VI with added DRL 5 sec LH 3 sec requirement.

The idea that a reinforcement schedule selectively reinforces specific inter-response times may be important in our understanding of the control which it exerts over behaviour. Of course, technically it reinforces a response which *follows* a particular IRT, thereby developing a characteristic overall rate of response. This selective reinforcement is further emphasised by reference to Fig. 15, which shows the behaviour of another rat (rat 1) in the experiment discussed above. In this case, the animal was transferred from the simple VI schedule to one in which only responses following an IRT of *less than* 0.3 seconds were followed by reinforcement according to the VI schedule. Again, the results of this procedure are represented by IRT analyses, histogram A being the distribution obtained from the simple VI schedule (expressed in 1 second bins), and showing an effect similar to the same condition in the previous Figure. Histogram B shows the effect of the additional requirement. Note that the bins in this histogram are 0.3 seconds only. The effect is dramatic; over 50% of all inter-response times are less than 0.3 seconds, and almost 80% of all IRTs are less than 0.9 seconds

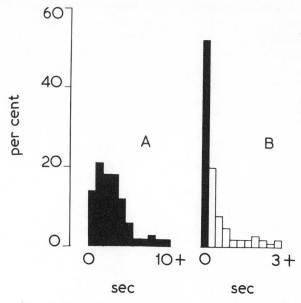

Figure 15 Frequency distributions of inter-response times. Left: VI 30 sec; right: same VI, but only responses emitted within 0.3 sec of a previous response might be followed by reinforcement. (Note the different bin durations for the two distributions.)

(i.e., in the first 3 bins), as opposed to approximately 15% in the first 1 second bin in histogram A. These data are reflected in the overall response rates obtained from this animal: on the simple VI schedule, this was approximately 40 per minute, but this increased to almost 80 per minute as a result of the change in the procedure.

Data such as these support the view that one may selectively reinforce specific inter-response times by appropriate scheduling arrangements, thereby controlling overall rates of operant responding. It follows that where such arrangements are not specifically made, chance effects may nevertheless become important (as we have seen so often already). Clearly, any overall response rate generated by a simple variable interval schedule can therefore be regarded as the chance result of the reinforcement of responses after a particular IRT, such an effect being generated and maintained in a way which we have previously regarded as 'superstitious'. With VI schedules, this does not seem a striking point: however, it may be extended to other schedules.

It will be recalled that variable ratio (VR) schedules generate and maintain consistent, high rates of responding. These schedules are formally specified, of course, in terms of the overall ratio of responses to reinforcements, or, in other words, without reference to time factors. Yet such time factors may nevertheless enter, in the form of the principle outlined above with variable interval schedules that particular inter-response times may be selectively reinforced. In the case of VR schedules, the training procedures effectively ensure that this should happen; the ratio is gradually increased on the basis of the animals' satisfactory adjustment to the previous value, i.e., if the animals are responding at a fairly high rate. In essence, changing the overall ratio may be not so much a successive approximation to the final run lengths of responses as the approximation to longer *durations*

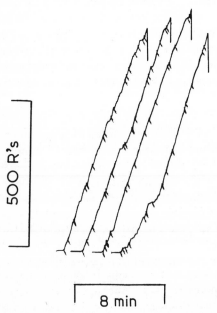

Figure 16   Ratio-like behaviour generated by a variable *interval* schedule with the added restriction that only responses emitted within 0.2 sec of a previous response might be followed by reinforcement.

of responding at a high rate. This case is supported by Fig. 16, in which are shown the collapsed cumulative records of a rat from another experiment (rat 2, Expt. 2; Blackman, 1968b). These records appear very similar indeed to those presented in Fig. 6 (p. 59) to depict typical VR performance. However, in the case of Fig. 16, the rat was exposed to a variable *interval* schedule (½ minute), with the added restriction that only a response occurring within 0.2 seconds of the previous response could be reinforced by the schedule. In this case, the rat emitted responses at an overall mean rate of 96 per minute, approximately 2 reinforcements being delivered each minute. The behaviour might be described as identical to that generated by variable *ratio* schedules, in this case, presumably, 'defined' as VR48 (the overall ratio of responses to reinforcements). This implies that the 'traditional' distinction between variable interval and variable ratio schedules may be no more than a difference in the formal arrangements for programming the schedules, reflecting no difference of any substance from a behavioural point of view.

The above argument becomes slightly more complicated if extended to a comparison of *fixed* interval and ratio schedules. We saw earlier that the typical pattern of behaviour maintained by fixed *interval* schedules included a pause in responding after a reinforcement had been delivered. This may be explained as the result of the reinforcer acting as a signal that no further reinforcement will be available for some time, i.e., signalling a period in which no response can be followed by a reinforcement, and in which the frequency of responding is therefore low. This pause gives way to responding, either by means of a gradual transition (which we shall not discuss here – but see Dews, 1970), or sometimes fairly suddenly. In the latter case, the behaviour resembles fixed ratio behaviour, except that the rate of responding just before reinforcement is much lower. Animals trained on fixed *ratio* schedules are usually first exposed to small ratios, which are then gradually increased. This tends to ensure that high response rates are generated by the chance relationships between some IRTs and reinforced responses following them. Increasing the ratio requirement may again be equivalent to increasing the *duration* of runs at a particular rate. However, as this procedure is developed, the interval between reinforcements inevitably increases, so that each reinforcement comes to signal a period of non-reinforcement. As a result, a pause in responding develops after each reinforcement, which gives way to a sustained run of responses at the rate which has been reinforced in the past. This, of course, makes it highly probable that the next reinforcement will (coincidentally) follow a response which was itself preceded by a short IRT, and so on. Such an account fits in reasonably well, of course, with the findings of Felton and Lyon (1966) discussed earlier that response rates differ little with different FR requirements, although the length of the post-reinforcement pause does.

Of course, this discussion does not detract from the findings outlined in the previous chapter which are the typical behavioural results of programming reinforcements in the various ways discussed there. If one carries out a typical experiment using a fixed ratio schedule, one observes typical fixed ratio behaviour. What is challenged, however, is that the four 'basic' schedules may be distinguished into two fundamentally different types, and that their behavioural effects reflect this. By recognising that a reinforcement increases and strengthens the frequency of more than just the lever press itself, but that it acts also on the behaviour immediately *preceding* that response (expressed in our terms by the inter-response time), it becomes possible to consider all patterns of behaviour maintained by reinforcement schedules within one conceptual framework.

There are many more schedules of reinforcement which might be discussed. For example, one may add a limited hold to a fixed interval schedule, so that the reinforcement is made available to a response for perhaps only 1 second every 2 minutes. This is usually achieved by gradually reducing the LH from an initially high value. The effects of such a procedure are to increase the running response rate, thereby making the behaviour appear more similar to that generated by FR schedules; but this can be predicted in terms of the above argument, as might many of the effects of other procedures not discussed here. The reader is referred to two books. The first, *Schedules of Reinforcement* (Ferster and Skinner, 1957) was a pioneering and detailed study of most of the effects discussed in this and the preceding chapter. The second, *The Theory of Reinforcement Schedules* (Schoenfeld, 1970) is a more recent collection of papers which indicates more recent research in this area. But we shall now move on to discuss how these various schedules may be used.

CHAPTER 7

The maintenance of behaviour

The two preceding chapters have shown that patterns of operant behaviour can differ widely as a function of the schedule of reinforcement to which an animal is exposed. It is now time to consider in more detail an important point which has been implied or assumed in the earlier discussion, namely that each schedule *maintains* its characteristic pattern of responding.

The cumulative records and other data given in the discussion of reinforcement schedules depicted not transitional effects (equivalent to learning), but rather the final patterns of behaviour which develop after prolonged exposure to the schedules. Although we considered the ways in which these patterns of behaviour are generated, the major emphasis was on the final result of these processes. This was possible simply because animals exposed to a consistent schedule of reinforcement in a controlled test situation eventually attain a state of equilibrium in their adjustment to the events in this environment. Their behaviour becomes progressively more consistent from one experimental session to the next, until we can *predict* with considerable accuracy the behaviour they will show in any subsequent session. So, one can predict how many times a rat will press a lever during an hour's exposure to a specified variable interval schedule on the basis of how many times that particular rat has emitted the response in previous sessions of that length.

It is only after a considerable number of identical experimental sessions that a consistent rate of responding develops on a VI schedule both within and between sessions. However, when this is eventually achieved, it is said that a *steady state* of behaviour has been produced (Sidman, 1960). Of course, a schedule such as fixed interval does not develop a consistent overall rate of responding throughout a session, but nevertheless this behaviour also eventually becomes predictable within fairly precise limits. Thus, the overall rate of responding may be effectively the same from one day to the next, and the post-reinforcement pause may also become consistent in this way. This too is then described as a steady or stable behavioural state. In the main, as seen earlier, the effects of the various types of reinforcement schedules are compared by referring to the steady states of behaviour which they support. Thus, the cumulative records shown in the two previous chapters are entirely typical of the subjects they represented.

The sensitive adjustment of emitted behaviour to the various reinforcement schedules demonstrated by these steady states of behaviour is indeed a phenomenon of some importance. There is something unusually powerful (at least in the context of psychology) about being able to predict fairly precisely how many reinforcements an animal exposed to, say, a VR100 schedule will obtain in one hour, for this reveals an unusual amount of experimental control over the behaviour. Steady states of behaviour emphasise once more the suggestion that behaviour may be interpreted as a function of the environment in which it occurs, or, in other words, as a function of observable events in the physical world. In the typical operant conditioning experiments, this world is made consistent by means of the careful experimental control of as many features as possible: the only events to occur are those programmed by the experimental arrangements. Of course, this consistency may be complex, determined by the rules of a complex reinforcement schedule, for example. In a situation which has such a degree of overall consistency, it is important that the behaviour associated with it also becomes consistent; if this were not so, the functional analysis of operant behaviour, relating behaviour to the environmental events of which it is a function, would be seriously limited.

Naturally, this predictability of behaviour is not absolute: for example, a pigeon which emits 6,002 operant responses per hour on one day may not emit *exactly* that number on the subsequent day. In practice, a steady behavioural state is normally claimed if a specified criterion is reached. For example, Schoenfeld, Cumming and Hearst (1956) employed a rigorous statistical test. They took six successive experimental sessions and calculated the average response rates for the first three and last three of these. If the difference between these means was less than 5% of the overall mean for the six sessions, they decided that the animal had reached a stable state. This criterion is severe, and Sidman (1960) has emphasised that 'only those experimenters whose laboratories are characterised by meticulous attention to details of experimental control will be able to employ the same stability criterion'. In a subsequent report, Cumming and Schoenfeld (1960) themselves cast considerable doubt on the efficiency of such a stringent criterion. Aware of the rather arbitrary nature of any criterion for stability, they resolved to record pigeons' performances on an intermittent schedule of reinforcement over a considerable period of time. The birds were exposed to between 197 and 223 experimental sessions, each of 20 minutes duration. Two kinds of variability in response rates were noticed throughout this experiment. A general, slight and unsystematic variability from day to day the experimenters described as 'noise'. However, there were also occasional rather abrupt changes in response rate, which it was not possible to correlate with any abrupt changes in the conditions in which the experiment was carried out. Characteristically, however, Cumming and Schoenfeld noted that they could not rule out the possibility of uncontrolled variations in the laboratory. This emphasises that whatever variability there is in a relatively stable pattern of behaviour is normally assumed to result from some uncontrolled change in the conditions rather than from any inherent variability in behaviour itself, for the latter assumption would weaken the argument that behaviour is best interpreted as a function of observable events.

Faced with observations such as these, many operant conditioners prefer to specify that a steady state of behaviour has been reached by means of an informal criterion, based on visual inspection of daily cumulative records and on an absence of any *systematic* pattern of variability from day to day.

Sidman (1960) has distinguished two major types of experimental interest in these steady states of behaviour. The first he calls descriptive, and it is this which has been used here in comparing the final effects of the various reinforcement schedules. These are *described* in terms of the steady behavioural states which they support. The second interest Sidman has termed manipulative. Steady states of behaviour may be *used*, not merely described, in order to assess the effects of additional experimental variables.

It has been seen that when a steady behavioural state is achieved it becomes possible to predict with some accuracy how an animal will behave. It follows that if an additional procedure is incorporated and the behaviour changes so that the performance is no longer within the bounds of the prediction based on past performances, then the new procedure has probably been responsible for this change. For example, if it is found that the overall response rate of an animal on a VI schedule is much lower than usual on a day when the animal is injected with a drug, this suggests that the drug is responsible for that drop in rate. If on the next day the animal's response rate returns to the previous predictions, the suggestion is further supported. The drug may be given to the same animal on subsequent occasions, and if the lower response rate is still a consistent feature it may be confidently proposed that the effect is indeed the direct consequence of the drug. In this way, the experimental control over behaviour revealed by a steady state may be used to advantage.

However, a procedure such as this differs markedly from the methods used more traditionally to investigate the effects of a variable such as a drug. Conventionally, this is achieved by an experiment which uses a *statistical* design. Instead of developing precise experimental control over the behaviour of individual animals, such procedures use less controlled situations, but compensate by using more animals. Put simply, one group of animals in an experimental situation is given the drug, but the other is not. A comparison is then made between the two groups, the argument being that if both groups have been treated identically, there is only a small chance that overall differences between them will emerge, any such difference reflecting the fact that there may be slight individual differences between the animals assigned to the two groups. Therefore, if any overall differences do emerge, these probably reflect the effects of the one difference between the groups from a procedural point of view, namely the administration of the drug. It is usual to call the drug group the *experimental* and the non-drugged animals the *control* group. Differences between them are assessed by the use of statistical techniques.

Sidman (1960) has argued that the research methods made possible by steady states of behaviour are preferable to the alternative statistical methods. He argues that the former need no statistics to establish whether the observed differences between a drug and control condition are 'real', for in such an experiment one is able to point readily to the differences between the two conditions. This is the direct result of the strong experimental control exerted, which makes it possible to predict the behaviour of an individual subject in the absence of the additional variable. Sidman attacks statistical designs as procedures which are used to 'cover up' the inadequacies of experimental control in group experiments. He believes not only that they are unnecessary, but that they reveal no psychological reality. His most extreme position is that behaviour is, in the final analysis, a characteristic of *individual* organisms, not of groups, so that if a phenomenon cannot be demonstrated within the behaviour of a single organism it has no psychological meaning or reality.

Sidman's position may be unnecessarily extreme, for it would seem that there are experimental effects of real significance in psychology which demand statistical comparisons between groups. This is especially the case when one is attempting to measure the effects of a variable which prove to be non-reversible. In our example above, the effects of a drug wear off, so that the previous steady state may be recovered; however, the effects of other variables of real importance may not be reversible in this way, and therefore not amenable to the steady state methodology. All the same, the more controlled experiments using individual subjects may indeed be preferable where they are possible. By repeatedly using one animal in an experimental (e.g., drug) condition and the same animal in control conditions, statistical procedures to control for chance effects become unnecessary.

The usefulness of steady states of behaviour is increased by many refinements discussed in detail by Sidman in his provocative book *Tactics of Scientific Research* (1960), which is in one sense a manual for designing experiments in which individual

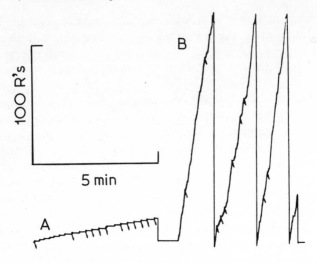

Figure 17   Cumulative record produced by a rat exposed to a multiple schedule of reinforcement. From Blackman (1968a).

animals act as their own experimental control in this way. One of the refinements is illustrated by the continuous segment of cumulative record shown in Fig. 17 (taken from rat 4, Blackman, 1968a). This rat was exposed to two separate schedules of reinforcement, each associated with its own discriminative stimulus and occurring within the same experimental session. A white light was illuminated for 5 minutes, during which time a DRL15 LH5 second schedule of reinforcement was in operation. This discriminative stimulus controlled a pattern of behaviour (marked A in Fig. 17) which has previously been described as the typical result of such a schedule: the record shows a consistently low rate of responding. The overall rate of responding was 4.6 per minute, and on average 2.4 reinforcements were obtained each minute (shown by diagonal marks in Fig. 17). At the end of this 5 minute period the recorder pen was reset, and the light extinguished. When the test cage was in darkness like this, no reinforcement schedule was in operation: appropriately, no lever presses were emitted during this time, again a phenomenon discussed earlier. After one minute of darkness, a red light was presented together with a hissing noise, these stimuli being in operation for 5 minutes, marked B on the record. As may be seen, these stimuli controlled a very high rate of responding (overall mean = 117.1 per minute), with on average 1.4 reinforcements per minute. These high rates of responding are reminiscent of variable ratio behaviour, but once more this behaviour is the result of a schedule specified in terms of temporal values, not in terms of a ratio of responses to reinforcements; this behaviour therefore strengthens further the suggestion that there may be no fundamental behavioural differences between the so-called ratio and interval schedules. The precise specification of the schedule controlling the behaviour marked B in Fig 17 is not important here, for the point being made is merely this: in the presence of a red light and a noise, the rat consistently emitted operant responses at a high rate. After the 5 minutes of schedule B, there followed another one-minute period without lights and noise during which no reinforcements were obtainable. After this, the whole cycle was repeated, four complete cycles being given in each experimental session.

Figure 17 provides a very clear indication that more than one pattern of behaviour may be controlled in an individual animal. In this case, not one but three steady states of behaviour were achieved: slow consistent responding, no responding at all, and extremely high rates of lever pressing. Each of these was under the control of an appropriate stimulus, and the experimenter could therefore in effect turn on or off either of two completely different patterns of behaviour, merely by presenting either of the discriminative stimuli. Experimental arrangements such as this are known as *multiple* schedules of reinforcement; two or more simple schedules, each associated with its own discriminative stimulus. The advantages offered by such schedules should be obvious. An experimenter is now able to compare the effects of an additional procedure such as a drug-injection on more than one pattern of behaviour, but still on the basis of data obtained from individual animals. So now each animal acts as his own control both in terms of the effects of a drug versus a non-drug condition, and in terms of differential susceptibilities to disruption shown by each pattern of behaviour. If, for example, a drug reliably affected one steady state of behaviour but not the other in an individual animal, the suggestion is emphasised that it is the nature of the behaviour which is important: it certainly cannot be an artefactual result of individual differences between animals, although there are other artefactual influences which must be guarded against when using such a design. In the case of the experiment from which the record in Fig 17 was taken, the effects of conditioned anxiety were measured against the two very different patterns of responding, and an interesting differential effect was established.

When multiple schedules of reinforcement are used, then, the power of steady state methodology may be considerably increased. But this is only one refinement; another example may be provided by the fact that a single animal may be exposed to a situation in which there are two levers, each one associated with its own schedule of reinforcement. Such an arrangement is termed a *concurrent schedule*, and has been widely investigated (see Catania, 1966). Further refinements will be introduced in subsequent chapters, which will discuss experiments in which steady states of behaviour have been used in the manipulative sense outlined in the latter half of this chapter.

CHAPTER 8

Conditioned reinforcement

In the first chapter of this book, it was suggested that it might be useful to formulate an account of behaviour by reference to observable environmental events rather than to inherently unobservable processes within the behaving organism. At that time, the implication was that *human* behaviour might be interpretable in such a way, as a function of the environment. However, it is now a long time since human behaviour was specifically discussed in this book; instead, the reader has been immersed (but, hopefully, not yet submerged) in detailed accounts of experiments which may appear to be far removed from general problems. Perhaps it is time to take stock briefly.

We are now considering *experimental* investigations of behaviour because such an approach offers a controlled way of isolating important variables. Further control and simplification is provided by using animals as subjects in these experiments. The discussion so far has shown that an act which may be executed simply and repeatedly may indeed be interpreted as a function of the environmental arrangements made by the investigator. Such emitted ('voluntary') behaviour of animals eventually reaches a state of equilibrium with the environment, this steady state depending on the schedule by which reinforcement is delivered and being expressed in terms of the frequency or patterning of the behavioural acts which are related to the delivery of that reinforcement. To this extent, the model of behaviour used in these experiments may be described as progressing reasonably well; the lever pressing behaviour of rats is recognised as being merely an arbitrary unit of behaviour which is convenient both to experimenter and to subject, but the orderliness of these emitted acts in a controlled situation suggests that this model may be useful in a general sense. But in all the experiments discussed so far, the environmental event of which behaviour has become a function has been the delivery of food to an animal which has previously been deprived of food for a short period; it is hardly surprising that the animal's behaviour should become determined by such a biologically significant event. The claim was made in Chapter 4 that this event is also arbitrary, food being used as a model for all events which may be described as reinforcers. Clearly, it makes sense to exploit as a model an event which is likely to be maximally effective, easy to deliver in a controlled way, and for which the appropriate antecedent conditions can be readily specified and varied. But it is now time to consider to what extent such a biologically crucial event may be taken as similar in its effects to other, less crucial but nevertheless effective, events.

This problem assumes even more importance, of course, when one attempts to use the operant conditioning model to help understand *human* behaviour. It is, after all, a truism to suggest that the complexities of human behaviour cannot be readily interpreted as the direct functions of such biologically important events as the delivery of food or water. If our behaviour is to be interpreted in environmental terms at all, it would seem that many other things must be included as reinforcers. Money, social approval, attention, honour, artistic appreciation: these are examples of reinforcers in the technical sense outlined in Chapter 3, none of which has the obviously beneficial effects of food for a hungry rat. Moreover, there are many aspects of our environment of which our behaviour would seem to be a function which may be counter-productive in a biological sense, such as cigarettes, sweets, fast cars, and danger. The reinforcing power of these things differs from one individual to another, apparently being based more on the past experience of each individual than on universal biological requirements. Is there any way in which the operant conditioning model, with animals as subjects, may be used to shed light on the power of these biologically less significant events?

This question has for long now been answered by suggesting that two types of reinforcement can be distinguished in animal conditioning experiments. *Primary reinforcers* have their effects on behaviour because of their biological significance; food and water provide the most obvious examples, but many theorists have also included sex. *Secondary* or *conditioned reinforcers* acquire their effects on behaviour by reason of their relationships to primary reinforcers. In fact, this concept of conditioned reinforcement was discussed earlier (Chapter 3), in connection with Skinner's paper on how to teach animals. In this case, immediacy of reinforcement was achieved by signalling that food had been obtained in a successive approximation procedure. The power of that signal to act as a reinforcer was acquired as a result of the initial training procedure, and it was therefore not a primary, but a conditioned, reinforcer. This distinction between the two types of reinforcement has often been elaborated in textbooks of psychology, but, although it is clear that there must be some truth in such an account, many writers have proved singularly unconvincing in their assertions that conditioned reinforcement provides a bridge between the controlled conditioning of animals and the complex behaviour of humans outside the laboratory. The trouble is that it is only too clear that some such concept as conditioned reinforcement is essential from a theoretical point of view, but the experimental demonstrations of the effect have not been forceful, for they seem to suggest that the effects of conditioned reinforcement are either transitory or slight. However, this lack of experimental support is currently being changed by research which manipulates steady states of behaviour. This incorporates events which are clearly not primary reinforcers into operant conditioning experiments, and studies the behavioural effects which these sustain. It is for this procedural reason that the topic is introduced here, immediately after the chapter on steady states of behaviour.

Early experimental investigations of conditioned reinforcement tended to use one of two basic procedures, sometimes described as the 'new response' and 'extinction' methods. The first of these is illustrated by Fig. 18 (taken from Skinner, 1938), which displays the cumulative records of the lever pressing behaviour of four food-deprived rats. These animals had first been exposed to the usual preliminary procedures for a typical operant conditioning experiment, an important part of which is the delivery of pellets of food regardless of what the animal does. This adapts him to the noise of the pellet dispenser, and allows this noise to acquire signalling or conditioned reinforcing properties, so that the animal approaches and eats the food as soon as it is delivered. The next procedure is normally, of course, to make the operation of the food dispenser (and thereby the delivery of a primary reinforcer) dependent on a lever press. However, in the experiment illustrated in Fig. 18, the first

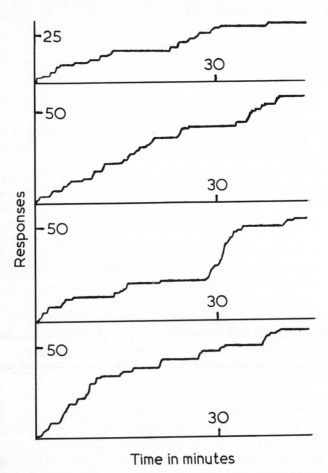

Time in minutes

Figure 18   Cumulative records of the lever pressing of four rats. Each response was followed by the operation of an *empty* pellet dispenser. From Skinner (1938).

normal consequence, but not the second, occurred after a lever press, for the operant behaviour was followed by the noise resulting from the operation of an *empty* pellet dispenser. The records show clearly that this conditioned reinforcer was sufficient to condition, or establish, lever pressing at a reasonably high rate, but that this effect was transitory, for the operant behaviour reverts to its previous very low rate of occurrence after 45 minutes or so. The extinction of this conditioned behaviour is not surprising, of course, for the effect of the conditioned reinforcer is diminishing all the time. This is because its previously reliable relationship with the primary reinforcer was broken at this stage of the experiment in order to investigate its effect uncontaminated by the primary reinforcing effects of food. Nevertheless, this 'new response' method is sufficient to establish that the noise of the pellet dispenser was a reinforcer in its own right for a short period, for it certainly strengthened and maintained for a short time an operant response upon which it was made dependent; the noise was therefore a *conditioned* reinforcer.

The second research design, described above as the 'extinction' method, tries to measure the influence of a conditioned rein-forcer in terms of its retarding effects on extinction, that is on patterns of behaviour whose frequency is reverting to a lower level because a primary reinforcer which was delivered previously is now withheld. Thus, an operant response is first conditioned by making the delivery of food dependent on it. Thereafter, extinction procedures are introduced so that the primary reinforcer is no longer delivered. If some animals are exposed at this stage to a situation in which nothing follows a response, but others to a situation in which stimuli which were previously associated with the delivery of food still occur (such as the noise of an empty pellet dispenser operating), then it can be shown that the latter group will emit more responses before they stop completely. This difference is usually assessed by comparing the number of responses emitted by the two groups of animals before reaching some criterion of extinction; this involves a statistical comparison, of course, and is clearly not a steady-state research design (see Bugelski, 1938, for example).

Wike (1966) has provided a detailed account of how these two general research designs may be used, discussing the appropriate control procedures. However, it is quite clear that designs such as these must inevitably provide firm evidence only for transitory effects of conditioned reinforcers; yet it is this rather fragile evidence that has conventionally been used to support the view that complex human behaviour may be interpreted as a function of conditioned reinforcers rather than primary reinforcers. It is not surprising that some psychologists with different theoretical orientations find this unconvincing. And yet, in spite of (or perhaps because of) a lack of really convincing data, two opposing theories of conditioned reinforcement arose. Both of these attempted to explain how a previously ineffective stimulus acquires conditioned reinforcing properties. The first theory developed from the writings of Hull (1943); it states the general principle that any stimulus which occurs in close temporal contiguity with a primary reinforcer will become a conditioned reinforcer in its own right. Thus, the noise of the pellet dispenser is invariably associated with the delivery of food, and so becomes a conditioned reinforcer because of the pairing of the two stimuli. The alternative theory came from Skinner (1938), and was developed into a clearly stated hypothesis by Keller and Schoenfeld (1950), who suggested that only discriminative stimuli become conditioned reinforcers. As explained earlier, a discriminative stimulus is something in the environment which sets the occasion for an operant response to be followed by a reinforcer. For example the noise of a pellet dispenser operating (after a lever press) sets the occasion for the rat to approach the hopper and to eat the food which has been delivered there. According to this argument, the lever press is maintained by a *conditioned* reinforcer, which is in fact the discriminative stimulus for a completely different pattern of behaviour (only the latter pattern being, formally speaking, strengthened and maintained by *primary* reinforcement).

This second theory now seems less comprehensive and attractive than it once did, but there is no doubt that it enjoys support from many areas of research. A discriminative stimulus certainly does appear to have reinforcing properties for a pattern of behaviour upon which it is made dependent. For example, it is easy to train a completely new pattern of conditioned behaviour in rats merely by following it with a stimulus which sets the occasion for reinforced lever pressing behaviour. If the lever pressing is reinforced (perhaps only intermittently) exclusively in the presence of, say, a noise, any other pattern of behaviour (such as washing, for example) may quickly be increased in frequency by making the noise dependent on such washing behaviour. The result is described as a *heterogeneous* chain of behaviour. In the chain described, the earlier part is effectively maintained merely by its association with the onset of the discriminative stimulus for lever pressing (which is itself, according to the above account, maintained merely by the discriminative stimulus which sets the occasion for approaches to the food hopper to be followed by primary reinforcement).

Chains of considerable length and complexity may be easily developed in this way; the guiding principles are to establish the chain from its final member first and to reinforce additional preceding patterns of behaviour by giving the discriminative stimulus which controls the next pattern of behaviour in the chain. Thus a stimulus (S1) may set the occasion for what is to become the final act of a chain (R1). Then another stimulus (S2) may be presented, which is superceded by S1 only when a particular pattern of behaviour (R2) is emitted. When this two component chain is established, a further stimulus (S3) is introduced, which gives way to S2 only when another new pattern of behaviour occurs (R3); S2 still changes to S1 when R2 occurs; R1 is emitted in the presence of S1, whereupon primary reinforcement is delivered, and then S3 is presented again. By building up such a sequence slowly and progressively, chains of remarkable complexity may be established, especially if successive approximation and intermittent reinforcement procedures are incorporated at each stage as well.

Pierrel and Sherman (1963) demonstrated the power of these techniques in an amusing way by training a rat to climb a spiral staircase, mount a platform at the top, push down and cross a drawbridge to another platform, climb an open ladder, jump into a vehicle which he propelled by turning a paddle-wheel to the foot of an additional flight of steps, which he also ascended. At the top, the rat ran through a tube, clambered into a model lift, the descent of which was started by raising a flag; when the lift reached the lowest level, the rat jumped out, and approached and pressed a lever, thereby receiving a pellet of food; whereupon, he set off on this journey once more! This feat of behavioural engineering was achieved largely by the use of conditioned reinforcers, for each act ended in circumstances which were appropriate for the emission of the next part of the chain.

The development of heterogeneous chains such as the above may demonstrate the power of the procedures employed, but does little to further a detailed analysis of conditioned reinforcement. However, it does have the advantage, in comparison with the more ephemeral 'new response' and 'extinction' procedures, of providing a situation in which behaviour is assumed to be *maintained* by conditioned reinforcers. Much work has recently been carried out on complex schedules of reinforcement which share this advantage. *Chain schedules* of reinforcement programme a sequence of reinforcement schedules, each associated with its own discriminative stimulus, only the final schedule of the sequence providing primary reinforcement. For example, a Chain FR10 FI 1 minute schedule provides the following sequence of events. One stimulus is present until the tenth lever press is emitted; this produces another stimulus, which stays present until the first response is emitted one minute after its onset, whereupon a pellet of food is delivered, and the first stimulus is presented once more. Thus the first stimulus is the discriminative stimulus for behaviour appropriate to an FR10 schedule, this pattern of responding being maintained by the onset of the second stimulus, the discriminative stimulus for FI behaviour. Such schedules have been investigated in various combinations, and, on the whole, their behavioural effects are much as would be expected (see Ferster and Skinner, 1957, for example).

Chained schedules such as the above begin to make it possible to measure the power of a conditioned reinforcer. By way of illustration, one might compare the performances maintained by Chain FR100 FI 1 minute and Chain FR100 FI 3 minutes. Here, the initial part of the chain is identical, but is followed by different consequences; therefore, any differences between the fixed ratio patterns maintained in these situations may perhaps be attributed to the differences in the strength of conditioned reinforcement provided by the discriminative stimuli for FI 1 and FI 3 minute schedules. However, some of the most interesting and meaningful data have been obtained from chained schedules in which the successive components are identical except for their accompanying stimuli, as, for example, with a Chain FI 1 FI 1 FI 1 minute schedule. Such an arrangement effectively provides a primary reinforcer at the end of each third FI pattern of behaviour, each of which is accompanied by a separate stimulus.

It is interesting to compare the behavioural effects of such a schedule with those resulting from a schedule which is programmed identically except that all components are accompanied by the *same* stimulus (this is called a *Tandem* FI 1 FI 1 FI 1 minute schedule). This experiment was carried out by Kelleher and Fry (1962), and its results may seem somewhat surprising. Pigeons were trained first of all in the tandem condition. Their behaviour took the form of positively accelerated responding between food reinforcements, there being increasing numbers of responses emitted in each successive (but undifferentiated) FI 1 minute component. However, when these birds were transferred to the chain condition, in which the responding in the first FI component was followed by the discriminative stimulus for the second and so on, their behaviour changed fairly quickly, until eventually the first component was characterised by very pronounced pauses in responding, these being sometimes longer than 30 minutes. As a result, the first response emitted in the presence of the first stimulus usually changed it to the second. Responding during the second and third stimuli remained positively accelerated, although the number of responses emitted during the second component of the chained schedule was rather less than had been emitted during the corresponding part of the tandem schedule. The prolonged pausing in the first stimulus inevitably led to a large fall in the frequency of reinforcement, so the introduction of the three discriminative stimuli had an overall adverse influence on the efficiency of the pigeons' behaviour. Kelleher and Fry argue that 'neither the rate nor patterning of responding in the first component indicated that the appearance of the second-component stimulus is a conditioned reinforcer'. However, they suggested that the positively accelerated responding during the second-component stimulus did support the view that the third-component stimulus *was* a conditioned reinforcer.

Schedules such as the chained and tandem FI discussed above have been described as *second order schedules* (Kelleher, 1966). Since each third FI component was followed by primary reinforcement, the schedule could be defined as FR3, where each FI component in the sequence is regarded as the unit of behaviour rather than one single lever press. So alternative definitions of the schedules used by Kelleher and Fry (1962) are chained and tandem FR3 (FI 1 minute). Kelleher (1966) has reported the effects of extended sequences of 15 4-min fixed-interval components, only the last of which was followed by primary reinforcement — FR15 (FI 4 minutes). In this experiment, however, the tandem condition was compared with a condition which was characterised by the presentation of a *brief* stimulus after the response which initiated the next component. Instead of associating separate stimuli with each of the 15 parts of the sequence, as each FI 4 minute segment was completed there was a flash of a white light which lasted for 0.7 seconds. The fifteenth component was terminated by the flash of light followed by primary reinforcement. In this case, the schedule with the brief stimulus is termed FR15(FI 4 min : S). This schedule proved highly effective in maintaining the key-pecking behaviour of the pigeons; almost all the 15 successive 4-minute intervals were characterised by the scalloped pattern of responding typical of ordinary fixed interval schedules. In contrast, the tandem procedure, which was identical except that the flash of light was not delivered, produced much lower overall rates of responding with no consistent patterning. The implication of this experiment is clear. Each presentation of the primary reinforcer was always preceded by the flash of light, so that these two stimuli were occasionally paired. Since the responding in each of the 15 components was maintained in a consistently orderly way by the brief light stimulus, it may be regarded as a reinforcer, its effect being conditioned perhaps as a result of its pairings with food.

The two experiments discussed above suggest that these complex scheduling arrangements make it possible to analyse the effects of stimuli in terms of the ways in which they maintain behaviour. They also appear to support the theory of conditioned reinforcement based on the suggestion that a stimulus acquires such power by being paired with a primary reinforcer. However, this second assertion is not in fact established, for an appropriate control condition for identifying the effects of the *pairing* of the light with food might be to end the first 14 FI periods with a brief stimulus, and to end the 15th with food but *without* the brief stimulus. Kelleher (1966) does in fact mention that he carried out such an experiment, and that its effect was similar to the tandem procedure (i.e., when no stimuli follow the completion of each FI component). However, there have been other reports in which brief stimuli which are never paired with food develop considerable powers over behaviour in similar second order schedules. For example, Neuringer and Chung

(1967) exposed rats to a VI schedule of primary reinforcement. Next, they maintained the same schedule of primary reinforcement, but also delivered a brief stimulus after every 11th response, taking care that this stimulus was never immediately paired with food. Response rates did not change appreciably as a function of this addition to the schedule; however, they increased dramatically when the procedure was changed to a second order schedule. Now every 11th response was followed either by food or by the brief stimulus, neither event occurring at any other time. This schedule was therefore a VI (FR11 : S), but the brief stimulus was omitted when a reinforcement was obtained. Neuringer and Chung called this a quasi-reinforcement effect, but in terms of the experiments discussed earlier, one might say that the brief stimulus has become a conditioned reinforcer, for it maintained behaviour in a way appropriate to the schedule of its delivery, yet the stimulus was not paired with a primary reinforcer, nor was it a discriminative stimulus in the normal sense. Stubbs (1971) has also reported conditioned reinforcing effects of a stimulus which is never directly paired with a primary reinforcer, using a number of different second-order schedules.

Another experimental technique which is being used increasingly in this area of research is an extension of chained schedules. This procedure was first used extensively by Autor (1960), and is known as a *concurrent chain* schedule. It makes it possible to measure an animal's preferences for the stimuli associated with various schedules of primary reinforcement, and is depicted in diagrammatic form in Fig. 19. A pigeon is faced with two keys, at either of which he may peck at any time. Figure 19A shows the sequence of events if the bird pecks consistently at the left key. At first, both keys are white, but according to a VI schedule, pecks turn it to green, at the same time extinguishing the illumination on the right key. When the left key turns green, a schedule of primary reinforcement comes into operation on that key. When the reinforcement is obtained, the two keys are illuminated by white lights once more. Figure 19B depicts the consequences of pecking at the right key only. In this case, the key turns to red after a peck, according to a VI schedule of the same value as that in operation on the left key when it is white (although these two identical VI schedules are independent). A peck to the right key which turns it red also has the effect of extinguishing the light on the left key. Pecks on

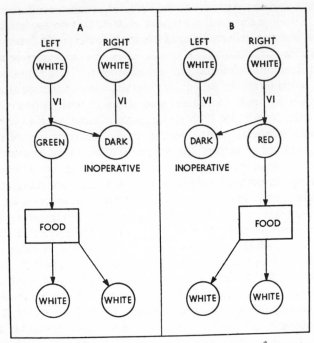

Figure 19 Diagram to show the sequences of events in a concurrent chain schedule. From Fantino (1969).

the red key obtain primary reinforcement according to some intermittent schedule, and after such a reinforcer, both keys revert to white once again. Pecks to either *darkened* key are entirely ineffective, and both VI schedules stop when either of the keys is dark. So an animal in such a situation is effectively exposed to the initial links of two chained schedules concurrently, but may choose which final link to enter.

Concurrent chain techniques provide an extremely sensitive indication of an animal's preference of the schedules in the final links. This can be expressed in terms of the relative rate of responding on the two white keys, for, of course, the choice is over once the animal produces the transition into one of the final schedules of primary reinforcement. Herrnstein (1964) found that these relative rates of responding are extremely sensitive to differences in reinforcement frequency associated with the final segments. For example, if the rate of reinforcement in the final segment is twice as high on the right key as on the left, then the rate of responding on the right key is twice that on the left in the initial links. Similarly, if reinforcement rates in the two final links are identical, the response rates in the initial link are identitical, on both keys.

It is obvious that such a precise measurement technique should prove useful in the analysis of conditioned reinforcement. One can, for example, pit a simple schedule of reinforcement against the same schedule with additional conditioned reinforcers in the final segment, assessing the subject's preference for either of these by means of the relative response rates in the initial segment. As yet, not a great deal of work has done this, but one notable exception (Schuster, 1969) certainly provides results of a most challenging nature. Schuster exposed animals either to a simple schedule of reinforcement or to the same schedule with a brief stimulus superimposed on it which was occasionally also paired with the primary reinforcer. Animals responded faster when exposed to the latter condition, suggesting that the brief stimulus was acting as a conditioned reinforcer. However, when animals were given the opportunity to choose between these two schedules by making them the final segments of a concurrent chain situation, they preferred the former. It would appear that the discriminative stimulus associated with the simple schedule was a greater conditioned reinforcer than the discriminative stimulus associated with the same schedule with additional conditioned reinforcers! Schuster attempts to explain this apparent paradox by developing what he describes as a functional analysis. Essentially, this involves the concept that a stimulus may develop control over a pattern of behaviour merely by reason of its providing information about the requirements of a schedule of primary reinforcement; in doing this, the stimulus does not necessarily acquire reinforcing properties in its own right. This is a very simplified account of Schuster's theoretical position, and it is clear that much further work is needed; however, it brings us to a consideration of another important concept in the study of conditioned reinforcement, namely that of *information*.

Interest in informative aspects of conditioned reinforcement stems mainly from some early experiments by Egger and Miller (1962, 1963). These employed the 'new response' and 'extinction' methods, but it was nevertheless possible to show that the pairing of a stimulus with a primary reinforcer is not sufficient for it to acquire conditioned reinforcing properties. In one experiment (1962), two stimuli were programmed: S1 lasted for 2 seconds, and S2 for 1.5 seconds. Both were delivered so that they ended simultaneously with the delivery of food, so that S1 came on just 0.5 seconds before S2. This latter stimulus was therefore largely redundant in terms of predicting the delivery of food. The subsequent tests revealed that S1 was the more effective stimulus as a conditioned reinforcer. On the other hand, if *additional* presentations of S1 only were made, divorced from S2 and food, the conditioned reinforcing power of S1 was appreciably reduced. These results, together with their later data (1963), led Egger and Miller to suggest that a stimulus must convey information about the presentation of a primary reinforcer in order to become a conditioned reinforcer; in these cases, information results from the predictive relationships of S1 and S2 to food.

In the light of experiments such as those discussed above, the information hypothesis is currently receiving much experimental attention, and as a result the two original hypotheses of conditioned reinforcement are becoming less adequate. In particular, the information hypothesis obtains support from experiments in which an animal emits a response which merely informs him of the schedule of primary reinforcement currently in operation. This observing response method has developed from the pioneering work of Wyckoff (1950), and is illustrated by an experiment by Steiner (1967). Animals were exposed to a Multiple FI Extinction schedule, that is to say, periods of a fixed interval schedule of reinforcement were mixed with similar periods when no schedule of reinforcement was in operation. The discriminative stimuli associated with these two components of the schedule were varied, sometimes being easily differentiated and some times being identical. In addition, the animal was able to emit another operant response (the observing response) which turned on further stimuli which were always very different, one being presented if an FI component was in operation and the other if an extinction component was then in force. Steiner found that his subjects would emit operant responses in order to obtain these additional cues, the effect being greatest when the discriminative stimuli associated with the periods of the two components were themselves very similar or identical. In other words, the animals would work to produce a stimulus which provided them with more information about the schedule of reinforcement to which they were currently exposed. In fact, the additional stimuli remained present in Steiner's experiment until the end of the component, so one of them was occasionally paired directly with food. However, this is not necessary for an informative stimulus to be reinforcing, for Kendall (1969) has reported an essentially similar effect with *brief* informative stimuli.

The term 'information' has been widely used in experimental psychology, as in 'information theory', where it has proved helpful in evaluating human performances in experiments on memory capacity and speed of reaction (see Brown, 1966). In such a context, information is a precise term, a measurement of the environment in terms of the probability of occurrence of events in that environment. One 'bit' of information is said to be provided by the occurrence of one of two equally probable events (as with an unbiassed coin falling head uppermost when tossed). Each time the number of equally probable events is *doubled*, one extra 'bit' of information is incorporated into the situation. It has been found that the efficiency of certain human performances varies as a function of the amount of information in a situation. However, in the context of conditioned reinforcement, it seems that the term 'information' is presently being used in a less precise way. It remains to be seen whether the informativeness of a conditioned reinforcer can be adequately specified merely in terms of environmental events, and whether the behavioural effects of such a stimulus are a direct function of such a measure; preliminary results have not been entirely in keeping with this formulation (e.g. Hendry, 1969b; Steiner, 1970). In the absence of such progress, the word information may easily mean no more than that a stimulus tells the inner animal how the outer animal should behave, a tendency which operant conditioners will surely resist.

Such a short review of conditioned reinforcement is inevitably highly selective. However, it shows that this area of research is currently developing quickly (see Hendry, 1969a), as much as anything because of the introduction of various sophisticated research designs. Chained schedules, concurrent chains and observing response procedures all make it possible to investigate the behavioural effects of stimuli other than primary reinforcers against controlled steady-state baselines. The earlier techniques for demonstrating such effects may be seen to lack the power of these more complex procedures. Any feelings that conditioned reinforcement has only ephemeral and slight effects must now be dismissed, for recent experiments demonstrate unequivocally the power of such a stimulus to play a significant part in the organisation and maintenance of operant behaviour. Such work also suggests the inadequacy of previous theoretical formulations: a stimulus need neither be paired with a primary reinforcer nor be a discriminative stimulus in the normal sense to acquire such power over behaviour, for brief stimuli never directly associated with a primary reinforcer may be effective if programmed to occur in certain ways. To this extent, the analogy between operant conditioning experiments and the richness of human behaviour in the real world may be said to be becoming more forceful. Human behaviour is not readily interpreted merely as a function of biologically significant events; but equally, the behaviour of animals in controlled environments may be dramatically affected by stimuli which have no direct biological significance. The need for a concept of conditioned reinforcement, which has been felt for so long, is now being supported by empirical demonstrations of its power.

CHAPTER 9

Stimulus control

The patterns of behaviour controlled by multiple schedules of reinforcement show that the animals are capable of distinguishing between the discriminative stimuli associated with the different component schedules. For example, the rat whose behaviour was displayed by the cumulative record in Fig. 17 (p. 88) must have been able to identify the various stimuli, for his behaviour adjusts to an appropriate pattern as soon as each stimulus is presented. Similarly, the effects of conditioned reinforcers discussed in the previous chapter show that the subject is capable of recognising or discriminating the various stimuli scheduled in these situations. Until now, our discussion has assumed that the animals are able to distinguish stimuli in this way, and the experiments reviewed have capitalised on the fact that different stimuli may control different patterns of behaviour. It is now time to examine this concept of stimulus control more carefully. In what conditions does a stimulus develop control over behaviour?; how general is its effect?; what stimuli can an animal detect or differentiate?

It might appear that the simplest way to develop discriminative control over operant behaviour would be to allow responses to be followed by occasional reinforcements in the presence of a particular stimulus. With a simple schedule of reinforcement, the whole test situation provides the stimulus which sets the occasion for responding in this way. However, it would be unrealistic to expect the animal to respond only in one test cage, for he would surely behave similarly in similar test situations. To what extent does stimulus control spread to other similar situations? Jenkins and Harrison (1960) investigated this; however, instead of testing their animals in cages of various shapes and sizes, they trained pigeons with a stimulus which was both distinctive and easily varied. They were trained to peck a key in a situation in which a tone of 1,000 cycles per second (now known as 1,000 herz) was sounded continuously, the birds being reinforced with food according to a variable interval schedule. This tone was therefore a discriminative stimulus (S^D). When this procedure had established a fairly steady pattern of responding, Jenkins and Harrison tested the effects of other tones on behaviour. This had to be done in extinction conditions, in which the key-pecking gradually became less frequent through lack of reinforcement, for if the schedule of reinforcement had remained in operation throughout all the tones, it might have contaminated the experiment by allowing each tone to act as a discriminative stimulus associated with the same schedule. On the other hand, the original training tone could not continue to be associated with reinforcement as before and only the other stimuli with extinction, for this might quickly develop a conditioned discrimination between the training tone and all other tones. By transferring the birds to an extinction procedure, the experimenters avoided these complications. Eight test situations were examined, and, since the key pecking behaviour was extinguishing progressively through lack of reinforcement, each was presented for short periods in a random order. The results of this procedure are shown in Fig. 20. The number of extinction responses in each stimulus is expressed as a percentage of the overall total number of extinction responses, the data for three individual birds being shown. Seven test tones were used (300, 450, 670, 1,000, 1,500, 2,250 and 3,500 hz.); these were equally spaced around the training tone of 1,000 hz. according to a logarithmic scale of frequency. It is clear that all three birds failed to made any distinction between the various tones; they failed to single out the previous discriminative stimulus as being different from the others and therefore worth more responses because of its previous status. The eighth test condition interspersed with the seven tones was a period with no noise at all (shown on the right in Fig. 20); these periods were also

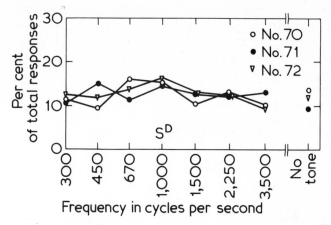

Figure 20   Generalisation gradients of responding obtained from pigeons after training with a continuous 1,000 hz tone. From Jenkins and Harrison (1960).

accompanied by approximately the same number of extinction responses. One may conclude, then, that the pigeons failed to pay any attention to the 1,000 hz. tone as a significant feature of the test situation; indeed, such data do not rule out the possibility that these three birds were deaf!

However, Jenkins and Harrison trained some other pigeons in a slightly different situation. Instead of having a 1,000 hz. tone and the VI schedule in operation continuously, these birds were exposed to a multiple schedule: periods of the tone accompanied the VI schedule, but were mixed at random with periods without the tone and with no reinforcement schedule in operation. This procedure developed the normal control over behaviour, the birds responding consistently when the tone sounded, but much less frequently in its absence. Conditions associated with no reinforcement (i.e., absence of the tone in this experiment) are often abbreviated as S^Δ. When these birds were eventually tested with different tones in extinction, a very different pattern of responding emerged, as shown in Fig. 21. They emitted many more responses during the previous S^D than during the other tones; they emitted few responses during the previous S^Δ (as a function of their training); and they showed different numbers of responses to the various tones, responding more during the tones

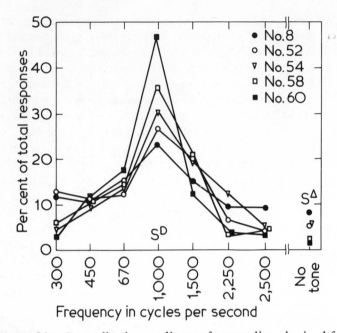

Figure 21   Generalisation gradients of responding obtained from pigeons after differential training (S^D = 1,000 hz, S^Δ = no tone). From Jenkins and Harrison (1960).

which were most similar to the previous S^D, and very little during the tones which were most different from the S^D.

Graphs such as that shown in Fig. 21 are known as gradients of *stimulus generalisation*, for they show the degree to which the animals generalise from one discriminative stimulus to other similar stimuli. The flat graphs in Fig. 20 are also, of course, gradients of stimulus generalisation; a comparison of the two figures shows that the shape of the generalisation gradient depends on the prior history of the experimental subject. The animals exposed to a non-differential training procedure show no evidence that the 1,000 hz. tone exerted any control over their behaviour, while the animals exposed to the differential S^D/S^Δ training showed that the stimulus dimension had developed considerable control — although this was not confined merely to the discriminative stimulus itself. The greater the stimulus generalisation, the less stimulus control is said to be exerted by a discriminative stimulus.

Data such as the above have been taken to indicate that differential training is necessary if a stimulus is to become a discriminative stimulus. To revert to a concept discussed earlier, it would seem that a discriminative stimulus must also impart information if it is to have a controlling effect on behaviour.

Many textbooks of psychology suggest that stimulus generalisation gradients always take the form of a symmetrical curve, with the amount of responding decreasing as a function of increasing distance from the training stimulus. However, it is misleading to suggest that such a curve is typical, for it has also been shown that the gradient of generalisation depends on many procedural variables. For example, it depends on the nature of the reinforcement schedule with which a discriminative stimulus is initially associated, and is even affected by the *value* of a variable interval schedule used in initial training, the gradient becoming flatter with larger mean intervals (Hearst et al., 1964). Moreover, it is possible to make the gradient so steep by means of differential training procedures that the 'typical' curve seems to be scarcely representative.

Gradients of generalisation have been investigated using many different stimulus dimensions. For example, Fig. 22 (taken from Bloomfield, 1967) shows gradients obtained from pigeons which were initially trained with a vertical line projected onto their pecking key as a discriminative stimulus. In the extinction test, short periods of this previous S^D were mixed at random with similar periods during which lines tilted at various angles were projected. The line joining the open points depicts the generalisation gradient after a differential procedure essentially identical to that reported above for Jenkins and Harrison; in this case, S^Δ was the absence of any line on the key. The generalisation gradient obtained after this training is similar to that which is often described as typical. However, the more interesting data in this Figure are depicted by the solid points. In this case, S^Δ was a stimulus on the same dimension as S^D (rather than the *absence* of any stimulus on that dimension): S^D was again a vertical line projected onto the key, but S^Δ was a similar line projected at an angle of 45° to the vertical, this line always being tilted in the same direction. In Fig. 22, S^D and S^Δ are identified by the two arrows. The important point to notice is that the gradient no longer has its peak associated with the previous S^D in this case. More responses were emitted in the

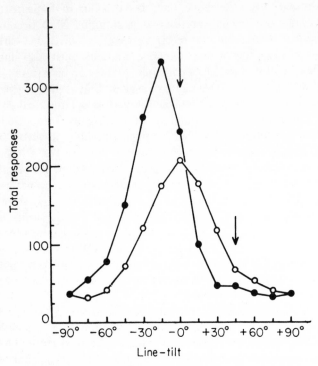

Figure 22 Distribution of responses to a selection of line orientations in a generalisation test (pigeons). Arrows show the S^D and S^Δ points, the latter being appropriate only for differential training (depicted by solid points). From Bloomfield (1967).

presence of a line tilted 15° away from the previous S^Δ than when the vertical line was projected. It is as if the whole gradient is shifted to the left; it is also asymmetrical, as a result of the suppressing effects of S^Δ on the right of the gradient.

This phenomenon of 'peak shift' is a well-documented consequence of differential training procedures in which S^D and S^Δ are both stimuli drawn from a particular dimension. In general terms, the peak of the stimulus generalisation gradient is displaced away from the previous S^Δ, so that the animal appears to favour a stimulus which was not in fact the previous discriminative stimulus. If S^Δ is merely the *absence* of any stimulus on the dimension from which S^D is drawn, then the peak of the gradient centres on the discriminative stimulus.

Before leaving stimulus generalisation, we may notice that almost all experiments in this area use an extinction technique similar to that now superceded in the study of conditioned reinforcement. Another technique, which is based on the chained schedule, has been used (Schuster and Gross, 1969), but as yet not extensively.

Although peak shift develops only as a result of differential training procedures in which S^D and S^Δ are both drawn from the same stimulus dimension, another phenomenon which may appear surprising can develop in *any* differential training procedure. This is known as 'behavioural contrast' (Reynolds, 1961a) and the effect is shown in stylised form in Fig. 23 (taken from Bloomfield, 1969). In these cases, differential training is not begun until after a number of non-differential sessions, in order to demonstrate the effect more clearly. Consider the lower segments of the diagram first. An animal is exposed to a schedule of intermittent reinforcement until its response rate becomes predictable within limits (lower left). Since any discriminative stimulus programmed by the experimenter is present continuously, this is a non-differential procedure; on the basis of Jenkins and Harrison's data (Fig. 20), we should not expect this stimulus to establish much control over behaviour. An attempt can then be made to increase its control by transferring the animal to a differential training procedure: the previous discriminative stimulus continues to be associated with the unchanged schedule of reinforcement, but periods of S^Δ are now interspersed which signal extinction periods. Predictably, the response rate in these S^Δ periods falls progressively, because of the absence of reinforcements (open points on lower right of Fig. 23). However, at the same time, the response rate in the S^D (solid points) *increases* above its previous stable level, although the schedule of reinforcements in its presence is unchanged. This is an example of the behavioural contrast phenomenon: a change in response rate during an unchanged discriminative stimulus as a result of the introduction of periods of another stimulus and schedule of reinforcement (Bloomfield, 1969). An alternative procedure is shown in the upper half of Fig. 23. Here, two stimuli are used from the beginning of the training procedure, each being associated (at different times) with the same intermittent

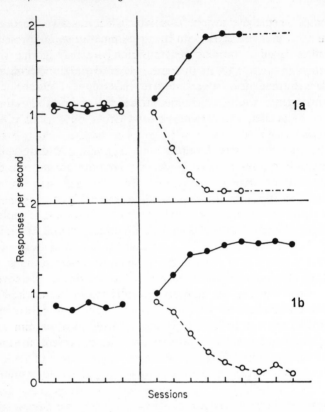

Figure 23   Two procedures by which behavioural contrast may develop: the response rate depicted by the solid points increases although no change is made in that component. From Bloomfield (1969).

schedule of reinforcement. As a result, approximately the same rate of responding occurs in both. When these rates have reached a steady state, the schedule of reinforcement associated with one of the stimuli is changed (to extinction, say), and the rate of responding in its presence declines. At the same time, the response rate in the presence of the other stimulus *increases*, although no change has been made to the schedule with which it is associated. This is the procedure which has been used by Reynolds (1961a), who originally defined behavioural contrast in the following way: 'If the rate of responding with a red key increases when the rate with a green key decreases (or decreases when the other increases), the change in rate during the presence of red is called a *contrast'*. If both changes occur in the same direction (as may happen in some circumstances), the phenomenon is termed *behavioural induction* (Reynolds, 1961b). The contrast effect may be demonstrated whether the two stimuli are drawn from the same dimension or whether there is only one stimulus which is present with one component schedule but absent when the other is in operation (Reynolds, 1961a).

The above discussion suggests that in order to increase the control of a stimulus over behaviour it is necessary to use differential training procedures. The strength of a specific discriminative stimulus (S^D), in terms of the behavioural control it exerts, is maximised if an S^Δ is incorporated into the training procedure. However, the introduction of S^Δ may have side effects. It may lead to changes in the behaviour controlled by the discriminative stimulus, as with behavioural contrast. Moreover, if S^Δ is drawn from the same stimulus dimension, it may lead to a situation in which an animal's behaviour may be more strongly controlled by a stimulus *other* than the discriminative stimulus, one which is displaced away from S^Δ (the peak shift phenomenon).

It is possible to avoid these side effects, however, and thereby show that they result from the *procedures* traditionally used to establish a discrimination' rather than the establishment of the discrimination itself. The traditional way to train an animal to discriminate two stimuli has been to use the differential procedures discussed above. A response is reinforced in the presence of one stimulus (S^D), but never in the presence of the other (S^Δ). Thus periods of reinforcement are mixed with periods of *extinction*, for the animal is normally left to discover for himself, as it were, the fact that one of the stimuli to which he is occasionally exposed either never accompanies reinforcement or ceases to accompany it (the two procedures shown in Fig. 23). Hence, the idea has arisen that an animal learns a discrimination by a trial and error procedure; occasionally his behaviour is successful, in that it produces a reinforcement (in S^D). However, every response emitted in the presence of S^Δ can be regarded as an error, for, in the absence of any possibility of a reinforcement, it is an inappropriate response. The discrimination is said to be established when the animal emits responses regularly during S^D, but rarely during S^Δ. Using such procedures, it was once assumed that the making of errors was an essential prerequisite for an animal to master a discrimination. However, Terrace (1963a) has reported an experiment in which he showed that pigeons could learn to discriminate a red key (S^D) from a green key (S^Δ) without making any error (or, at least, with very few errors indeed). This was achieved by what amounts to a successive approximation procedure. When conditioning an animal, the experimenter can either wait for the spontaneous occurrence of the behaviour to be increased (thereby allowing the animal to do the 'wrong' things before this happens), or he can shape his final behaviour by reinforcing behaviour which increasingly approximates this response. The traditional method of establishing a discrimination is analogous to the first procedure: one allows the subject to work the problem out for himself, thereby making errors. Terrace's method develops control over behaviour by gradually approximating the situation to the final discrimination task.

The 'errorless discrimination learning' procedure which enabled pigeons to differentiate the two stimuli began in the very first experimental session. Fairly long periods of bright red light on the pecking key (S^D) were interspersed with periods of darkened key which were at first of very short duration, but which became progressively longer (S^Δ). Some care was taken at first to ensure that the periods of darkness began when the bird was not in a very favourable position to peck the key (for example, when his head was turned away momentarily); however, this restriction was quickly relaxed. When periods of red S^D were alternating with 30 second periods of darkened key (S^Δ), the latter were shortened back to 5 seconds. However, during these 5 second periods, the key was now illuminated in green, at first very dimly indeed, but with gradually increasing brightness, until the red and green lights were of equal intensity. The final stage of the procedure was once more to increase the duration of S^Δ (now the green light), again progressively, until eventually the key was being lit with equal brightness and duration either in red (S^D) or green (S^Δ). While these changes were occurring in the programming of S^Δ periods, the schedule of reinforcement during S^D was adjusted from continuous reinforcement to VI 1 minute.

This progressive procedure was successful in developing appropriate discriminative control by the red and green stimuli.

However, this was achieved with only very few 'errors', these tending to occur either at the very beginning of an S^Δ period as a carry over from the S^D responding, or very occasionally just before the end of an S^Δ period. Subsequent experiments established this red/green discrimination in several birds without a single error at any stage (Terrace, 1963b), this improvement being the result of slight refinements in the procedure. In this second set of experiments, animals were subsequently transferred from the red/green discrimination to a discrimination between a vertical and a horizontal white line. These new stimuli were first projected onto the pecking key by superimposing them on the red and green backgrounds, and then the colours, which were previously S^D and S^Δ, were slowly and progressively faded out. As a result, the animals transferred from the old to the new discrimination, again without making errors. Since the latter discrimination is normally regarded as more difficult for pigeons to master by traditional techniques, its acquisition without errors is even more striking. Difficult discriminations can be developed without errors if animals are progressively moved through a sequence which first establishes an easy discrimination and then slowly fades this into the more complex.

Terrace's findings are exceptionally important, for they challenge any theory of discrimination learning which assumes that errors are crucial in the acquisition of differential control by two stimuli or in sharpening the stimulus control exerted by a discriminative stimulus. However, his discussions of these theoretical implications from a historical point of view will not be elaborated here (see Terrace, 1966). Of greater relevance in the present context are a number of empirical differences between the behaviour established by traditional and by errorless procedures. First, the *final* performance maintained after a progressive training appears to be superior to the final performance learned by trial and error, for animals trained in the latter way may never stop responding completely during S^Δ periods; they tend to make occasional bursts of errors even after very considerable exposure to the two stimuli. A second difference is that there is no evidence for behavioural contrast when progressive procedures are used: in other words, the rate of responding in S^D appears to be entirely unaffected by manipulations of S^Δ. For example, if, after progressive training, S^Δ is withheld so that S^D is presented continuously, the frequency of operant responding during S^D does not change; nor does it alter when S^Δ periods are subsequently reintroduced. On the other hand, animals trained by trial and error procedures show a decrease in S^D response rate if S^Δ is discontinued, and a subsequent increase when S^Δ is incorporated once again — the behavioural contrast phenomenon (see Terrace, 1963a). A third difference between the behaviours established by the two procedures is to be seen during S^Δ periods. With traditional procedures, it has often been reported that animals tend to become emotional during S^Δ periods: pigeons often strut about their cages noisily, flap their wings and vocalise. A number of possible reasons come to mind in an intuitive way. S^Δ periods seem to make an animal angry or frustrated or inhibited: it seems quite clear that animals do not like them. However, animals who have learned without errors show no such histrionics; they appear merely to wait patiently for the next period of S^D. This discussion is, of course, too free and unquantified, but it receives some effective experimental support from a further study by Terrace (1963c), in which the effects of drugs on discrimination performance were investigated. It had previously been reported that the drugs chlorpromazine and imipramine disrupt discriminations by producing many more errors, i.e., responses in S^Δ. One possible reason for this is that the drugs interfere with the *perceptual* processes; in other words, the animals are no longer able to 'see' the difference between S^D and S^Δ. However, Terrace showed that this could not be the true reason, for pigeons trained on an identical discrimination by the progressive method were not at all affected in S^Δ by the same doses of these drugs: they still made no errors. A more plausible hypothesis for the effects of the drugs on traditionally trained animals takes into account the generally relaxing effects of these drugs. In general terms, Terrace argued that the disruption of 'normal' discriminations resulted from the fact that the drugs reduced the aversiveness or 'nastiness' of the S^Δ. Since pigeons trained by errorless procedures did not find S^Δ aversive at all, these effects could not occur, and therefore the discrimination was unaffected. This experiment, then, supports the view that there is a general difference in the patterns of behaviour generated by the two procedures, conveniently summarised by the suggestion that conventional procedures result in an aversive S^Δ which produces 'emotional' behaviour, but that progressive procedures result in a non-aversive S^Δ through which the animal waits patiently.

A final difference between the discrimination engendered by the two procedures concerns the peak shift phenomenon explained earlier. Terrace has shown (1964) that animals which are progressively trained to differentiate an S^D from an S^Δ drawn from the same stimulus dimension show no peak shift in the generalisation gradients produced subsequently in extinction tests. In this case, S^D was a light of 580 millimicrons (which is a slightly orange yellow); S^Δ was a light of equal intensity but of a different wavelength (540 millimicrons – a slightly green yellow). Animals were trained either by progressive or trial and error procedures. Generalisation tests were conducted in extinction using 15 different stimuli, from 490 millimicrons (a bluish green) to 670 millimicrons (towards the red end of the visual spectrum). The generalision gradients obtained revealed that birds trained traditionally showed a peak shift, emitting more responses to a light of 590 millimicrons than to the previous S^D, i.e., a shift away from the previous S^Δ. On the other hand, birds trained by Terrace's progressive methods showed a peak at the previous S^D, although their previous S^Δ was also drawn from the same stimulus dimension.

This finding, taken in conjunction with the previous discussion concerning the aversiveness of an S^Δ produced by trial and error procedures, strongly suggests that the peak shift phenomenon also results in some way from the animal's dislike of the previous S^Δ. Thus, the peak is shifted as a result of the animal's distaste for the S^Δ, and therefore the peak of the gradient moves from the S^D to a stimulus farther away from that S^Δ. This view is supported by an experiment by Grusec (1968). He trained pigeons to discriminate colours either by trial and error or by progressive procedures. Stimulus generalisation gradients were then obtained, these being similar to those reported by Terrace (1964): a peak shift was again the consequence of traditional procedures, but not of errorless training. Then Grusec delivered occasional slight and brief electric shocks to some of the pigeons during the periods of S^Δ, his reasoning being that this procedure should contribute to the aversiveness of that S^Δ stimulus. The result of this was that the peak shift increased in size for the traditionally trained birds, and a peak shift away from the S^Δ occurred for the first time with the birds trained by the errorless procedure. This is a strong indication, then, that the traditional trial and error procedures for teaching a discrimination produce an aversive S^Δ, which generates emotional behaviour; this in turn contributes to side effects on the behaviour in the presence of S^D, such side effects being mimicked by delivering painful stimuli during S^Δ to an animal which has been trained by procedures which until then protected S^Δ from becoming aversive.

The implications of all this work for teaching discriminations to children and adults will be discussed in a later chapter. For the moment, it indicates that the making of errors is *not* necessarily fundamental to the establishment of a discrimination. Indeed, a procedure which generates errors may also generate undesirable consequences for behaviour; however, these may be effectively avoided if progressive shaping techniques are used to establish differential control of behaviour.

So far in this chapter on stimulus control of behaviour no attention has been paid to the *capabilities* of animals to discriminate; instead, the processes have been considered which contribute to the development of control by stimuli which are in any case discriminable. It may, however, be appropriate here to outline some experimental work on the perceptual capacities of animals. There is little to gain here by ennumerating what some species of animals can see or not see, for this would not contribute to the general aims of this book. Besides, the preceding discussion suggests that these capabilities depend to a large extent on the procedures used to investigate them. For example, Terrace succeeded in teaching a difficult discrimination without errors ever being made. One might expect the smallest differential effects to be generated by the most efficient training procedures; an animal might be able to discriminate more successfully between very similar stimuli if his 'attention' is progressively focussed by an errorless training procedure. For this reason, the ensuing discussion centres on the appropriate techniques for investigating the perceptual capabilities of animals, and the implications of some of this work.

A major contribution to the study of animals' perceptual processes has been the work of Blough (e.g., 1958). Using operant conditioning techniques, he has been able to plot the visual threshold of pigeons; the birds perform in a way which makes it possible to say with complete precision what is the minimum intensity of light that they are able to see. Not surprisingly, such a complex requirement demands a sophisticated experimental technique. In essence, Blough decided to ask the pigeons to respond differentially on two keys: if a light could be seen, key A was to be pecked, but if the light could not be seen, the pigeon was to peck key B. A problem, of course, arises when appropriate reinforcement schedules are incorporated to maintain such key-pecking behaviour: how can the experimenter know when he may reinforce a peck on either key if only the pigeon knows what he can or can't see? After all, this is the whole point of the experiment. The solution to this difficulty depends on Blough's certainty that a pigeon is unable to see a light which isn't there! In other words, Blough decided to reinforce pecks on key B only when that light definitely could not be seen because it was hidden from the animal by an automatic shutter. This, of course, will maintain pecking on key B whenever the light stimulus is either hidden physically or is present but is too dim for the pigeon to see. By never reinforcing the animal at all if the stimulus is in fact present, the schedule of reinforcement for an invisible light becomes intermittent. On the other hand, a peck on key B can also never be reinforced at all if the pigeon *is* able to see the light. The final step in the process is to transfer pecks to key A when the bird *can* see the light. This cannot be done by reinforcing the bird in a similar fashion, i.e., by providing a reinforcement only for pecks on key A which occur when the light is so bright that it *must* be visible, for this might quickly establish a discrimination between this light and other lights which are less bright but nevertheless visible. Blough's ingenious solution to this difficulty depends on the processes of conditioned reinforcement outlined earlier. Pecking on key A can be maintained by the delivery of the discriminative stimulus for pecking on key B, namely by the light becoming invisible. If pecks on key A progressively reduce the intensity of the light, the pigeon will be able to 'decide' for himself when the light has become invisible, and therefore switch to key B. If pecks on key B in turn lead to progressive *increases* in the light intensity, the pigeon will switch back to key A when the light becomes visible, and so on. In this way the pigeon plots his own visual threshold.

This procedure is illustrated in Fig. 24. The pigeon is facing the two keys. Pecks on key A move an optical wedge through which a light is shining, thereby reducing the intensity of the light in front of the pigeon. Pecks on key B have the opposite

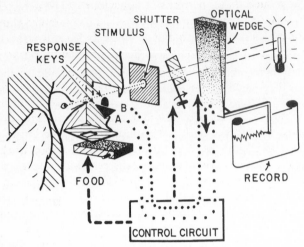

Figure 24   System for determining the visual threshold of a pigeon. From Blough (1958).

effect, progressively *increasing* the intensity of the stimulus by moving the optical wedge in the other direction. Occasionally, when the bird is judging that the stimulus is invisible (by responding on key B), a shutter is placed between the source of the light and the pigeon, thereby making it 'safe' for the experimenter to reinforce a response on key B. Finally, by keeping a record of the position of the optical wedge, the experimenter is able to say at which stages the bird judges whether the light is visible or not. In this way, he is able to determine the pigeon's visual threshold, the intensity of illumination which is just enough to be seen by the subject.

This experimental technique is very complex, and Blough has admitted to a number of failures to develop appropriate stimulus control. For example, it is possible that a bird might merely disregard the stimulus to which he was supposed to be responding, but just peck for a while on key A, switch to key B for a period, then back to A and so on. In other words, the stimulus would not have developed control over behaviour, but the bird would nevertheless have formulated a strategy which was adequate for him to obtain occasional reinforcement. A number of such complications may arise, and it is not possible to consider here how they may best be avoided. However, it is easy to suggest how such 'false' patterns of behaviour can be detected if they do develop. For example, one could interpose the shutter continuously for a period; an animal whose behaviour was under appropriate stimulus control would peck consistently on key B, whereas an aberrant bird would continue to allocate his pecks between the two keys as before. Another test procedure is illustrated by the record shown in Fig. 25. This shows the visual threshold plotted by a pigeon tested in the above procedure after being transferred to the dark test situation from a period in the light. The initial fall in the threshold demonstrates what in humans is known as dark adaptation, the phenomenon whereby our ability to detect faint lights increases as we remain in darkness for a period. Expressed in another way, dark adaptation results in a progressive decrease in the visual threshold, causing a decrease in the minimum intensity of light required to be detected. Figure 25 shows that pigeons show the same process, for the bird drives the intensity of his stimulus down progressively; his responses on key B still occur, and drive the light

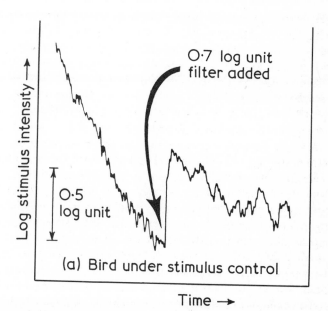

Figure 25   Dark-adaptation in the pigeon, and the effect of interposing a filter between the bird and the source of light. From Blough (1958).

intensity up when it becomes sub-threshold, but the *overall* tendency is for more responses to be emitted on key A, thereby plotting a gradual decrease in the visual threshold. The arrow in Fig. 25 shows the effect of interposing an *additional* filter between the optical wedge and the pigeon. The pigeon immediately compensates for the resultant decrease in the intensity of the stimulus available to him, by responding on key B until the adjustable wedge allows enough light through for him to see it once again and thereby prompt him to switch to key A. The additional light allowed through the adjustable wedge exactly compensated for the amount of light blocked by the additional filter. Figure 25 shows, then, the very precise nature of the stimulus control exerted by light, first in terms of an adjusting threshold as the pigeon adapts to darkness, and second by the compensation in the adjustment of the optical wedge as the result of an additional filter.

This degree of experimental control over an animal's behaviour is most impressive, and the ability to plot such complex perceptual phenomena as dark adaptation in infra-human species offers considerable hope for the study of perception in general. Using similar techniques, Blough (1961) has been able to study what amounts to a visual illusion, still using pigeons as subjects. This is known as the brightness contrast effect: if two spots are of equal brightness, the one which appears on a dark background appears to be brighter than the one with a light background. Blough discovered that pigeons are also misled by the different backgrounds. In this case the pigeon was required to adjust the brightness of two spots which he could see simultaneously, that is he was trying to match them. The pigeons set the spot on the light background to a lower brightness than the spot on the dark ground. It is interesting to be able to show that pigeons are subject to illusions in the same way as humans, and work like this promises to be helpful in identifying the causes of such misperceptions, for the past experience of animals can be much more adequately controlled than that of human subjects.

Techniques such as Blough's show that the behaviour of animals can be brought under the precise control of complex stimulus conditions. This, together with the ability of operant conditioning experiments in general to produce consistent steady states of behaviour, suggests the interesting possibility that animals could be used to carry out some of the repetitive, but skilful, tasks at present entrusted to (sometimes unwilling) humans. To take an example, the ability of pigeons to distinguish red from green has been discussed repeatedly in this chapter. Given that each of these stimuli (or their absence) may develop predictable control over pigeons' behaviour, one might suggest that the birds would make excellent train drivers, for the human driver is doing essentially the same thing, responding differentially according to red and green signals. If this prospect seems too bold, the pigeon might at least be an effective substitute for the human inspector in automatic systems such as that on the Victoria Line of the London Underground railway, where, one is led to believe, the 'driver' does not drive in the usual sense, since the running of the train is almost totally automated (presumably by expensive apparatus). Suggestions such as these are normally met with open derision, an outcome which is amusingly outlined in an article by Verhave (1966). We are not attuned to the belief that we can trust in the behaviour of infrahuman species: pigeons cannot be as reliable as humans. Yet experiments in operant conditioning, especially those of Terrace and of Blough discussed in this chapter, show that animal behaviour can be extremely reliable even in complex circumstances. In his paper, Verhave points out that automation by machine has not yet been very effective in tasks which demand the ability to discriminate one stimulus from another (e.g. on the basis of colour, shape, size, regularity, etc.). Therefore, humans are asked to do boring, repetitive tasks, especially in the context of routine inspection of products such as cigarettes, drug capsules, electronic components, and so on, where some products are rejected on the basis of their appearance. Verhave suggests that for a nominal sum, one may purchase an 'organic device' which has an average life of 10 to 15 years, is extremely flexible to specific circumstances, has visual acuity at least as good as the human eye, and is extremely sensitive to slight differences in colour — the pigeon! Cumming (1966) went so far as to interest a manufacturer of electrical diodes in the possibility of releasing humans from hum-drum inspection tasks, replacing them with pigeons who appear to be much 'happier' in such situations. In this case, the task was to reject inadequate diodes on the basis of unsatisfactory coats of paint on their covers. It is easy to see in principle how pigeons can be trained to do this: they could be kept in cages with transparent windows, past which individual diodes might be fed. Perfect diodes might be developed as discriminative stimuli for one response, the consequence of which might be to channel that diode to the packing station. Any form of imperfect diode would 'produce' another response, which in turn could open a trap-door to a rubbish bin (or back to the paint shop). The established discrimination could be maintained, as in Blough's experiments, by allowing access to food only when the response *must* be appropriate, perhaps by automatically interposing known duds or satisfactory diodes occasionally. A cheaper suggestion (first made by Verhave, 1966) would be to allow access to food only if two or more trained pigeons *all* agreed that the sample object was acceptable or to be rejected. This would have the advantage of 'holding in' appropriate behaviour without additional automation, for if only two pigeons each have an error rate as high as 1 out of 100, the probability of two birds agreeing to accept what they were originally trained to reject would be 1 in 10,000 samples! The rate of inspection could be controlled at a high frequency by means of a suitable schedule of reinforcement.

One need not elaborate details here, for the principles involved have been outlined already. Cumming (1966) went further, however; he set up a mock production line on the above basis, and demonstrated to his own satisfaction that such an innovation would work. His pigeons were easily trained to 'reject' a diode which had unpainted spots as small as 2.5 mm. in diameter. Further progress was halted not by limits in the pigeons' ability, but by the abrupt termination of the project by the sponsoring organisation. Cumming's opinion is that this decision was prompted not by any failure in the preliminary work, but by its very success! Executive decisions loomed into sight which it was felt were best avoided, such as the reaction of the human labour force to being replaced by such an 'inferior' organism. Indeed, this seems to be the major obstacle to any sort of progress in this area of 'applied animal psychology': humans believe that they are intellectually superior to the less 'intelligent' pigeon or monkey. This is doubtless true in many senses, but we have seen that even Descartes acknowledged animals as superior to humans in certain respects. As for the suggestion that animals would be unreliable in such situations, this can hardly be sustained, for there can be no reason to doubt the extreme predictability of animals' behaviour in well-controlled environments.

Of course, this final discussion is slightly whimsical, but it is introduced here for a very good purpose. It is now beyond dispute that the behaviour of animals may come under the precise control of their environment, if that environment is itself controlled. Moreover, considerable perceptual skills may be developed in animals by appropriate training procedures. The combination of schedules of intermittent reinforcement and techniques for developing stimulus control provides a most powerful technique for the study and control of operant behaviour.

CHAPTER 10
The effects of punishment on behaviour

So far we have discussed the ways in which the behaviour of animals may be controlled by consequences which we might assume were in some sense pleasant. The fact that animals will work in order to obtain a reinforcer (or rather, because such behaviour has been associated with reinforcement in the past) might be taken as an indication that the consequences of behaviour are pleasant in these situations, although it should be noticed that there is no necessity for them to be pleasant in terms of the formal definition of a reinforcing event. In this chapter, however, the focus of attention will be the effects of unpleasant stimuli on behaviour. If a stimulus which we presume to be unpleasant is associated with behaviour, the procedure is recognisable as punishment, as encountered in the relatively unstructured environment provided by home or school. This is obviously an area of considerable controversy in our society; educationists, psychologists, and laymen have long disputed the advantages and disadvantages of using corporal punishment to 'correct' behaviour. The current attitude seems ambivalent. 'Spare the rod and spoil the child' is a view which is not as much advocated in public as it once was; and yet it seems to be accepted that in a few dire circumstances punishment of some kind (not necessarily corporal) cannot be avoided. This implies a belief that punishment may be a more effective procedure for changing behaviour than methods based on pleasant consequences for appropriate behaviour, but that it is to be avoided whenever possible because of its unpleasantness for both punished *and* punisher.

In this discussion, the rights and wrongs of punishment techniques will not be discussed. Instead, we shall attempt to discover whether punishment really is an effective procedure for eliminating a pattern of behaviour — does experimental evidence support the assertion that punishment is either more or less effective than procedures which do not include unpleasant stimuli? Again, this question will be examined on the basis of controlled experimental investigations in which animals act as subjects. Since punishment is supposed to reduce the probability or frequency of a pattern of behaviour, operant conditioning experiments provide a useful test situation, for schedules of intermittent reinforcement can establish predictable patterns of behaviour characterised by a high frequency of arbitrary responses. Animals are used in such experiments because the procedure can be controlled and adjusted in a rigorous way. In addition, it is perhaps a little less morally reprehensible to use animals to investigate the bases of punishment than humans, although, of course, their use nevertheless remains extremely offensive to many. However, such work is carried out in the hope of isolating variables of general behavioural importance, so that we may gain more insight into factors important at a human level too.

The attitudes of society in general to punishment techniques have been closely mirrored in the development of psychological theory. For example, Thorndike, who was one of the earliest researchers to investigate learning behaviour systematically (and from whom the phrase 'trial-and-error learning' may be traced), at first adopted a view of punishment much in accord with a 'common-sense' outlook. He suggested (e.g., 1913) that both rewards and punishments have simple effects: behaviour was said to be strengthened if followed by a 'satisfying' state of affairs, but weakened if followed by an 'annoying' state of affairs. However, Thorndike abandoned this balanced 'Law of Effect', when he subsequently discovered that punishment did not always have a clear-cut effect (e.g., 1932); he therefore concentrated his theories on a truncated law of effect which laid stress on the efficacy of satisfying states of affairs to modify behaviour. Since that time, further inconsistencies in the effects of punishment have been revealed (some of which will be reviewed later), and some writers of textbooks in psychology have largely avoided discussing this important problem, or have contented themselves with mysterious comments about the complexities, or even the paradoxes, of punishment procedures.

There are three separate concepts involved in a common definition of punishment: a *reduction* in the strength or frequency of behaviour which is *followed* by an *unpleasant* stimulus. In this discussion, the last of these three will be accepted as fundamental for the moment; in other words, the effects of noxious or aversive stimuli will be examined, without any determined attempt to define exactly what a noxious stimulus is (for this will be considered later). In the experiments to be reviewed, the punishing stimulus is invariably one which is readily interpretable as unpleasant, often taking the form of a brief electric shock. Shock is, of course, an 'unnatural' stimulus for most animals, but it has the advantage of being readily adjusted by the experimenter in terms of its intensity and its duration, and it is therefore used as a model of aversive stimuli in the same way that food is used as a model of pleasant stimuli. However, the other two concepts in the common definition of punishment need careful consideration, for the idea that punishment reduces behaviour has been challenged, as has the assumption that punishment is essentially the association of a *response* with an aversive stimulus.

Early experimental work in this area (as in others already considered) was for some time handicapped by a lack of procedural sophistication, and a consequent reliance on data obtained from such situations as extinction tests. Nevertheless, data obtained in this way appeared challenging and important, and have been widely quoted. Figure 26 shows the results of one such experiment (Skinner, 1938). Two groups of hungry rats were trained to press a lever on an intermittent schedule of food reinforcement. They were then tested for 2 hours on each of two subsequent days, during which no reinforcements were delivered (i.e., in an extinction condition). However, in one of the groups, each lever-press in the first ten minutes of the first of these extinction sessions produced a sudden rebound of the lever (caused by the other side of the lever being knocked down-

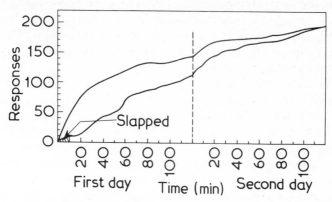

Figure 26   The effects on extinction of a mild punishment administered at the beginning of the extinction period. From Skinner (1938).

wards), which produced an unpleasant slap on the front feet of the rat; in other words, the first ten minutes of the extinction procedure were accompanied by a mild punishment procedure. The curves in Fig. 26 are cumulative records of the performance of the two groups of animals on these two days. The upper curve is for extinction without punishment: there is a progressive decline in the rate of pressing the lever, which is slightly disrupted by a temporary increase in response rate at the beginning of the second session. This curve is, then, a typical extinction curve. In comparison, the responses of the punished group were markedly suppressed during the ten-minute punishment period. However, when the punishments were discontinued, the lever pressing of this group of rats showed a compensatory increase in rate. By the end of the second day, the behaviour of both groups had almost completely extinguished, but the punished group had made as many responses in the extinction period as had the unpunished control group, in spite of the initial suppression of their behaviour.

This result has been taken to illustrate two effects of punishment: first, that it causes suppression of behaviour when it is introduced; but second, that it does not 'eliminate' behaviour, for the behaviour of the punished group completely compensated for their initial suppression when the slaps from the lever were discontinued. Skinner's experiment was followed by an influential series of investigations by his colleague Estes, and published in 1944. His general conclusion was that 'a response cannot be eliminated from an organism's repertoire more rapidly with the aid of punishment than without it'. A response can only be permanently weakened, according to Estes, by a sufficient number of unreinforced occurrences, and a response which is suppressed by punishment can in fact be protected from this process of extinction, thereby prolonging the *time* required for extinction to become complete. It is important to emphasise here that Estes was reporting merely the long-term effects of *temporary* periods of punishment on the number of *extinction* responses. His punishment procedures did suppress behaviour while they were in operation (as did Skinner's). These limitations may be easily overlooked, and, as a result, his findings may be unduly extended to a suggestion that punishment is generally ineffective.

It was in this series of experiments that the necessity for a close relationship between *behaviour* and an aversive stimulus was challenged in the context of punishment. On the basis of one of his experiments (Experiment I, 1944), Estes suggested that a close temporal relationship between a response and an aversive stimulus was no more effective in suppressing behaviour than a procedure which delivered aversive stimuli completely independently of behaviour. It appeared that it was the association between the noxious stimulus and the *discriminative stimulus* for lever pressing which was important. Estes went on to argue that the association between any stimulus present and the aversive stimulus was sufficient to establish an emotional reaction in the animals, and that the (temporary) suppression of their behaviour was the indirect consequence of 'anxiety' or fear. If true, this assertion would attribute the suppression of behaviour by punishment to a conditioning process which related *stimuli* (as in Pavlovian conditioning). It would also have important practical implications, for, in social conditions, a person who punishes is himself one part of the environment as the aversive event is delivered, and so *any* behaviour for which the first person may act as a discriminative stimulus is also likely to be suppressed. In Estes' words: 'Whipping a dog, for example, is quite as likely to result in the conditioning of fear and withdrawal reactions to the sight of the trainer as in the weakening of the undesired behaviour. And the emotional state is as effective in depressing the strength of other behaviour which would normally occur in the situation in question as in depressing the strength of the punished response' (Estes, 1944).

It is not unnatural that data and conclusions such as those of Estes should be interpreted as casting considerable doubt on the social desirability of any form of punishment. Punishment appeared to be both ineffective and fraught with dangers of undesirable side-effects. However, the study of punishment procedures is now benefitting from the more sophisticated experimental techniques which have been so useful in the study of conditioned reinforcement. Indeed, there is an increasingly close relationship developing between these two fields of study, which is due to the use of maintained patterns of behaviour and steady state designs in both.

There now seems little doubt that behavioural differences *do* result from situations in which aversive stimuli are delivered either immediately after an operant response or independently of behaviour. Preliminary evidence was reported to this effect by Hunt and Brady (1955), and it seems to be established incontrovertibly in an experiment reported by Azrin (1956) which uses a very sophisticated design when one considers the early date of the experiment. Azrin compared two variations of both the two procedures, using them in a way which made it possible to compare their effects on individual animals (pigeons) acting as their own controls. Each subject was exposed to all four conditions, individual animals encountering these in different orders to control for possible sequence effects. The pecking of the food-deprived birds was first stabilised on a VI 3 minute schedule of food reinforcement, during which 2 minute periods of blue light on the key alternated with similar periods of orange. Then the crucial experimental work was begun, the VI schedule of food reinforcement remaining unchanged. The four experimental conditions, and their effects were as follows:

a) *FI uncorrelated shock.* A shock was delivered to the subject one minute after the beginning of each period of orange light, independently of his behaviour. Responding became progressively less frequent until the shock was delivered, but thereafter showed a progressive acceleration.

b) *FI correlated shock.* Here, a shock was delivered immediately after the first response to be emitted after one minute of each period of the orange light. The responding maintained by this condition typically decreased in frequency during the first minute, usually stopping completely just before shock would have been delivered. Very few shocks were delivered in this condition as a result of this pattern of behaviour. The pigeons began to peck again as soon as the blue light reappeared.

c) *VI uncorrelated shock.* Shocks were delivered during each period of orange light, regardless of the pigeon's behaviour. However, in this condition, the moment of shock was unpredictable, as was the *number* of shocks in any particular period of orange. In this part of the experiment, the birds showed a consistent decrease in responding during the orange light (in comparison with their response rates in the presence of blue).

d) *VI correlated shock.* Shock was delivered immediately after a response, but its occasion was unpredictable, as in condition c). In this condition, the pigeons did not respond at all during the orange stimulus.

These results establish unequivocally that shocks delivered only immediately after a response (and which an animal may therefore avoid by not responding) have a greater suppressive effect on responding than do shocks which are delivered unavoidably and entirely unrelated to responding. These results are therefore not consistent with Estes' conclusions reviewed above. Azrin suggested that Estes had been unable to distinguish between his two procedures because of the brevity of his 'punishment' conditions: the different effects of the two procedures may not have had time to develop. Azrin's experiment therefore emphasises the advantages of steady state experiments in this area of research. In his report, Azrin discusses the different *patterns* of responding during the orange light. He concluded that 'the findings of the investigation are consistent with the view that aversive stimuli act in a direction opposite to that of reinforcers'. Thus the FI condition was typified by the opposite of the FI scallop that we saw when discussing schedules of food reinforcement. Azrin's interest in the effects of *scheduling* aversive stimuli is again, in some senses, before its time: these problems will also be discussed later.

So, it would seem, considerable behavioural differences result from giving shocks only immediately after an operant response and delivering them independently of behaviour. The term 'anxiety' will be used to characterise the results of the latter procedure (which also caused some suppression of behaviour in

Azrin's experiment), and the term 'punishment' reserved only for the procedure in which shocks are dependent on responding. The question now to be considered is whether punishment procedures invariably have consistent suppressing effects on maintained operant behaviour in a steady state research design.

One common finding in experiments on punishment is that the effects of shock wane as the experiment progresses. This is shown very clearly in Fig. 27, which is taken from another report by Azrin (1960). This shows the cumulative records of key pecking by a pigeon which was exposed throughout this experiment to a VI 1 minute schedule of food reinforcement (delivery of reinforcement is not shown). This pigeon's stable performance without punishment is shown in the top left segment of Fig. 27 (0 volts). The remainder of the top row of records shows the

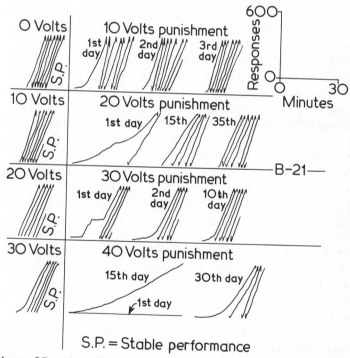

Figure 27   The effects on VI behaviour of continuous punishment procedures. Delivery of reinforcement is not shown. From Azrin (1960).

effect of delivering a very brief shock of 10 volts immediately after every response throughout each experimental session. It can be seen that on the first day this punishment procedure had an immediate suppressive effect; however, this wore off quite quickly. On the second day there was a limited amount of suppression initially, but this was confined to the first 10 minutes of the session. On the third day, the effect was even less pronounced. By the fourth day (shown as the record to the left of the second row) punishment by a shock of 10 volts had no detectable effect on behaviour, for this was again identical with the original. The punishment was then increased to 20 volts, and this produced a very marked suppressive effect on the first day. However, this effect also diminished progressively (although more slowly), and by the 35th day of this procedure had effectively disappeared. When behaviour was again stable with the 20 volt punishment, the intensity was increased by a further 10 volts, which produced much the same effects — an initial disruption but an eventual return to the original response rate without punishment. However, these 30 volt shocks did continue to cause some suppression at the beginning of each session. When the shock intensity was increased to 40 volts, the same cycle was repeated yet again — initial gross disruptions were eventually superseded by response rates as high as those which had been seen in the 0 volt condition.

These results show that the suppressive effects of punishment may become substantially reduced as the procedure is continued: aversive stimuli which at first suppress behaviour may lose their power. Clearly, this is an important feature to be taken into account when considering punishment in general. Nevertheless, Azrin (1960) has shown that as shock intensity is increased beyond the values considered above, a sustained suppressive effect occurs. For example, Fig. 28 shows sample cumulative records obtained by Azrin from a pigeon which was exposed to a VI schedule of food reinforcement together with a punishing shock after each response. It may be seen that the degree of suppression in the final steady states is in fact a function of the intensity of the aversive stimulus used to punish responding. These data suggest that sustained punishment is capable of suppressing behaviour when the schedule of reinforcement maintaining the behaviour remains unchanged. However, even though the final degree of suppression is related to the intensity

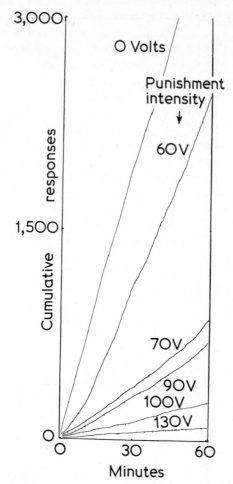

Figure 28   Cumulative records showing response rate as a function of punishment intensity. From Azrin (1960).

of the punishing stimulus, the importance of initial adaptation effects must always be considered.

There is now much supporting evidence for the above generalisations (e.g., Appel, 1963b), and it is established that *consistent* punishment procedures which use relatively severe shocks may suppress behaviour for as long as they are continued. If the intensity is such that *complete* suppression results, this may have the effect of eliminating behaviour although no change in the conditions of reinforcement have been made. However, responding which is only *partially* suppressed soon reverts to its previous rate (or an even higher rate) when the punishment procedure is discontinued (Azrin and Holz, 1966).

The effects of a punishment procedure may vary when it is superimposed on patterns of behaviour maintained by different schedules of reinforcement; similarly suppression may be sustained by *intermittent* punishment procedures (see Azrin and Holz, 1966). These findings add considerably to the complexity of any account of punishment, but involve no inconsistency with the results discussed above. However, a number of experimenters have reported results which seem at first sight difficult to incorporate into a systematic theory of punishment.

Perhaps the most celebrated 'paradoxical' finding is that reported by Muenzinger as long ago as 1934. In accord with the predominant research interests of that time, Muenzinger was interested to discover the effects of punishment in a *learning* situation. Groups of rats were taught a discrimination in a T-shaped maze; at a choice point they were faced with one lit and one dark arm (these being to left or right in a random order). The lit arm always led to food, the dark arm never did so. This discrimination was learned by means of a 'trial and error' procedure, the behaviour under study being the speed of learning (number of errors in the first 100 trials, and the number of trials required to master the problem). Muenzinger found that animals which were rewarded at the end of the lit arm but *punished* by slight shock when running through the dark arm (i.e., when making an error) learned more quickly than rats which were merely rewarded for correct responses. Such a finding could be accommodated within the 'common-sense' law of effect as originally formulated by Thorndike: rewards strengthen correct responses, and punishments weaken errors, thereby leading to faster learning than the strengthening of correct responses alone. However, the surprising finding of this experiment was that punishing *correct* responses also led to faster learning than did reward alone! Muenzinger concluded that these results 'flatly contradict that part of the law of effect which deals with the after-effects of annoyers'. He considered that shocks (no matter where they occurred) made his animals respond more readily to the significant features in the learning situation, a view which has been elaborated from a theoretical point of view (see, for example, Church, 1963).

This, and other apparent anomalies in the study of punishment, appears paradoxical only if one insists *a priori* that aversive stimuli must reduce behaviour; but this may reflect a confusion in the normal *definition* of punishment, for it is surely an empirical matter to determine the effects of aversive stimuli which are delivered in close association with behaviour. Moreover, Muenzinger's results can be readily accommodated within the analysis of behaviour formulated by operant conditioning experiments. In Muenzinger's study, the punishment for a correct response took the form of shock administered as the rat ran through the lit arm of the maze, that is after the animal's choice, but *before* his access to food. The shock could therefore acquire conditioned reinforcing properties (this could apply with any of the theories of conditioned reinforcement: the shock reliably preceded the food, it acted as a discriminative stimulus, or it provided the rat with early 'information' about his choice and access to food). The paradoxical nature of these results is reduced if one considers that the punishing stimulus is nevertheless a stimulus which may in some senses be regarded like any other.

This point is strengthened by more recent research on discriminative aspects of punishment procedures. Holz and Azrin (1961), for example, exposed pigeons to alternating periods of a variable interval schedule of reinforcement and extinction. No S^D or S^Δ was programmed to accompany these periods so the animal did not 'know' which was in effect at any moment. It was found that a very mild (20 volt) shock delivered after every response emitted in the extinction periods led to a marked and sustained decrease in the rate of responding during these periods. In other situations (as we have seen), such a stimulus may have no consistent suppressing effects on behaviour. It appears, then, that the suppression in this experiment may be largely attributed to the fact that the mild shock provided 'information' that a period was in operation when reinforcement was impossible. Conversely, when each response during a period of the reinforcement schedule was followed by a shock, the response rate during those periods *increased* (Holz and Azrin, 1961), another 'paradoxical' effect. It seems that any suppressing effect of the shock is more than counterbalanced by its conditioned reinforcing properties (for each response is followed by a shock which is differentially associated with a schedule of reinforcement, as is a discriminative stimulus). In these experiments similar effects might have been predicted if flashes of light or some other innocuous stimulus rather than shock had followed each response. This has been shown to be the case, except that very high intensities of shock may cause *suppression* of behaviour in spite of the discriminative properties which they could acquire by reason of their relationship to reinforcements such as food (Holz and Azrin, 1962).

The possible discriminative properties of punishing stimuli have often been overlooked. The work on punishment of extinction responses outlined earlier failed to take this possibility into account, and these results may equally be as much an indication of the discriminative properties of the stimuli they used as of their suppressing effects. For example, Azrin and Holz (1966) replicated (in general terms) the punishment condition used by Skinner (1938) and by Estes (1944). On this occasion, a pigeon was trained to respond on a schedule of intermittent reinforcement. It was then transferred to an extinction condition, but each response was now followed by a brief flash of green light on the key. This produced a fairly rapid decrease in response rate. When the green light was discontinued (extinction still being in operation), the response rate quickly *increased* to the previous rate during reinforcement, and then gradually and progressively subsided once more. One might argue that the green light, like shock in Estes' experiments, merely suppressed behaviour, but did not eliminate it. This was because the green light acted as an 'informative' stimulus, for it was introduced only when the extinction procedure was begun; when it was discontinued, the stimulus conditions reverted to those previously associated with intermittent reinforcement, and the previously appropriate behaviour then gradually extinguished as a result of the subsequent absence of reinforcement. This experiment by Azrin and Holz is not in any sense adequate for complete comparisons to be made between 'punishment' by shock and by other stimuli, for only one pigeon was used and this was exposed only to the conditions outlined above. Nevertheless, it provides a very forceful demonstration that the discriminative properties of stimuli must be considered when we try to evaluate much of the earlier research on punishment.

Complications such as these make it impossible to provide a

short answer to the original question as to whether punishment is an effective procedure, for this clearly depends on the circumstances in which it is used. However, a number of points may be made. First, aversive stimuli (as other stimuli) have their maximum effect on behaviour if they are made dependent on that behaviour, although shocks delivered independently may have similar, but less marked, effects. Second, confusion results from the assumption that aversive stimuli inevitably decrease the frequency of the behaviour with which they are associated. To this extent, 'common sense' cannot be sustained, for it is an empirical matter to determine whether response-dependent shocks, for example, do suppress behaviour; the procedure must be distinguished from its effects. Third, if an aversive stimulus follows responses in such a way that it cannot acquire discriminative properties, then it may suppress behaviour. Even then, however, the initial degree of suppression is likely to be much decreased as the procedure is continued, thereby making it necessary to advance to relatively severe punishers if the behaviour is to be kept suppressed. Fourth, if an aversive stimulus is presented in such a way that it may acquire discriminative properties, then it may fail to suppress behaviour, or may even *increase* its frequency or strength. Once more, however, relatively *severe* punishment may suppress behaviour despite such discriminative properties. Finally, partial suppression of responding which results from punishment procedures quickly disappears when the punishment is removed.

The above conclusions apply primarily to situations in which the schedule of reinforcement which *maintains* the behaviour is still in force when the punishment procedure is introduced. This would presumably be the case in many human situations. If punishment *and extinction* procedures are introduced simultaneously, and maintained, behaviour extinguishes more quickly than if only the extinction procedure is instituted; however, with mild punishment, this may be as much a result of the punishment denoting a change in the conditions as of the use of an *aversive* stimulus *per se.* If such a punishment is discontinued during extinction, the conditions revert to those previously in operation when responding was reinforced, and so response rates rise abruptly, and then subside once more as the extinction progresses; the net result may therefore be no decrease in the total number of extinction responses or no decrease in the time before the animal stops responding in comparison with a simple extinction procedure.

One situation in which punishment procedures may be useful, however, is that in which an alternative response is available by means of which a reinforcement may be obtained. Holz and Azrin (1966) review evidence that pigeons' responding on one key may be readily eliminated if a punishment procedure is introduced for such responses, while others on another key which are equally effective in producing reinforcement remain unpunished. The implications of such findings are obvious, although again it is difficult to separate discriminative and punishing aspects of the procedure.

Some further provisos should now be added. There have been occasional reports of behaviour being completely disrupted when a punishment procedure is instituted (e.g., Holz and Azrin, 1963) even though the aversive stimulus was apparently quite mild. For example, Appel (1961) reported that the operant behaviour of squirrel monkeys was almost completely eliminated when a punishment condition was introduced which used a shock of only 1 ma. intensity. What is more, Appel was unable to reinstate this behaviour in any sustained way even when the punishment procedure was discontinued for 50 experimental sessions. The monkeys appeared 'fearful', and would not even eat pellets of food delivered to them in the test chamber. Such a mal-adaptive reaction is obviously undesirable from any point of view. It is unlikely that it reflects a greater sensitivity of this species of animal to an aversive stimulus; it is more probably the result of some other as yet unexplained aspect of the control of behaviour by aversive stimuli (perhaps related to the phenomena discussed in the next chapter). The effects of mild stimuli have often disappeared as punishment procedures progress, as we have seen; this indicates that relatively severe punishment may be the more efficient. However, Appel's data suggest that relatively severe punishment should certainly not be introduced at the outset of the punishment condition, for this increases the risk of such a mal-adaptive result.

Even though Estes' (1944) explanation of *punishment* is incorrect (because of the differences in the effects of response-dependent and independent shocks), it certainly remains true that the association of a person with an aversive stimulus which he uses in an attempt to suppress behaviour may result in his acquiring some aversive properties himself, as in Estes' example of whipping a dog. This complication assumes greater importance from a practical point of view in social settings, in which punishment is often used with humans. Another complication is provided by the finding that a painful stimulus may make an animal behave aggressively (see Ulrich, et al., 1965), a side-effect which should also be considered when a punishment procedure is contemplated.

Punishment is indeed a complex (although perhaps not a paradoxical) procedure. Lack of space inevitably precludes a discussion of many important findings. Nevertheless, some of the more basic findings have been reviewed, and principles have been established which must apply to any attempts to control behaviour by means of punishment. For further consideration of the effects of punishment, the reader is referred to two books. The first (Boe and Church, 1968) presents a collection of papers which have been influential in this field both from a practical and theoretical point of view. The second (Campbell and Church, 1969) is the report of a conference on this and related topics, and therefore provides a good indication of present research interests; it also includes a useful and comprehensive bibliography on punishment.

Finally, we should note that in an important paper Azrin and Holz (1966) have suggested a definition of punishment which is rather different from that prompted by common sense. Instead of defining punishment as the reduction of responding by aversive stimuli delivered after a response (which we have seen produces many difficulties), Azrin and Holz *define* it as 'a reduction of the future probability of a specific response as a result of the immediate delivery of a stimulus for that response'. In other words, for Azrin and Holz punishment *is* the suppression of behaviour by response-produced stimuli; and, what is more, their definition does not include any reference to aversive stimuli, but merely stimuli. It follows that if shocks do not suppress the behaviour they follow, then they are not punishing, according to this definition. On the other hand, if a green light *does* suppress the behaviour it follows, then it *is* a punisher.

At first glance, Azrin and Holz's definition may seem strange. However, it has some distinct advantages. One of these is that the definition of punishment now becomes rather similar to (though the obverse of) the definition of reinforcement we discussed earlier. You will recall that a stimulus is said to be a reinforcer not if it is nice or pleasant but *merely* if it increases the future probability of the behaviour which it follows. We saw that it is an empirical matter to discover the circumstances in which a particular stimulus acts as a reinforcer. Food is not always a reinforcer: it is not usually a reinforcer for an animal that has recently had plenty of food, to take an obvious example. Similarly, according to Azrin and Holz, a stimulus is not to be regarded as a punisher just because it is nasty or unpleasant, but *only* if it decreases the future frequency of the behaviour which it follows. So shock is not always a punisher: when delivered in certain circumstances or (as we shall see later) to animals with certain experimental histories it does not suppress behaviour. These definitions of reinforcement and punishment both avoid any kind of appeal to 'inner animals' which like or dislike the stimuli they experience. Both direct attention towards identifying the circumstances in which a stimulus will act as a reinforcer or as a punisher. Azrin and Holz's definition moves us away from the crude expectations that nasty stimuli ought to suppress behaviour in all circumstances simply because they are nasty. Such stimuli do not always have this effect on behaviour — and this is one of the most important points to emerge from this chapter.

CHAPTER 11

The effects of conditioned anxiety

We saw in the previous chapter that in some situations aversive stimuli are better at suppressing behaviour if they are made dependent on the emission of an operant response. Nevertheless, shocks delivered independently of behaviour also produce suppression. This procedure was earlier said to generate 'anxiety' and this chapter provides a brief outline of the relevance of operant conditioning techniques to the study of such emotional aspects of behaviour.

Sidman has noted that 'anxiety is almost impossible to define' (1964). It is a concept, however, which has been used very freely in experimental psychology, frequently at an explanatory level. In such circumstances, the anxiety is inferred from its assumed effects on behaviour, but is usually not measured directly at all. Here we shall confine ourselves to one field of research in which the concept of anxiety has been invoked, but one which has the advantage of having been specifically designed for this purpose and which incorporates an unusual degree of quantification. Once again, these advantages come from the use of operant conditioning techniques in steady state research designs. The original investigation was reported by Estes and Skinner (1941) in a paper which they entitled 'Some quantitative properties of anxiety'. They established consistent patterns of lever pressing in rats by means of a schedule of intermittent food reinforcement. Then, without changing this schedule of reinforcement in any way, they introduced periods of a tone. As each of these periods ended, a brief unavoidable shock was delivered entirely independently of the rats' behaviour. The result of this procedure was eventually a decrease in the rate of operant responding during the pre-shock tone, a disruption of behaviour which Estes and Skinner attributed to a state of anxiety which they argued was the consequence of the tone's relationship to the shock. In this way, any suppressive effects on behaviour of independently programmed shocks are greatly increased.

Results such as these have been widely replicated, and the phenomenon is illustrated by the segments of cumulative record shown in Fig. 29. These were produced by a rat which was exposed to a VI 30 sec schedule of food reinforcement (reinforcers are shown as usual by small diagonal marks). In the middle of each seven-minute period, an additional stimulus was presented for one minute, during the whole of which time the

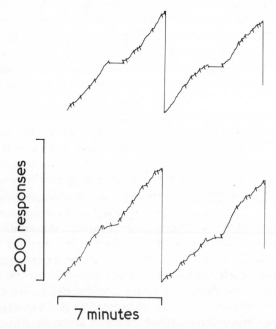

Figure 29   The effects on VI behaviour of a stimulus which precedes an unavoidable shock (conditioned suppression). The response pen is offset during the pre-shock stimulus.

pen on the cumulative recorder was deflected downwards, although it could still be stepped across the paper by an operant response. At the end of each of these one-minute periods, a very brief shock was delivered, and the pen reverted to its normal line. The two segments of record at the top of Fig. 29 show that a consistent rate of operant responding maintained by the VI schedule was completely disrupted during the pre-shock stimulus, for the record becomes horizontal during the one-minute deflection, which indicates, of course, that no responses were emitted during that period. The behaviour recovers shortly after the unavoidable shock has been delivered. The two segments of record shown in the lower half of Fig. 29 were obtained from the same animal in exactly identical circumstances, except that the intensity of the shock was lower. In these cases, the responding did not cease completely during the pre-shock stimulus, although the response rate did fall considerably as indicated by the shallower slope of the record during the period of deflection. Since the VI schedule was still in operation during these periods, responses could still be occasionally followed by a reinforcer, which indeed happened, being denoted in this instance by a brief *upward* mark on the record.

Data such as these suggest, then, that anxiety can be measured in terms of its disrupting effect on maintained patterns of operant behaviour. So, the rat whose records are shown in Fig. 29 became more anxious during a stimulus which preceded the greater intensity of shock, for the upper records show the more disruption. Such a result agrees with our intuitions about anxiety. The *amount* of disruption in these experiments may be measured by comparing the rate of responding during the pre-shock stimulus with the response rate in its absence. This measure is known as a *suppression ratio*. The behavioural phenomenon itself is now often termed *conditioned suppression*, for this is a more objective description of what may actually be observed in such experiments: 'anxiety' itself cannot be seen from the cumulative records, but suppression of behaviour is seen to develop as a function of the experimental conditions. Nevertheless, it seems reasonable to attribute the suppression of responding to a state of anxiety or to a *conditioned emotional response* (CER) on the part of the animal (see Brady and Hunt, 1955). This interpretation is supported by the finding that animals may show other signs of emotion during the pre-shock stimulus, such as defecation, urination or a 'freezing' posture of immobility; however, such patterns are not always seen. Certainly this procedure may be formally distinguished from the punishment operation discussed earlier, for the shock is not dependent on behaviour. Moreover, with punishment procedures, the resulting suppression of responding achieves a lower frequency of punishing aversive stimuli, and is therefore adaptive in some senses. However, the suppression of responding which occurs during a stimulus which precedes an *unavoidable* shock does not have this obvious adaptiveness; it seems to be a less specific emotional reaction on the part of the animal.

The advantages of this model of anxiety need not be emphasised here, except to say that this procedure makes it possible to turn on and off an emotional state which may therefore be repeatedly measured using the same subject in various experimental conditions. At one time, much interest was shown in the phenomenon as a model which made it possible to evaluate experimentally some of the treatments for human anxiety conditions which are used in clinical practice. The work of Brady and his associates is particularly important in this context. For example, in 1956 Brady reported the effects of drugs on a conditioned emotional response established by the above procedure. He found that amphetamine (a stimulant drug) increased this anxiety, for an animal emitted fewer responses during a pre-shock stimulus when injected with this drug than in identical control conditions. This decrease in responding was seen in spite of an *increase* in the normal (baseline) rate of responding which is a typical consequence of the injection of stimulant drugs. The drug reserpine had the opposite effect, for although it produced a decrease in the baseline rate of responding, the number of responses emitted during the pre-shock stimulus actually rose in comparison with control days; it was therefore concluded that reserpine attenuated anxiety (the conditioned emotional response). These results are summarized by the cumulative records shown in Fig. 30, taken from Brady (1956). The pen was offset during the pre-shock stimulus, and reinforcements are not shown; the effects of the drugs on the responding of a single animal may be seen clearly. This report by Brady is of exceptional importance, for he concluded that the conditioned suppression phenomenon makes it possible to assess the effects of possible therapeutic procedures on emotion or mood while

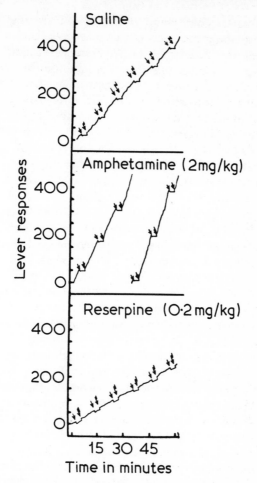

Figure 30   Cumulative records showing the effects of drugs on conditioned suppression of a rat's VI behaviour. From Brady (1956).

controlling adequately for non-specific side effects on general activity which might result from such procedures.

However, since this early report there has been a succession of conflicting or ambiguous results which have led to a change of emotion on the part of the experimental investigators! Early

enthusiasm has given way to extreme caution or even to pessi-
mism concerning the general relevance of conditioned suppression to clinical anxiety states. For example, Kinnard, Aceto and
Buckley (1962) have suggested that conditioned suppression is
not a true model of anxiety, because drugs which attenuate
clinical anxiety did not have clear-cut effects on suppression in
their experiments. On the other hand, Ray (1965) has argued
that the failure of certain drugs to attenuate conditioned suppression in his experiments indicates that these drugs do not achieve
their clinical effects by acting directly on anxiety!

This confusing situation probably results in part from insufficient heed being taken by experimenters in this field of possible
interactions between 'anxiety' and the behavioural baselines
through which it is shown in the conditioned suppression
phenomenon. Of particular importance here is an experiment by
Appel (1963c), who reported that a dosage of reserpine which
reliably reduced the amount of conditioned suppression when
the shock was of an intensity of 0.8 ma. failed to give consistent
results when the shock was increased only to 1.0 ma. This implies
that, at present, any attempt to make generalisations about the
effects of this drug on 'anxiety' are premature. What is needed is
a greater understanding of the important variables in the behavioural phenomenon itself. Recent work has shown that these
are complex. It is not perhaps surprising that the degree of
behavioural suppression depends on the intensity of the aversive
stimulus, and on the intensity of the pre-shock stimulus or its
relationship to the shock, for such findings are consistent with
principles of *Pavlovian* conditioning which cannot be elaborated
here (see Kamin, 1965). However, Stein, Sidman and Brady
(1958) have shown that the amount of conditioned suppression
resulting from a specified shock and pre-shock stimulus also
depends on the frequency with which this combination of stimuli
is presented. Animals whose behaviour is completely suppressed
during a pre-shock stimulus presented relatively rarely may show
much less behavioural disruption when it is presented more
frequently within a session, even though the physical specifications of the two stimuli are identical in both conditions. Stein et
al. reported that their animals showed complete conditioned
suppression only to the extent that they did not thereby lose
more than a certain proportion of the maximum possible reinforcements programmed by a VI schedule; if suppression would

result in too great a loss of such reinforcements, the animals continued to respond during the pre-shock stimulus. Further complications are provided by findings that animals' behaviour is more disrupted by an identical procedure if they obtain a relatively low frequency of reinforcement from the schedule which maintains their baseline behaviour, and that an animal is more disrupted if he responds at a high rate than at a low rate, all other variables being controlled (Blackman, 1967, 1968b).

This last finding is worth considering in more detail, for it emphasises the complexity of the apparently simple phenomenon of conditioned suppression. In one of the experiments (1967), rats were exposed to a variable interval schedule of food reinforcement, which remained in operation throughout the experiment. However, as was discussed in Chapter 6 and shown in Figs. 14 and 15 (pp. 78, 79), the response rates of these animals were manipulated by differentially reinforcing either short inter-response times (thereby generating high response rates) or relatively long inter-response times (which resulted in sustained low rates of responding). In this way, response rates which were initially of the order of 40 per minute were changed to 80 or 90 per minute. When an *identical* conditioned suppression procedure was superimposed on these various baselines, it was found that the animals responded least often during the pre-shock stimulus when their response rates were very high, and that the lowest response rates were hardly disrupted during the pre-shock stimulus. So the *amount* of behavioural disruption was seen to depend critically on the *nature* of the behaviour being disrupted. This finding has some immediate implications. For example, these data bear a striking resemblance to those reported earlier by Brady (1956), shown in Fig. 30. The behavioural baselines in both experiments were affected in similar ways, in Brady's as a result of the 'non-specific side-effects' of the drugs, and in Blackman's by reason of the selective reinforcement of responses which followed specified inter-response times. But responding during the pre-shock stimulus *also* changed in similar ways, although no drugs were involved in Blackman's experiment: in both cases, high response rates showed most disruption, and low response rates least, during the same pre-shock stimulus. Such similarities suggest that Brady's findings do not necessarily establish his assertion that the drugs had a specific effect on anxiety *despite* their peripheral effects on activity: on the contrary, these changes in baseline response rates may have *contributed* in part to the differences during the pre-shock stimulus (Blackman, 1968c).

The above comments in no sense detract from the importance of Brady's experiments. No discussion can change the fact that the drugs used in his experiments had important effects on 'emotional' *behaviour* (see Blackman, 1972). However, they do call into question the value of explaining conditioned suppression in simple terms as the behavioural effect of anxiety, for data such as the above provide a dilemma. The original assertion was that the degree of conditioned suppression reflects the amount of underlying anxiety. In this case, such anxiety is determined not merely by such obviously important features in the environment as aversive stimuli, but also by the nature of ongoing behaviour. Put crudely, this suggests that one changes the amount of anxiety by changing the nature of the behaviour which the anxiety-procedure disrupts. An alternative to this statement would be to assert that the amount of anxiety 'felt' by an animal is indeed determined solely by environmental events like shock, but that some patterns of responding are more resistant to disruption than others. In this case, the suppression ratio is in no sense *the* quantification of anxiety, and an animal's behaviour does not necessarily reflect accurately how anxious he is. If this latter argument is adopted, anxiety may quickly disappear as an observable or quantifiable entity in behavioural terms: the question then posed is whether it reappears in terms of other observable phenomena, or merely acts as an unquantifiable, but convenient, explanatory concept.

One suggestion that might be made is that anxiety could reappear as quantifiable changes in the physiological activities of the subject, or in patterns of internal behaviour which are not usually measured in conditioned suppression experiments. For example, it seems plausible that the unavoidable shocks delivered in such an experiment will *elicit* certain changes in an animal; since the pre-shock stimulus invariably precedes the shock, the situation is very similar to any Pavlovian conditioning experiment. The pre-shock stimulus may therefore become a conditional stimulus and therefore come to elicit the reactions previously elicited by the shock alone (as does the bell which precedes the delivery of food in other classical conditioning experiments). If these conditioned responses are incompatible with operant lever-pressing, such emitted behaviour will inevitably decrease in frequency during the stimulus which precedes shock. So these conditioned responses could be regarded as 'anxiety', and the difficulties discussed above would be resolved by assuming that some rates of operant responding are more readily disrupted than others. Why this should be remains a problem for behavioural analysis, and a number of minor problems for this account are posed by experiments in which an identical anxiety procedure actually causes an *increase* in some patterns of responding while causing the more usual suppression of other patterns (e.g., Blackman, 1970a, b). However, the chief problem with such an account lies in providing experimental, quantifiable support for it. A recent experiment by Brady, Kelly and Plumlee (1969) is particularly challenging in this respect. They tried to correlate changes in certain autonomic, or elicited, activity with suppression of emitted behaviour by measuring heart rate and systolic and diastolic blood pressure. Using rhesus monkeys as subjects, Brady and his associates were certainly able to detect changes in these activities during a stimulus which preceded unavoidable shock, as well as a suppression of operant responding. However, they were unable to isolate systematic patterns of co-variation in operant and autonomic behaviour. For example, suppression of lever-pressing consistently developed *before* any detectable changes in the other patterns of behaviour being monitored, a finding which is clearly difficult to interpret as the theory would demand. With one monkey, it was consistently observed that changes in heart rate were most affected when behavioural suppression was least severe, and vice versa. Even the two forms of blood pressure showed divergent patterns of conditioned reactions on frequent occasions. On the basis of these data, Brady and his associates concluded that all these effects were causally independent, although doubtless related in complex ways; in other words, it was not possible to claim that the behavioural suppression was *caused by* or was a *function* of, changes in cardio-vascular activity. It would be more accurate to describe all these changes as being the independently conditioned results of the same environmental events.

The data reviewed above might be used to support several points, not least of which would be the great advantages offered to psychophysiological workers by operant conditioning techniques. In the present context, however, they serve to emphasise that there is little *evidence* at present for the view that 'anxiety' is to be identified as one particular pattern of behavioural changes, for all these effects might be described as 'anxious behaviour' (including the suppression of operant responding). Even though one might suggest that *other* patterns of elicited autonomic behaviour might vary systematically with the suppression of operant behaviour, the evidence of Brady and his associates makes this appear less forceful as an *explanation* of disruptions in emitted behaviour.

A number of other possible explanations for conditioned suppression have been offered. Perhaps the most important is found in the original report by Estes and Skinner (1941), and which has been developed by Estes (1969). This can be termed a motivational theory. It suggests that anxiety is a motivational force with a negative value; the baseline operant behaviour is said to be maintained by positive motivations such as hunger or thirst. When a pre-shock stimulus is delivered, this is said to cause the two forms of motivation to interact, the net outcome being a reduction in the positive motivation available for responding (and thereby a decrease in the rate of operant responding). This theory is difficult to discuss fairly in the present context, since this book has attempted to develop accounts of behaviour without recourse to non-observable motivational forces within a behaving organism but solely in relation to observable phenomena. There are undoubtedly some advantages in the motivational account of anxiety, and some testable predictions may be generated by this theory. (See Millenson & de Villiers, 1972). Nevertheless, it is clear that the theory must be adjusted to take into account the complications that a specified anxiety procedure has different effects on different patterns of behaviour which are maintained by the same hunger motivation (see above); moreover, a number of further difficulties have been discussed elsewhere, including failure to support one of Estes' specific predictions (see Blackman, 1972). Briefly, this concerns the effects of anxiety on patterns of behaviour which are themselves maintained by 'negative motivation' (discussed in the next chapter); the motivational theory of anxiety predicts that such behaviour should not be suppressed (Estes, 1969), but this has been shown not to be so in certain circumstances (Blackman, 1970b, 1972).

Of course, there are many models of anxiety in experimental psychology, and this discussion has included only one of them. However, the model first described by Estes and Skinner has advantages, some of which may have emerged in this short discussion. The biggest single problem in any discussion is provided by a lack of agreed definition of what anxiety is. This can be best overcome by attempting to secure agreement as to the *situations* which are said to generate anxiety, in which case, the prefacing of a noxious stimulus by a harmless stimulus might seem to be basic. However, the present discussion establishes that even this simple *procedure* may result in behavioural effects which are difficult to systemize.

In discussing contributions to a symposium on psychopathology, Schoenfeld (1957) was led to complain: 'One of the central difficulties is "fear"; our thought stumbles and gropes while this term assumes many faces and shapes by popular demand. "Fear" is a response, a drive, an emotion, and possibly even a stimulus, at the same time'. The same is true of 'anxiety' (indeed, many unhappy hours may be spent in arguing the relationship between 'fear' and 'anxiety'). Semantic confusions have hindered scientific progress in the analysis of the effects of aversive stimuli. It is especially unfortunate that this is so, for clinical psychologists have traditionally looked to experiments on aversive stimulation in an attempt to find experimental models of clinical abnormalities in human behaviour. No attempt is made, therefore, in this chapter to go beyond the observable effects of a specifiable procedure. Some may call this 'anxiety', some may wish not to do so. It may not be clear how this model relates to other examples of anxiety. But at least the experimental analysis of behavioural phenomena resulting from this procedure may be attempted with rigour, and functional relationships sought which may eventually be of practical significance. Without doubt, the *explanatory* power of the concept of anxiety must depend on adequate experimental evidence relating anxious behaviour to the environment which supports it.

To conclude this discussion, one can do no better than reiterate another statement made by Schoenfeld (1950): 'It remains to be seen whether what is termed anxiety by the laboratory worker has relevance to speculations about anxiety in man. Certainly we do not understand from the clinical standpoint precisely what anxiety is in man, whereas the laboratory worker can specify a meaning. To borrow the word anxiety for our experiments reflects the judgement that the experiments contain the basic features of what is believed, though without adequate proof as yet, to be involved in human anxiety'. Although written twenty years ago, this is still true.

CHAPTER 12
Schedules of aversive stimuli

In all the experiments reviewed so far, patterns of operant behaviour have been established and maintained by the delivery of reinforcers such as food or water to suitably deprived animals. It has been shown that such behaviour may be considerably affected by also delivering other stimuli, either of a non-aversive kind (as in most studies of conditioned reinforcement) or of an aversive nature (as in experiments on punishment and anxiety). However, aversive stimuli are also capable of developing considerable control over emitted behaviour even in the absence of any positive reinforcers, and this chapter provides a short review of such effects.

Perhaps the simplest experimental situation in which responding will come under the control of aversive stimuli is provided by *escape* conditioning. Here, an operant response may terminate an aversive stimulus which is presented independently of the animal's behaviour. This procedure has been investigated in many experiments, and there is no doubt that animals will emit an operant response if this is immediately followed by the termination of an aversive stimulus. Indeed, this may provide a convenient *definition* of an aversive stimulus, i.e., one which maintains any operant behaviour which terminates it. Such a definition avoids any claim that an aversive stimulus is 'disliked' by any 'inner animal' — again, we define a class of stimuli in terms of its effects on behaviour, as with reinforcers and punishers. The behaviour generated by this simple escape situation can be measured by the time between the onset of the aversive stimulus and the response which ended it. However, it is also possible to *schedule* the offset of the stimulus intermittently, in ways which are analogous to the scheduling of food delivery. Thus, one might specify that every fourth response will turn off a shock, a procedure which could be described as FR4 escape; such a schedule will develop and maintain a pattern of behaviour during a shock which is similar to an FR4 schedule of food reinforcement. However, it is, of course, not possible to produce sustained rates of responding for the duration of an escape experiment, for clearly each fourth response must remove the shock for an appreciable period of time, and the length of this time is an important controlling variable. Nevertheless, this limitation should not be allowed to detract from the basic similarities between the behaviour maintained by intermittent schedules of food reinforcement and identical schedules of escape. Dinsmoor and Winograd (1958), for example, studied the effects of a variable interval schedule of escape, in which responses were effective in turning off a slight shock only after it had been on for varying intervals which averaged 30 seconds, the effective response being followed by a 2-minute period without shock. This procedure generated moderate, but sustained, rates of lever pressing whenever the shock was on, a pattern of behaviour which resembles that generated by VI schedules of food reinforcement. Dinsmoor and Winograd were also able to show that the rate of this escape responding was a function of the intensity of the shock.

The study of escape from aversive stimuli such as shock has not been carried out very frequently with intermittent schedules, perhaps because more meaningful experiments are possible using escape from a stimulus *associated* with shock. Before discussing these, however, it may be helpful to consider briefly what use may be made of experiments in which animals emit operant responses to escape from shock itself. A good example of this is to be found in a series of experiments carried out by Weiss and Laties and their associates. They used a titration schedule, in which the intensity of a shock became progressively greater, but in which an operant response reduced this intensity by a pre-set amount. Thus, animals could not escape from shock completely, but could bring it to a level so low that it did not maintain further escape responses (i.e., was no longer aversive). This technique was used to measure the effects of analgesic drugs such as morphine and aspirin, usually with the expected effect, namely that the animals allowed the shock to reach higher intensities before responding if they had been given one of these drugs (e.g. Weiss and Laties, 1961). So this technique may be useful for screening new drugs which are intended to alleviate pain.

Schedule effects on escape behaviour are most easily seen, as noted above, when animals are given the opportunity to escape not from shock itself, but from a stimulus which is not aversive in its own right but during which occasional brief shocks are delivered. In this way, the animal is not exposed to undue amounts of shock, but the effects of intermittencies can be readily studied. Such experiments support the view that schedules of escape from these stimuli produce patterns of behaviour strikingly similar to similar schedules of positive reinforcement. For example, Kelleher and Morse (1964) studied the effects of a multiple FI FR schedule of escape from a stimulus occasionally associated with shock: each escape response was followed by 2.5 minutes in which no stimuli or shocks were present. During the stimulus with which the FI escape schedule was associated there was no responding at first, but this was followed by a progressive increase in response rate during the period (producing a scalloped cumulative record). The first response after 10 min turned off the stimulus (FI 10). In the FR component, the thirtieth response to be emitted produced the 2.5 minute time-out, and this generated behaviour typical of an FR 30 schedule of food reinforcement. Cumulative records illustrating these effects are shown in Fig. 31. The behaviour of monkey S-1 was maintained by this schedule of food reinforcement, while that of S-26 was maintained by escape from a stimulus associated with occasional shock. At the beginning of the records, the FI 10 minute schedules were in operation in the presence of a white light. The pen reset when the appropriate reinforcement was delivered, whereupon the 2.5 minute period of time-out (TO) was instituted. When this ended (denoted by the small mark on the record), a red stimulus was presented which signalled the FR30 schedule. Again, the pen reset when the reinforcement was obtained, and there was a 2.5 minute time-out, after which the FI schedule was presented once more

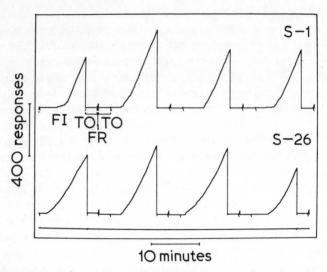

Figure 31   Effects of a multiple FI FR schedule with a time-out (TO) between components (squirrel monkeys). Top: food reinforcement; bottom: escape from a stimulus associated with shock. From Morse and Kelleher (1970) after Kelleher and Morse (1964).

(the beginning of the FI period being denoted by the small mark again). The similarity of these two performances needs no emphasis.

In these experiments, the stimulus associated with occasional shocks is sometimes called a *conditioned aversive stimulus* (CAS); although this stimulus was originally not aversive, it acquires aversiveness by reason of its relationship to the shock, and thereby becomes capable of sustaining a pattern of behaviour which terminates it. The power of a stimulus to acquire such conditioned aversive properties has been used to explain another area of interest in the control of behaviour by aversive stimuli, namely *avoidance* conditioning. It has been established for many years that animals may emit responses which *prevent* the delivery of an aversive stimulus. Such a finding provides considerable difficulties for an account which seeks to explain behaviour in terms of its consequences, for avoidance responding by its very nature prevents the delivery of the stimuli to which one would wish to relate the behaviour. How then can avoidance responding be said to be a function of a stimulus whose delivery does not occur? According to some theorists, this difficulty is to be overcome by suggesting that the avoidance of shock is really no more than the side-effect of the animal *escaping* from stimuli which are associated with shock and which have therefore become conditioned aversive stimuli.

To understand the force of this suggestion, it is necessary to consider in some detail the typical avoidance conditioning procedure. These experiments are often carried out in an apparatus known as a 'shuttle-box'. A rat is placed into one side of a rectangular box. After a while, a light comes on, and five seconds after this the floor of that side of the box is electrified. The rat can *escape* from this shock by running to the other end, which also has the effect of turning off the light and the shock on the first side. After a further period, a light comes on in the second side of the box, and after a further five seconds, the floor on this side is electrified. Again, the animal may escape from this shock by running to the other end. This sequence is continued. If, however, the rat runs to the opposite end of the box during the first five seconds of light, this turns off the light and avoids the shock. In this situation, animals eventually learn to shuttle from one end of the box to the other whenever the light comes on, thereby avoiding a very high proportion of the shocks. Any crossing responses which occur in the absence of the light are ignored in this procedure. It was Schoenfeld (1950) who suggested that the avoidance behaviour was really no more than *escape* from the light, a stimulus which has acquired aversive properties by reason of its relationship to shock before the animal has learned the avoidance response. Schoenfeld's account was offered as an alternative to a theory proposed by Mowrer (1947) which invoked the concept of 'anxiety' to explain avoidance behaviour. Mowrer suggested that the light became an anxiety-arousing stimulus because it preceded a shock in the early stages of training; so an avoidance response was maintained because it reduced the anxiety within the animal by turning off the light. This is known as a two-process theory of avoidance conditioning, for it was argued that the light aroused anxiety because of its pairing with shock (a *classical* conditioning procedure), and that the reduction of this anxiety provided the reinforcement for the *emitted* behaviour of running to the other side of the shuttle-box.

Theories of this sort look less convincing in the light of a series of experiments by Sidman in which animals learned to emit responses and thereby to avoid shock although there was *no* warning signal from which the animal could be said to escape or which could be considered to arouse anxiety (Sidman, 1966). Sidman (e.g., 1953) simply placed animals in a standard operant conditioning test chamber, to the floor of which brief shocks were delivered at regular intervals (described as the shock-shock interval — S-S). If, however, the rat pressed a lever, this instituted another interval which was usually longer (the response-shock interval — R-S). The rat could press the lever whenever, and as often as, it 'chose', each response having the effect of introducing a new R-S interval. For example, if the S-S interval was 5 seconds and the R-S interval was 20 seconds, shocks were delivered every 5 seconds, unless the rat pressed the lever, in which case the stream of shocks was interrupted for 20 seconds. Any operant response ensured that the next shock could not occur for 20 seconds. There is no warning signal programmed whatsoever in this schedule, and yet animals learn to emit operant responses in these circumstances, as is shown in Fig. 32. This is the 'collapsed' cumulative record of a rat exposed to the above schedule for three consecutive hours. Each response stepped the pen across the paper in the usual way, but in this case the diagonal marks denote the delivery of a very brief shock. This rat had been exposed to this schedule for many daily sessions, so this is not a

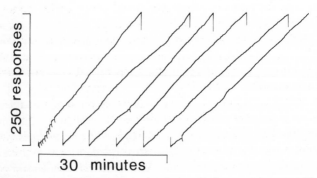

Figure 32   Cumulative record of a rat's free-operant avoidance behaviour. Diagonal marks denote the delivery of an unavoided shock.

record which shows avoidance *learning*, but the steady state of operant behaviour which is eventually achieved. As can be seen, this animal failed to avoid only 11 shocks, and of these, 9 occurred in the first ten minutes or so (a typical 'warm-up' effect with such schedules). This behaviour is therefore highly efficient in terms of the proportion of shocks avoided, for the theoretical maximum is over 2,000. Moreover, it may be seen that this animal emits his responses at a fairly consistent rate, which averages approximately 7.6 per minute over the entire session. The consistency of this responding is obvious, although, as it happens, the same number of shocks could in principle be avoided by a response rate only half of that recorded: it will be recalled that the R-S interval was 20 seconds, and so if the rat pressed the lever exactly every 19 seconds, he would avoid all the shocks. Clearly this rat 'prefers' to keep himself well away from any imminent shock by instituting a new R-S interval approximately every 8 seconds on average. It must be emphasised once more that there was no change in the stimulus conditions throughout the experiment, except for the delivery of the 15 unavoided shocks; it is therefore difficult to sustain explanations of this efficient behaviour in terms of *escape* from any conditioned aversive stimulus. Anger (1963) has suggested that each operant response reduces conditioned aversive *temporal* stimuli (CATS); he argued that after each response, internal stimuli become more and more aversive as time passes, and are reduced by any response which is emitted. One might suggest that these CATS are a form of anxiety — but such accounts suffer from the great disadvantage that they are unable to identify either the CATS or the anxiety, and may therefore be no more than a rephrasing of the observable phenomenon, the behaviour itself.

A further interesting phenomenon may be observed if a slight modification to Sidman's original procedure is incorporated which makes it rather more similar to the traditional avoidance conditioning experiments. This can be done by introducing a stimulus just before a shock is due to be delivered. Figure 33 shows the cumulative record obtained from a rat in identical circumstances to those discussed above, except that a noise was introduced 5 seconds before a shock was due to be delivered (i.e., throughout the shock-shock interval, or 15 seconds after a response). The stable state achieved by this rat is at first sight even more impressive than that produced by the previous rat.

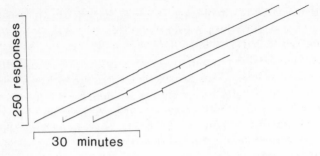

Figure 33   Cumulative record of the behaviour generated by a free-operant avoidance schedule in which a noise stimulus is introduced for the last 5 sec of each response-shock interval. Diagonal marks denote the delivery of an unavoided shock.

There is no warm-up effect at the beginning of the session, and in this case the rate of responding is even more consistent and lower, being approximately 3.5 per minute overall. This reflects the fact that this animal waited for the noise to come on before pressing the lever; indeed, from a total of 627 responses in the three hours, no less than 606 occurred in the presence of the noise. With this schedule the rat could press the lever at any time and thereby introduce a new response-shock interval, and so avoid the *noise*, but in fact the animal preferred to wait for the noise to occur. This noise was inevitably present whenever a shock was delivered, from the very beginning of this experiment, and would therefore seem to satisfy the requirements to become a conditioned aversive stimulus. One might expect then that the rat would 'prefer' to avoid it too, in the way that the previous rat avioded shock in the absence of changes in stimulus conditions. The finding that it did not suggests that this noise is better regarded as a discriminative stimulus setting the occasion for a response to be emitted rather than as an aversive stimulus. This view is supported by the fact that animals in this situation show no visible signs of anxiety or distress; they wait quietly for the noise to come on, and then press the lever in what appears to be a quite casual way, thereby turning off the noise for a further 15 seconds. An account such as this would, of course, apply to the shuttle-box situation as well.

Just as escape behaviour may be maintained by a reduction in the intensity of an aversive stimulus rather than its complete removal, it has recently been shown that animals will consistently emit operant responses which reduce the frequency of brief shocks rather than eliminate them completely. For example, Herrnstein and Hineline (1966) reported 'avoidance' behaviour in a situation in which shocks were delivered only at a lower (but not zero) frequency after a response. Two separate and independent programmes delivered brief shocks randomly in time. One of these entailed a higher frequency of shocks than the other, and was in operation if the rat failed to press a lever. However, any lever press had the effect of switching the animal (without any accompanying stimulus change) to the programme with the lower frequency. The experiment reverted to the higher frequency programme whenever a shock from the lower frequency programme was delivered. Therefore lever presses did no more than reduce the overall frequency of shocks. Moreover, this procedure made it inevitable that the rats would occasionally be shocked only a very short time after a response (for example, by switching to the lower frequency programme just before this was due to deliver a brief shock); such a possibility cannot arise in the avoidance experiments discussed above, for each response was there followed by a period free of shock for a specified period. In spite of this unusual feature, responding was generated and maintained consistently by the schedule of shock-frequency *reduction* rather than shock *avoidance*. On the basis of such findings, Herrnstein and Hineline suggested that the crucial specifiable determinant of 'avoidance' responding is the overall reduction of shock frequency produced by such behaviour. This view represents a considerable change from previous assertions that such behaviour is maintained by the reduction of anxiety or by escape from a conditioned aversive stimulus, and it directs attention away from hypothetical internal processes to events in the environment which may be observed in any avoidance conditioning experiment (see Herrnstein, 1969, for a review of these theoretical implications). The generalisation that a class of behaviour is increased and maintained if it is associated with a reduction in the frequency of aversive stimuli becomes in itself an explanation for this behaviour, in the same way as does an assertion that behaviour is generated and maintained if it is associated with a positive reinforcer. It seems that concepts such as anxiety in the analysis of schedule control by aversive stimuli may serve no more useful a purpose than does an assertion that reduction of *hunger* explains the control of other stimuli over behaviour; both are unobserved, and both may be effectively replaced by emphasising the important roles of observable environmental events.

If, after avoidance behaviour has been established, the shock generator is disconnected so that shocks can no longer be delivered, the rate of operant responding decreases very slowly. This is often described as the extinction of avoidance responding, by analogy with the similar behavioural process resulting when positive reinforcers are no longer delivered. However, some writers (e.g., Morgan, 1968) have suggested that a more appropriate analogy to the latter would be a procedure in which previously effective avoidance responses no longer lead to a reduction in shock frequency. It is argued that this would be more similar to the procedure whereby operant responses are no longer followed by food reinforcers after having been previously effective in producing them. However, it seems that a pattern of avoidance behaviour may in fact be *sustained* by delivering unavoidable shocks in this way. For example, Sidman, Herrnstein and Conrad (1957) trained monkeys to emit operant responses which avoided shock. They then transferred the animals to a condition in which an *unavoidable* shock was delivered every ten minutes. During the five minutes preceding each shock, a clicking noise was presented. When the avoidance schedule was disconnected, so that only the unavoidable shocks and clicker periods occurred, it was found that the monkeys' lever pressing was maintained for far longer during the clicker than in the other five-minute periods.

This work provides a bridge to another area of research which has recently received some attention. This is sometimes called the *response-produced shock* phenomenon, and is illustrated by an experiment reported by McKearney (1969). Squirrel monkeys were trained to avoid shocks in the situation described by Sidman. When this behaviour was stable, they were transferred to a procedure in which the avoidance schedule was still in operation but in which a fixed interval schedule of shock *presentation* was also incorporated: the first response after each period of ten minutes was followed by a shock in exactly the same way as responses are followed by food on an FI 10 minute schedule of food reinforcement. Then the avoidance schedule was removed, leaving the FI 10 minute schedule of shock presentation as the

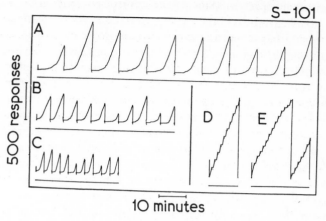

Figure 34   Maintenance of behaviour when its sole consequence is the production of a shock according to a fixed interval schedule. – from McKearney (1969).

only consequence of responding. It was found that, in these circumstances, the schedule maintained scalloped patterns of responding which appear identical to those maintained by FI schedules of food reinforcement. This effect is shown in Fig. 34 in which are displayed segments of cumulative record obtained from a later stage of McKearney's experiment (phase 7). In this part of the investigation, the FI schedule of shock presentation was set on different occasions to 10 minutes (record A), 5 minutes (B), 3 minutes (C), or 1 minute (records D and E). The recorder pen reset to the baseline after each shock, except in the latter condition. It may be seen from these records that the monkeys responded in a consistent and organised way according to the specification of the schedule. And yet it must be emphasised that the sole consequence of this responding was the intermittent presentation of a shock; the animal would have received no shocks if he had not emitted operant responses! These patterns of responding were maintained over 70 experimental sessions without showing any sign of disappearing, and these fixed interval scallops are indistinguishable from those which result from identical schedules of food presentation (given an appropriate period of food-deprivation, of course).

   This striking behavioural phenomenon is particulary surprising. One's first thought might be that the monkeys are perversely working in order to shock themselves when they could readily stop, and thereby end the presentations of shock. However, when discussing behaviour maintained by schedules of *food* reinforcement, we have explained such apparently purposive behaviour by reference to events in the past, and there seems no good reason why this should not be insisted upon in the present context. Another possible 'explanation' is that the animals have been tricked; they *think* that they are still exposed to the avoidance schedule but that they fail to respond efficiently enough to avoid all the shocks. Put another way, it may be that the avoidance schedule resulted in shock becoming a stimulus which set the occasion for responding, a function which is 'superstitiously' maintained by the FI schedule of shock presentation superimposed on avoidance responding. Any attempt to explain this behavioural phenomenon, however, has to take into account the fact that it must be related to the past history of the animal, for the schedule would not normally be expected to maintain behaviour in this way if it were presented alone from the beginning of the experiment. Nevertheless, the behaviour is the orderly consequence of the schedule when it replaces an avoidance schedule, and also in certain circumstances even with animals who have had no prior experience of shock-avoidance (see Morse and Kelleher, 1970). Much more work is needed in this field to establish unequivocally the sufficient conditions for such patterns of behaviour to be developed and maintained by intermittent schedules of shock presentation (see Stretch, 1972). However, these data are certainly challenging in themselves. They emphasise yet again that the effects of stimuli such as electric shock depend on the way in which these are scheduled to occur and also on the past history of the experimental subject. Such a view leads us once more away from motivational accounts of behaviour (according to which this behaviour appears to be clearly paradoxical) and towards explaining behaviour in terms of observable procedures and events. This will assume greater importance in the next chapter, in which the effects of drugs on behaviour will be discussed.

For the moment, then, this chapter shows that substantial control over operant behaviour may be exerted by stimuli such as shock even in the absence of any positive reinforcers such as food. The situations most studied are provided by escape schedules (either from shock itself or from stimuli associated with it) and by avoidance conditions. However, given animals with appropriate experimental histories, schedules of shock *presentation* also appear capable of maintaining patterns of operant behaviour.

CHAPTER 13
Drugs and behaviour

Throughout this book there have been a number of references to the effects of drugs on operant behaviour. We are now in a position to consider this research in its own right, and this chapter reviews the contribution made by the techniques of operant conditioning to an area of research which is known either as *psychopharmacology* or *behavioural pharmacology*.

The first thing to be stressed once more is that schedules of reinforcement *maintain* behaviour. This may be easily overlooked by those who accept the connotation of 'conditioning' as a change in behaviour or as transitional states. However, it is important, for psycho-active drugs are usually used not in learning situations, but in the everyday situations in which human behaviour has become adjusted and attuned to the environment in which it occurs. For example, drugs used in clinical psychology are rarely intended to produce changes in learning, but a general invigorating or sedative effect, or to change levels of anxiety and so on. The stable behaviour resulting from schedules of intermittent reinforcement provides a controlled situation in which the important variables are reasonably well identified, and is therefore suitable for investigating the effects of drugs on behaviour.

The general research strategy made possible by steady states of behaviour was discussed in the context of drug effects earlier (Chapter 7) and is therefore not repeated here. However, a number of specific points should be made. First, steady states of behaviour can extend over very considerable periods of time; for example, in the previous chapter, cumulative records were discussed which showed the control of reinforcement schedules over periods of three hours. Such maintained patterns of behaviour are ideal for investigating the effects of a drug over time. Using such a procedure, one can detect a drug effect which begins to take hold only one or two hours after the injection and can plot effects as they increase or decrease over time. Clearly, the time-course of a drug's action is an important consideration.

A second point which should be emphasised is that operant conditioning experiments make it possible to control for peripheral effects of a drug when assessing the influence of that drug on behaviour. One difficulty in psychopharmacology when animals have been used as subjects is that the effects of a drug on general behaviour may sometimes have resulted from its interfering with perceptual processes, for example. We met this problem earlier when discussing Terrace's work on errorless discrimination learning. You will remember that at one time it was assumed that chlorpromazine (a tranquillising compound) disrupted discriminations by affecting the visual system; Terrace's work suggested that this was not the case, because the identical discrimination was not impaired if the animal had acquired it by a progressive, errorless procedure (Terrace, 1963c). The converse may also apply: careful selection of behavioural baselines can make it possible to conclude with confidence that certain drugs *do* affect perceptual processes. For example, using his sophisticated experimental design, Blough (1957) was able to show that doses of lysergic acid diethylamide (the hallucinogenic drug LSD) affected the visual threshold of pigeons at doses which did not produce gross effects on motor activity and which did not disrupt the discriminative control exerted by light and dark stimuli.

A third advantage of operant conditioning is provided by the fact that steady states of behaviour with individual subjects can be maintained over many consecutive experimental sessions. This makes it possible to detect whether repeated injections of the same dosage of a specified drug always produce the same effect on behaviour, or whether tolerance builds up so that ever larger doses are required if a particular effect on behaviour is to be sustained. For example, Schuster, Dockens and Woods (1966) reported that small doses of dl-amphetamine (a central nervous system stimulant) had progressively less effect on a pattern of behaviour maintained by certain schedules of reinforcement. More specifically, DRL behaviour became resistant to the effects of the drug; however, FI behaviour (maintained with the same subjects by means of a multiple schedule) did not develop tolerance in this way. Schuster and his associates put forward the suggestion that behavioural tolerance develops only if a drug disrupts an animal's performance in meeting the schedule requirements for reinforcement. In other words, the drug initially increased DRL response rates, which led to a *decrease* in frequency of reinforcement; this is the sort of situation in which tolerance may develop. Increases in response rate on the less stringent FI schedule had no effect on reinforcement frequency and so tolerance to the drug did not develop. Similarly, the drug increased response rate in a shock-avoidance experiment, but because this did not lead to any detrimental effects (such as an increase in shock frequency), behavioural tolerance did not develop. So this work suggests that the development of behavioural tolerance is likely to occur only in specified circumstances, a finding of considerable importance.

The use of operant conditioning techniques in psycho-pharmacology has led, in general terms, to a much greater emphasis on the behavioural side of this combination of interests (see, for example, Thompson and Schuster, 1968). In the past, experimenters have often been much more interested in the chemical nature of the pharmacological substances themselves and their effects on the physiological system. It is now quite clear, however, that the effects of behaviourally-active drugs do not depend merely on their chemistry and on the physiological states of the animals, but also on the nature of the behaviour being investigated, and on the schedules of reinforcement which maintain the behaviour when the drug is given. An early experiment by Dews (1955) illustrates this point. He trained pigeons either on an FI 15 minute or an FR 50 schedule of food reinforcement, and investigated the effects of various doses of pentobarbital, a drug which is sometimes described as a depressant and which in larger doses can be used as an anaesthetic. Dews found that both patterns of operant behaviour were depressed by dosages of 4 or 5.6 mg. of the drug, as would be expected from the classification of pentobarbital as a

depressant. The fixed-interval responding was also markedly
reduced in frequency by smaller doses (1 and 2 mg.); however,
the responding maintained by the fixed-ratio schedule was, if
anything, *increased* by these smaller dosages. Doses even smaller
than these produced increases in both patterns of responding.
The first important point demonstrated by these data is that the
effect of a given dosage of the drug depends on the nature of the
ongoing behaviour, and through this on the schedule of reinforcement maintaining that behaviour. Second, even the *direction* of a
drug's effect on behaviour should not be too readily predicted
from a general description of the drug, for the 'depressant'
pentobarbital was shown to enhance response rates in certain
circumstances. Combining these points, whether a 'depressant'
decreases or increases response rates depends to a large extent on
the dosage used *and* the behaviour against which it is being
assessed.

Of course, Dews' experiment does not isolate the crucial factor
which determines the differential effects of drugs, for the FI and
FR schedules he used resulted in widely different rates of
responding and in very different frequencies of reinforcement.
However, early findings such as these were followed by much work
on the interactions between schedule controlled behaviour and
drugs. It is now accepted that it is not possible to talk of *the*
effects of a drug on behaviour, but that one should consider the
interactions between various dosages and different patterns of
behaviour. At present one important determinant of the behavioural effect of a drug seems to be the rate of responding in
non-drug conditions (a view first suggested by Dews in 1958).
For example, if the rate of responding in control conditions is
relatively low, amphetamines (classed as stimulants) may increase
that rate; however, if the control rate is high, the same drug at
the same dose may decrease it. There has also been growing
evidence that the importance of the baseline response rate is even
greater than the nature of the stimulus maintaining the behaviour. Kelleher and Morse (1964) investigated the effects of
drugs on the behaviour generated by the multiple FI FR
schedules of reinforcement discussed in the last chapter. It will
be recalled that monkeys were exposed to multiple FI FR
schedules, but for some these scheduled food while for others
they programmed escape from a stimulus associated with occasional shocks; the performances maintained by these schedules

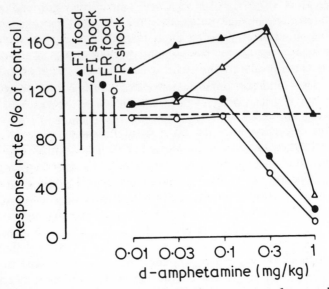

Figure 35   The effects of amphetamine on rates of responding maintained by multiple FI FR schedules of food presentation and escape from stimuli associated with shock. From Kelleher and Morse (1964).

were indistinguishable in spite of the different reinforcing events (Fig. 31, page 160). Morse and Kelleher administered the 'stimulant' drug d-amphetamine to these animals in various dosages, and the effects are shown in Fig. 35. The response rate after the drug is expressed as a percentage of the control rates of responding in the various conditions. It will be seen that the dose-effect curves are substantially similar when similar schedules are compared. For example both FR response rates maintained by food and escape were not greatly affected by doses of d-amphetamine up to 0.1 mg. per kilogram of body weight, but were *decreased* by greater doses. In contrast, both patterns of (slower) FI responding were enhanced by the smaller dosages, this effect being lost at the largest dose given (1 mg./kg.). Of course, the curves are not exactly the same; this might reflect slight individual differences between the three monkeys exposed to each of the two sorts of schedule. Nevertheless, it is clear that the effects of this drug depend more on the *schedule* of reinforcement than on the nature of the event which it schedules. Figure 35 also demonstrates the differential susceptibilities of different patterns of behaviour maintained by the same reinforcer. For example, a dose of 0.3 mg./kg. increased the relatively low rates of responding maintained by the FI schedule of food presentation, but decreased the higher control rates generated by the FR schedule of food delivery. The same finding applies to the FI and FR schedules of escape.

The determinants of this differential sensitivity to drug effects were further investigated by Morse and Kelleher on the basis of these data. They plotted the relative rate of responding after a drug injection of 0.3 mg./kg. against the control rate of responding in the escape conditions, and their results are shown in Fig. 36 (taken from Kelleher and Morse, 1968). The open and closed points indicate data from two different sessions. The triangles denote the effects of the drug on FR 30 behaviour:

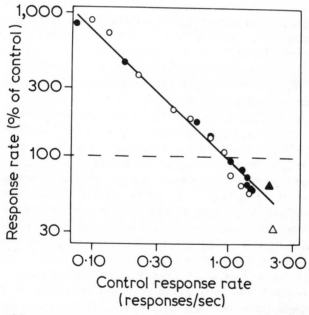

Figure 36   Response rates after administration of amphetamine expressed in comparison with control rates. From Kelleher and Morse (1968).

control rates which were normally between 2 and 3 responses per second were substantially reduced by the drug, as we have already seen. The circles depict the response rates in successive minutes of the FI 10 minutes components; since the typical performance on this schedule is a pause followed by a gradual transition to fairly moderate rates of responding, the response rates in the successive parts of the interval show a progressive increase, thereby shifting the data points to the right in the diagram. However, when the effects of the drug are plotted for these successive periods (in terms of the rate after the drug as a percentage of the control rates), it emerges that the greatest enhancing effect was on the lowest response rates, and that this effect becomes progressively less as the control rate increases to about one response per second, whereupon this pattern of behaviour also becomes suppressed by the drug. The straight line drawn between these points suggests, then, that there is a strong relationship between control response rates and the effect of the drug: rates lower than one per second are enhanced, this effect being greater with lower response rates; however, response rates higher than one per minute are proportionally decreased by the 'stimulant' drug. The fact that the FR data (triangles) fit approximately to the line suggests that the formal specification of the schedule is less important than the response rate which it maintains (a view we considered much earlier when discussing schedules of reinforcement).

This orderly relationship between response rate and the effects of a stimulant drug have also been reported by McKearney (1972). He used fixed interval schedules again, but in his experiment the event maintaining behaviour was either food for food-deprived animals or a *response-dependent* shock with animals previously exposed to an avoidance schedule. Scheduling either of these events according to the same FI schedule generated more or less identical, scalloped patterns of responding, and McKearney reported an orderly drug-effect substantially similar to that discussed above.

This work suggests, then, that the effects of psychoactive drugs depend on the schedule of reinforcement maintaining the behaviour rather than on the nature of that reinforcement; this effect is mediated through the response rates which are differentially maintained by the various schedules. Many of the implications of this theory remain to be examined (for example, could the effects of drugs on conditioned suppression be explained in this way?). However, for the moment it may be noted that yet again these data direct attention away from the traditional explanations of behaviour in terms of underlying motivations. In the past, many investigators have attempted to compare the effects of drugs (as of other variables) on patterns of behaviour which are 'positively' or 'negatively motivated', situations in which animals or humans may be said to *want* something to happen or want it *not* to happen. Patterns of behaviour maintained by food 'reward' or in shock-avoidance experiments have been used more or less indiscriminantly to investigate such questions. These investigations often assume that differences in the detailed characteristics of the resulting patterns of behaviour are unimportant in comparison with the differences in the assumed motivational systems. The work reviewed here suggests that this may be wrong, and that many of the differences (if not all of them) which have been reported by such programmes may in fact be schedule effects.

Operant conditioning techniques are also becoming increasingly important in investigating drug addiction. Although it is true that addiction is often associated with changes in the physioloigcal system of the addicted person, the problem is also a behavioural one. It is brought about in the first place by patterns of behaviour which produce (or are followed by) a drug, and it would seem that much more knowledge is required about these behavioural processes. What is more, the act of administering a drug to oneself is an example of operant or emitted behaviour, for it cannot be said to be elicited by any stimulus in the normal sense of that term. This operant behaviour may therefore be considered in terms of its consequences, which may then be identified as a reinforcer. The problem may then be considered in terms of operant behaviour in a situation in which reinforcers (the drug) are scheduled in various ways.

One method for studying the phenomenon in this way is discussed by Stretch and Gerber (1970). A squirrel monkey is placed in a typical operant conditioning chamber, where in front of him is a small lever, the depression of which provides an arbitrary operant response. The monkey has a tiny catheter or tube permanently inserted into his jugular vein, and this tube is led to a small box which the monkey wears on his back. In order to stop the animal damaging himself by tampering with the tube which is connected directly to his blood stream, he is fitted with a padded leather jacket, which he wears continuously and on which the back-pack is mounted. This pack can be connected by means of a further tube to a small infusion pump mounted above the test chamber. This can pump measured amounts of a drug solution through the tubes and thereby into the animal's blood stream with little delay. It is necessary to restrain the animal from moving about the cage when he is connected to the pump, and he is therefore seated in a chair which secures him at the waist. Using this arrangement, the direct infusion of a drug can be made immediately after a response in the same way as re-inforcers such as food. Moreover this arrangement has the advan-tage that the monkey is completely unrestrained when he is not being tested, and from his behaviour in his home cage it is quite clear that the surgical intervention (which is carried out under complete anaesthesia, of course) and the jacket cause him no discomfort or inconvenience. This technique has been used to show that monkeys will emit operant responses which are followed by small infusions of d-amphetamine. These animals had no prior experimental histories, but were first placed in a situation in which every lever press was followed by an infusion of 0.1 mg./kg. of the drug, this being accompanied by a green cue light above the response lever. They were then transferred to a ratio schedule of drug infusion, but one in which the number of responses required became progressively larger. The first response was followed by the drug, but three responses were required before the next infusion, then a further five for the next, ten for the fourth and thirty for the fifth infusion. Thereafter, thirty responses were required before further infusions, but if the monkey produced eight infusions within 45 minutes, a time-out of 50 minutes was instituted in which responses had no conse-quences and the stimuli associated with the reinforcement schedule were switched off. Each experimental session lasted for two hours and it was found that this schedule sustained responses at fairly high rates. It was shown that the drug was indeed the reinforcer in this situation by disconnecting it from the pump and delivering inert isotonic saline instead, a procedure which did not sustain responding. So these animals 'chose' to emit operant responses whose sole consequence was infusion of amphetamine, which can therefore be described as a reinforcer in the technical sense. The advantages of such a procedure are considerable, for it becomes possible to study the effects of treatments which are intended to alleviate drug-dependence. It is also possible to determine in what circumstances an animal may be led to administer other pharmacological substances to himself, and how the control of these drugs develops. In the case of the experiment reported above, the animals voluntarily administered d-amphetamine to themselves without other procedures being required, but it is possible that other drugs may develop their ability to control behaviour only in certain circumstances, which may, of course, be simulated experimentally.

Using rats in a similar procedure, Pickens and Thompson (1968) have shown that cocaine will act as a reinforcer without special prior training. It was found that the rates at which rats would respond depended on the size of each drug infusion, and the frequency of its delivery, the animals behaving in such a way that the mean hourly intake of cocaine was roughly constant.

The effects of morphine have also been studied in a number of similar experiments. In one of these (Thompson and Schuster, 1964) rhesus monkeys were first made *physically* dependent on the drug by infusing it regularly but independently of behaviour (although it has since been reported that morphine is also capable of developing control over behaviour without this procedure: Thompson and Schuster, 1968). These animals were then trained to emit responses which were followed by morphine infusion according to a Chain FI 2 minutes FR 25 schedule, a combination of requirements which produces a rich variety of behaviour, incorporating periods of no responding, periods of delicate transition to moderate rates, and periods of high response rates. This schedule maintained behaviour for periods as long as six months. The behaviour was shown to be a sensitive and reliable measure of changes induced by depriving the animals of the drug for a while, or of giving booster doses of the drug, or of injecting nalorphine, which is a morphine antagonist. In this experiment if was also discovered that other patterns of operant behaviour which were concurrently maintained by schedules of food reinforcement or shock avoidance were severely disrupted if the monkeys were deprived of the opportunity to produce their normal morphine infusions, but this disruption was rectified by only one self-infusion of the morphine solution.

This very brief review shows that the techniques of operant conditioning may make considerable contributions to the study of drug abuse. But it is not merely the technique which should be stressed here. The orientation within psychology expressed throughout this book may be particularly useful at a conceptual level when it comes to analysing some aspects of drug addiction, for this field is one in which motivational and physiological explanations are frequently used. As ever, there is nothing *wrong* with accounts of this nature, but they may not necessarily be the most useful. For example, it is clear that considerable *behavioural* dependence may be established without detectable signs of *physical* dependence (Thompson and Schuster, 1968) and it would seem that environmental variables of relevance to behaviour in general should not be overlooked. But certainly the technique opens up new possibilities for controlled investigations of measures which are intended to reduce an individual's reliance on psycho-active drugs, regardless of how one believes that addiction is caused.

CHAPTER 14

Applications to education

The preceding discussions have dealt almost exclusively with experiments in which animals acted as subjects. The remaining pages show how the approaches and techniques of operant conditioning may be used at a human level. In the space remaining, it is possible only to be selective, and so the implications of experimental findings on separate topics, such as the use of drugs or of punishment procedures, will not be considered formally; on the whole, these are fairly apparent. Instead, we shall deal with three separate, but general, aspects of operant conditioning. Some of the earlier chapters considered the ways in which new patterns of behaviour may be *acquired* by animals, either in the form of 'tricks' or in situations which show their potential capabilities to the full. The principles isolated by these experiments are now to be considered in the context of human education. A second major emphasis in the earlier chapters has been the repeated demonstration that patterns of behaviour may be *maintained* as a function of environmental events and the way in which these are scheduled to occur. The importance of this will also be considered briefly in terms of general and organisational problems in educational settings; however, they are applied more comprehensively in the following chapter to problems of abnormal human behaviour. The third important aspect of all the previous chapters has been the repeated assertion that behaviour may be considered most usefully in terms of the environment in which it occurs, and this more general *orientation* in psychology is discussed in the next and the final chapter.

Educational institutions are provided primarily, of course, to *teach*, most often with children as the learners. However, the specific goals of the teaching programmes are often poorly formulated, and are usually specified in fairly abstract terms such as 'knowledge' or 'understanding' rather than in terms of specific behavioural performance. Teachers rarely tend to consider that they are trying to produce changes in *behaviour*, by making new patterns of behaviour occur in appropriate circumstances; such a view is replaced by accounts of more general cognitive changes (although these are normally measured in terms of the pattern of behaviour which they support). In experiments in which animals act as subjects, on the other hand, our discussions are normally confined to observable behaviour which occurs in certain circumstances as a result of the training procedures. One could claim that a pigeon has been taught *how* to tell the difference between red and orange lights, but operant conditioners would prefer an account in terms of observable and environmental events: environmental circumstances are said to have resulted in the development of two separate patterns of behaviour in the presence of the two stimuli, rather than in an abstract ability. Similarly, they would hope to identify the purposes of education in concrete terms whenever possible. This is a difference in general orientation within psychology, of course, but it may be specially relevant in the context of teaching.

This general problem apart, we have seen that a number of basic principles are important in teaching animals. First, a reinforcer is required. Second, the reinforcer should be made dependent on the emission of a desired pattern of behaviour, and should be delivered immediately after that act has occurred. Third, if the behaviour to be developed is unlikely to occur spontaneously (so making it impossible to make reinforcements dependent on it), a procedure of successive approximation may 'shape' the desired behaviour effectively and quickly. When we turn to many classroom situations it is not always possible to identify these three principles at work. Many textbooks do bear a resemblance to successive approximation procedures, especially in subjects such as mathematics or foreign languages. The better books begin simply, with patterns of behaviour which do occur in appropriate circumstances, and gradually add more units to the students' repertoire while attempting to maintain the previous patterns as well. It is also true, however, that many lessons and even some books do not secure *progressive* increases in repertoire, but proceed in more *ad hoc* ways (perhaps because the final performance required has not been adequately specified). The most noticeable lack in many classrooms, however, is of identifiable environmental events which occur immediately after a pupil has emitted an appropriate pattern of behaviour. Indeed, in some cases (especially in lecture-halls), the only person who seems to be actively emitting any patterns of behaviour which have environmental consequences is the teacher; university students are only too often to be seen in serried ranks, their major requirement being to keep silent and to emit occasional patterns of behaviour which may be identified as reinforcers for the *lecturer's* behaviour! Occasionally, tasks are set which do demand the participation of pupils. If these are in the form of verbal questions, the teacher may generate more activity from his audience, but he is clearly not able to keep all his students 'in play' simultaneously and can deliver social approval dependent on the behaviour of only one of them at a time. If written assignments are set, the environmental consequences for an individual who completes them are often minimal and are frequently delayed: when a pupil finishes his class-work, he may be told merely to check his workings until others have finished, and the 'corrected' work may be returned as long as a week later.

Of course, one of the major difficulties in the typical teaching situation is that one person normally has to teach many pupils at the same time. A compromise is usually reached by proceeding through a successive approximation procedure at a speed which is judged to be adequate for most, if not all, of the students, but there is clearly a conflict of interests here. Since the teaching programme is not adjusted to the development of each child, periodic examinations are conducted. These grade the pupils in terms of those who have assimilated most, or least, information. Another difficulty of the group setting is simply that of finding any reinforcing events. It frequently appears that not all pupils *want* to learn, and so a major problem is that of motivating these individuals. In the past, the use of aversive stimuli (or the threat of their use) was important in this respect. More recently 'competition' was fostered as a normal part of the teaching situation, often backed up by relatively aversive consequences for the less 'able' students. However, the artificiality of such procedures in providing reinforcement for the individual has been shown by more progressive procedures in which children are encouraged to learn through their own experience and by their own successes and mistakes. If traditional drills are replaced by more 'humane' approaches to education, it has been found that a child may be adequately motivated (or reinforced) by 'finding things out' for himself or with others. With such an approach the children are certainly *doing* things and are less regimented. However, the teacher is now faced by an infinitely more demanding task, as he attempts to guide rather than coerce. Some critics have been heard to suggest that these techniques do not provide the pupil with an adequate grounding in the basic concepts of certain disciplines (the latter is an appropriate word it seems). A popular retort to this is that the more liberal systems of education provide a grounding for *life* rather than a training for academic life.

Problems of education rightly make for heated argument. It cannot be the purpose of a brief review such as this to resolve conflicts by providing a panacea. Our purpose in these turbulent waters is merely to investigate contributions that experiments in operant conditioning could make to the less structured world of the educational establishment. In these terms, the major problem would seem to be to identify a reinforcer which may be made immediately dependent on each pupil's behaviour, and to harness its power within a progressive procedure which successively approximates to a desired educational goal. More liberal systems provide evidence that the accumulation of knowledge may act as an adequate reinforcer in certain circumstances. One attempt to use this reinforcer effectively in a structured educational programme has been provided by *teaching machines*. Put in non-doctrinaire terms, these devices are intended to enable an individual to work at his own pace through a carefully graded *programme* of information, obtaining immediate knowledge as he progresses as to whether he has understood each additional item of information.

Teaching machines vary widely, but the reader probably has some idea of their basic characteristics. Normally, each machine is located in its own small cubicle, so that the pupil is removed from sources of distraction. With most machines there is a small window, through which an item of information is displayed.

Each display is known as one *frame* of the programme. The student is required to read this, and then to make some response, usually to a question which is based on the information given in that frame. The nature of this response varies with different machines, as will be discussed later; however, when it has been made, the machine advances the programme to the next frame, in which the pupil is told whether his previous response was correct or not, and in which further information and questions are to be found. This process is continued until the end of the programme is reached. Sometimes, a specially designed book may take the place of the machine, but the basic principles are the same: information is given in small amounts which become gradually more complex, questions are asked at each stage, and the pupil is told immediately whether his answer is right or wrong.

It is often suggested that programmed learning is a direct application of operant conditioning techniques. Certainly, one of its leading advocates has been B. F. Skinner, whose ideas and research were so fundamental in the development of modern operant conditioning. It is also apparent that programmed learning shares a number of characteristics with that research: responses are immediately followed by environmental consequences, and there is a process of successive approximation to an ultimate goal. However, some forms of programmed learning are more closely modelled on operant conditioning than others. The differences are to be found not so much in the hardware (the machines) as in the nature of the programmes used in them. Two general systems of programming may be distinguished: *linear* (advocated by Skinner) and *intrinsic* or branching (associated with Crowder).

As we have seen, in programmed learning a limited amount of information is given in each frame, which also incorporates some form of question. In the case of intrinsic programmes, a number of possible answers to this question are also given, and the pupil is asked to select the correct one from these. He does this by pressing one of a number of buttons. If he chooses the correct answer, this advances the programme to the next frame, which tells the student that his answer was correct, and which then gives another block of information together with some more possible answers. If he is wrong, however, the programme is advanced to another frame which tells him this and which probably explains why his answer is incorrect. The student may then be returned to the original frame and asked to select another of the possible answers, or he may be sent off on a special remedial sequence of frames which is intended to help him grasp a principle which his original answer indicated he had not adequately understood. So the person who consistently selects the correct answers will reach the end of the programme in fewer frames than one who makes mistakes. Intrinsic programmes take over one of the most important roles of the teacher, namely diagnosing the pupil's strengths and weaknesses and providing him with additional information if his performance shows that he needs it. On the other hand, the capable student who has grasped a point may be sent on to more advanced material without being held back by information which is not necessary for him. When intrinsic programmes are used in book form, they are usually provided as a 'scrambled' text, the student being directed to particular pages of the book as a consequence of his selected answer. This can lead to frenetic flipping to and fro, which is sometimes trying. However, the programmes are usually interesting, and even fun to use, and so can sustain concentration and motivation.

The linear programme usually gives rather less information in each frame, and does not provide a multiple choice from a number of possible answers. Often the student is asked to write in his answer to a question, or fill in a missing word. Whatever his answer, the programme advances to the next frame, in which the correct answer to the first is contained. If the student had given the wrong answer, he would not be told why it was wrong, for the second frame merely provides the *correct* answer to the first. In this way, each pupil progresses through all the frames, there being no short cuts for correct responses or remedial detours after errors. For this reason, linear programmes are relatively easy to automate, and are often presented in book form, each frame being placed immediately after its predecessor in the series. However, such programmes sometimes seem unadventurous in comparison with the multiple choice procedure of intrinsic programmes. This is because the programmes are constructed in such a way that errors are very rarely made, if at all; the questions are structured so that the student can be expected to supply the appropriate answer; each step is therefore small and cautious.

Both linear and intrinsic programmes have a number of advantages as teaching devices. First, both allow individual students to work at their own pace without slowing others or being held back by others. Second, the very fact that a great deal of effort has to be expended in developing and writing programmes tends to ensure that the ultimate goal of each one is precisely identified, and that there is a logical progression from beginning to end; it follows that the 'teacher' is always adequately prepared for a lesson once the programme has been formulated. Third, and perhaps most important of all, both systems make it possible to keep a record of each student's performance on any programme. In the case of intrinsic programmes, the pupil's problems and speed of progress can be accurately defined. In the case of linear programmes, which are designed so that errors should never occur, frames may be isolated which are inadequate in this respect, so that steps may be taken to amend those which generate an undue number of mistakes.

We cannot compare in detail the practical advantages of the two types of programme: the reader is referred to two comprehensive source books which give further details and evaluations (Lumsdaine and Glaser, 1960; Glaser, 1965). There is no simple answer as to which is the more effective; it depends to a large extent on the circumstances. However, both intrinsic and linear programmes have achieved considerable success in widely differing subjects. In spite of their obvious similarities from a procedural point of view, however, they differ fundamentally in their interpretation of the learning process itself. Intrinsic programmes mimic the traditional teacher to a large extent: they diagnose the student's capabilities and take remedial action where necessary. Linear programmes on the other hand, make no attempt to diagnose difficulties; indeed, they are explicitly designed to progress at such a pace that the students who use them make no mistakes at all. This reflects Skinner's repeated assertion that behaviour is increased in frequency by reinforcements made dependent on that behaviour. The learning process is not interpreted as a trial-and-error procedure at all (although critics often still seem to assume this); behaviour changes as a function of trial-and-*success*. Such a view has been advocated for many years, but the more recent studies of errorless discrimination learning in animals have provided strong empirical support for this assertion in addition to the support of traditional successive approximation procedures. They show that quite fine discriminations can be established between different colours, for example, merely by reinforcing responses to the appropriate stimulus and progressively 'fading in' a negative stimulus, in which case pigeons make no inappropriate responses; moreover, a difficult discrimination can be established without errors by gradually fading out the stimuli of an acquired discrimination and progressively replacing them by the new stimuli. A similar procedure can be seen in many linear programmes, for example in the teaching of spelling. Students are first asked to copy a word, a pattern of behaviour established by earlier teaching; then the word is provided in various sentences, but with letters missing, which the student supplies. The number of missing letters is gradually increased, until eventually the pupil is asked to write in the whole word in an appropriate sentence. Similar techniques may be used to teach a student geographical locations on maps, or anatomical structures (see Holland, 1960).

This approach to teaching may seem strange to many, for it makes everything 'too easy'. We are used to being assigned challenging tasks which are likely to induce errors. This may be largely an attempt to foster motivation in classroom settings, a problem which is overcome in different ways by programmed learning. Difficult tasks are also sometimes set because the student is to be taught to think beyond the material which is being given to him; however, this is sometimes little more than a rationalisation for confusing presentations. If constructive thinking really is to be taught, there seems no reason why this should not be accomplished by progressive programmes — but in this case, 'creative thought' must be adequately specified in terms of the behaviour which it is to support, and a careful programme constructed.

A powerful demonstration of the effects of errorless procedures has been provided by Sidman and Stoddard (1967). They tried to teach a rather complex discrimination between circles and ellipses to retarded children. The purpose of this investigation was to compare two methods of teaching this somewhat arbitrary skill. The children were all between 9 and 14 years old, but none of them had an intelligence quotient greater than 40, most of them being mongols or hydrocephalics. All of them had been confined to hospital for between 3 and 13 years. The task posed was to pick out a circle from a number of ellipses, and an automated teaching procedure was used. The children sat in front of a matrix of nine translucent panels on which the circles and

Figure 37 Some of the stages in a training programme to develop a discrimination between a key with a circle on it and other equally illuminated keys. — from Sidman and Stoddard (1967).

ellipses could be back-projected. The centre panel was always dark, but in the first phase of the experiment, one of the remaining eight panels was illuminated and had a black circle projected onto it; the other seven panels remained dark. If the child touched whichever panel was illuminated, a small chocolate was immediately delivered. Touching a dark panel had no consequence, but when confronted with this situation the children tended to touch the one illuminated panel, and they quickly learned to touch this wherever it appeared on the matrix from one trial to the next. As this continued, the panels which had no circle on them were gradually made slightly brighter, as shown in Fig. 37, until eventually the circle would appear on any one of eight equally-illuminated panels. This gradual progression resulted in errorless performance in seven out of ten children, who consistently touched the panel with the circle. This was called the form discrimination: these children had learned to discriminate a panel with a form projected onto it from seven identical panels with no form. These children were then exposed to the progression of stimuli shown in Fig. 38. As may be seen, the circle continued to occur at random on one of the keys, but was now accompanied by ellipses on the other keys. These were at

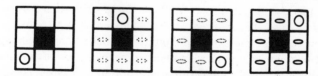

Figure 38 Some steps in 'fading-in' an ellipse in order to develop a discrimination between that symbol and a circle. From Sidman and Stoddard (1967).

first very faint, but eventually became as distinct as the circle. The seven children continued to touch the key with a circle on it, whenever it occurred, and so in the end were discriminating between a circle and ellipses of equally distinct lines projected onto panels of equal brightness. In other words, these children could tell the difference between a circle and an ellipse.

In contrast, of nine similar children who were placed into the final situation without a progressive procedure, only one learned to tell the difference between the circle and the ellipses. The remaining eight were then transferred to the final form discrimination shown in Fig. 37, which six of them eventually succeeded in learning. These six were then returned abruptly to the final circle/ellipse discrimination, but still only three of them were able to learn the correct response.

This experiment, although no more than a preliminary demonstration, has a number of important implications, not least of which is the suggestion that retarded children of such limited 'intelligence' may be taught this precise 'cognitive' skill in favourable circumstances; this, of course, inevitably emphasises that a child's ability to adjust his behaviour must be defined in terms of the procedures used to educate him. However, the experiment also suggests possible general advantages of using procedures which develop learning without errors. In particular, there may be advantages in using this kind of technique with specific difficulties which some normal children have. For example, some children have great difficulty in discriminating b from d and p from q; these problems may easily become surrounded by emotional complications for the child, perhaps because of the mistakes he makes. Errorless procedures may be helpful with such difficulties.

Programmed learning systems (both in linear and intrinsic form) are now being used in many educational settings. It is often suggested that they lead to faster learning and better immediate and long-term retention. Programmes have been devised to teach topics as widely ranging as reading, writing, spelling, a sense of rhythm, and the development of simple abstract concepts on the one hand, to neurophysiology, electronics, critical appreciation of literature and (inevitably) psychology on the other. There are, of course, enormous difficulties in evaluating the contribution of programmed learning fairly — which programmes should be compared with which teachers? Some of these problems are discussed in the general introduction to pro-grammed learning provided by Kay, Dodd and Sime (1968). However, linear programmes in particular also have wider impli-cations for educational assessment itself. For example, if an effective programme is evolved which all pupils finish without making an appreciable number of errors, one might ask to what extent terminal examinations are necessary. These ceremonies sometimes seem to be conducted as much in an attempt to generate 'motivation' as anything else, and this they sometimes achieve to an extent which is itself a problem, if university health centres before examination periods are any guide; yet their motivational effects (whether desirable or undesirable) are usually seen only in short periods preceding the examination. It is also claimed that examinations make it possible to tell how much each pupil has learned. However, there is continuous dis-cussion about the suitability of traditional examinations for this task. With effective linear programmes, on the other hand, indivi-duals might be 'assessed' merely in terms of their current posi-tions in a developing series of programmes (these varying, of course, by reason of the self-paced progress possible in such situations).

However, such a radical change in educational techniques would accentuate problems of individual differences in study habits. No matter how efficient these teaching techniques are, they cannot be effective if the pupils do not study and if they do not place themselves in the situation in which learning can occur. This problem is one of educational management rather than of teaching, and is similar to the difficulties which some university students encounter when they leave the relatively structured environment of their school and enter the less-organised world of further education. But this organisational requirement is never-theless a behavioural problem, and may therefore be tackled by means of operant conditioning. The problem becomes one of describing existing patterns of study, and then attempting to shape these into more effective patterns of behaviour by arrang-ing that events which might be reinforcers are made dependent on them. At the university level, it is clear that study rarely occurs in easily identifiable circumstances: it is not under good stimulus control. Lectures and tutorials are arranged to occur at various times throughout the day, an inevitable result of the individual combinations of subjects. It is not uncommon to have one commitment in one part of the university followed by another in a different place which begins an hour later. The intervening periods are often wasted from the point of view of study, for there are many other things to do, such as simply taking coffee or chatting. Frequently, study itself is regarded as aversive and is done in relatively large chunks, the beginning of each being characterised by relatively ineffective work until one 'gets into the swing' of the subject. Much of the time is inevitably spent in reading, and often notes are taken or sentences underlined in the textbook. There are a great many 'how-to-study' manuals available, but although many of them seem plausible, they usually seem to demand more self-discipline than is available.

In considering these problems, Fox (1962) decided that the principle requirements were to bring patterns of study under some improved form of stimulus control, and to maintain appropriate patterns of behaviour in this situation. He therefore carried out a small experiment in an attempt to see to what extent this could be achieved by procedures similar to those used in operant conditioning experiments. Selected volunteers who were experiencing difficulty in studying were instructed to go to a particular room at a fixed time daily, taking only books which were relevant to the task in hand. Each student was told that he *must* leave the room if he became bored or began to day-dream, and must do something which he regarded as pleasant instead (such as taking coffee); however, once he had decided to leave, he was to read *one* more page, or complete one more simple problem, and then leave even if he no longer wanted to. Then the amount of work to be completed after this decision was slowly increased, until he was reading about five pages. When this was established, the student was told that he might do the same amount of work again, but only after taking a separate decision each time, and he should not work for longer than an hour in any circumstances. When this regimen had been in operation for some time, another course was introduced at a separate time daily and in a different room, the behaviour being built up in the same way as outlined above. The result of this was to build up much more regular patterns of study behaviour.

Fox claims that this simple procedure made use of four well-established principles of behaviour. First, it exploited strong reinforcers which were freely available in the students' environment but which were now made dependent on the emission of a specified amount of work, which at first was very small indeed. What is more, the procedure stressed to the student that this was exactly what was required of him, and there was therefore no reason for the reinforcing events to lose their potential power to modify behaviour (there was no reason for this to be limited by feelings of 'guilt'). Second, the principle of successive approximation was employed by requiring the student to complete only very small assignments of work which then became gradually larger. Third, by breaking the assignments into small chunks and demanding a positive decision to stay at the end of each, Fox argued that he was providing a relatively small fixed-ratio schedule, one which generates high rates of behaviour. Fourth, the procedure always occurred in identical circumstances, thereby giving a specified set of environmental stimuli the opportunity to become discriminative stimuli. In this way, they set the occasion for appropriate behaviour, and this heightened the stimulus control of the procedure; studying occurred 'naturally' in these circumstances.

Fox used similar techniques to develop and maintain specified types of study behaviour as well as specified periods of studying. He took up an earlier suggestion that effective study consisted of surveying the material to be mastered, posing questions, reading in order to answer these self-posed questions, reciting what has been read after only small sections, and then reviewing that section to check on one's recitation. The important point here is that the global concept of study had been broken down into smaller components, and Fox tackled each separately using techniques of successive approximation within each block of time for which the student opted to stay (thereby using the same ultimate reinforcements).

Of course, the above procedures are hardly revolutionary, but it is important to recognise that Fox did not appeal to his students to work harder, nor did he interpret the initial problem as a motivational one. Difficulties in study were not helped by sympathy and exhaustive personal interviews. For him, the matter was to be regarded 'merely' as a behavioural problem, and was therefore considered to be amenable to environmental control as with any other operant behaviour. One might note, for example, that his procedures made it exceedingly unlikely that ineffective behaviour in a particular environment would be followed by reinforcement: the students obtained pleasant consequences only after periods of appropriate study, however short these might be initially. Contrast this with the constant temptation to break from study when things begin to go badly and to finish when a difficulty is encountered, both of which may lead to an increase in the frequency of poor studying.

These general, organisational procedures based on principles of behaviour are at least as important a contribution to education made by operant conditioning as is the use of teaching machines. For example, Keller (1968) has discussed a scheme in which college courses are restructured on the basis of these general principles. Small, graded tasks are given to individuals and further assignments are provided only when these have been completed, and competence in them briefly demonstrated. This is not achieved by *competitive* tests, merely by the opportunity for each student to demonstrate that he has completed the previous assignment. The expectation, then, is that students should be able to take these small tests in their stride. Lectures or demonstrations are programmed to occur relatively rarely and are intended to be 'inspirational' rather than didactic. Attendance at them is entirely optional, but only students who have reached a point where they have demonstrated that they will be able to profit have the *opportunity* of attending them. The lectures are also recorded, so that they can be heard at the appropriate time by those who had not originally qualified for them. Examinations are given at the end of this course, but count for far less than the number of units completed. Keller reported that a much higher proportion of students obtained good grades than one expects from more traditional courses. A detailed account of a similar procedure has also been reported by Johnston and Pennypacker (1971), who provide evidence that such programmes are extremely popular with students, and generate considerable enthusiasm (as shown by their behaviour); it was suggested by some that 'it's an easy course, but you really have to work for it'. One could envisage similar techniques being used at earlier levels of education, and one can readily see how the advantages of teaching machines or programmed texts might be exploited when appropriate.

Two common objections raised to approaches to education such as these are that they treat children like animals, allowing no scope for individuality and challenge, and that they lose the human touch of the teacher, replacing him by 'cold' machines. However, these objections seem wide of the mark. In the first place, the approach is intended to avoid regimentation and emphasises the individuality of each child by allowing him to work at his own pace and even according to his own work-schedule. There is certainly no down-grading of humanity inherent in this. Perhaps the first objection is intended to emphasise that educational technology is not capable of developing the essential attributes of the human — his ability to conceptualise and to think creatively or critically. This view would also seem to be unfair, however, for the requirements of the techniques discussed here make it essential that the education has a final purpose which must be specified. Vague goals such as 'critical appreciation' may be translated into sub-components, and procedures of successive approximation may then develop the behavioural repertoires which are taken to be critical for those who have this ability. There is nothing in this chapter which is at all contrary to the development of the refined capabilities characteristic of humans only. As for the teacher, it is certainly true that his rôle may change, but this is again, one would have thought, to the advantage both of himself and of his pupils. He would become more of an educational manager, and, released from many of his present chores, could afford to be a real person instead of the caricature which some teachers are forced to become by reason of the present demands made on them. He would find himself in a position to interact with individual students more, and thereby act as a counsellor who may devote time to any special problems, whether academic or personal. In addition, he would be able to act as a dispenser of greater 'treats' than at present, such as leading genuine discussions and developing some of the special interests and aptitudes of his pupils.

However, as I have said before, this chapter is *not* intended to provide a panacea for education. In discussing possible applications of behavioural principles to educational settings, the intention is not to suggest a stereotyped change in teaching techniques. Whatever organisational procedure is used, there are principles of general importance which help to identify the role of any teacher, human or machine. The purpose of the teaching should be clearly identified in unambiguous terms. A child's present repertoire needs to be carefully assessed in as far as it is relevant to the final goal. The transition from initial to final performance is best achieved by progressive approximations. It is not necessarily a good thing to generate errors from which a student is to learn, for behaviour is most effectively generated by a trial-and-success procedure. Success at each specific task usually acts as a reinforcer in the technical sense, as long as it is indicated immediately after the appropriate behaviour. Whether or not these principles were *generated* by operant conditioning experiments, they receive powerful support from them and may therefore be seen in a clearer light in the context of human education.

Finally, even the traditional problems of educational discipline may be appropriately analysed in the behaviouristic terms outlined here. The traditional classroom situation provides an excellent example of this. Teachers often encounter difficulties in maintaining discipline if they are not sufficiently aware of basic behavioural principles. The dismissal of a class is usually reinforcing, in the technical sense, to students, particularly if the lesson is dull or ineffective. For this reason, patterns of behaviour occurring immediately before the class is dismissed are likely to increase in frequency in that situation. Inadvertently allowing the class to go when behaviour is undesirable is therefore likely to have a detrimental effect on classroom discipline. More beneficial effects can be obtained by establishing an invariant relationship between acceptable behaviour and dismissal, techniques of successive approximation being exploited once more. This should not be taken to imply that the teacher should announce his strategy, for this may provide additional discriminative cues to the class; when the teacher publicly demands silence at the end of the lesson, he may easily achieve this while having no effect on general patterns of classroom behaviour.

Other problems of individual discipline may result from techniques which 'leave well alone' by giving a student little attention when he is behaving satisfactorily, but singling him out when he misbehaves. This type of behaviour on the part of the teacher which is intended to be aversive may in fact act as a reinforcer and *strengthen* the aberrant pupil's behaviour, for it is at least a form of attention, and one which is likely to be much approved of by the fellow pupils and therefore be followed by other reinforcers. The power of attention to maintain unacceptable patterns of behaviour has been demonstrated by Zimmerman and Zimmerman (1962). They discuss the tantrum behaviours of an eleven year old boy who kicked and screamed and was generally difficult in class. He frequently had to be coerced into the classroom and would often throw himself on the floor before the door, a pattern of behaviour which naturally produced a great deal of attention from both teachers and pupils alike. This behaviour was effectively reduced merely by ensuring that it was ignored, and that acceptable behaviour secured the attention and interest of the teacher. At first this was achieved by *allowing* him to scream and shout, and only giving him attention when he had been quiet for a while. Then this requirement was gradually increased and an intermittent schedule of attention introduced. For example, when the child was sitting appropriately in class, he was occasionally asked a question which he could answer, and for which he might therefore reasonably be praised in that situation. This simple expedient was successful in eliminating the undesirable patterns of behaviour, which therefore suggests that his previous behaviour was being maintained by the attention which followed it, and by the previous relative lack of attention for acceptable patterns of behaviour.

Again, this latter example may seem to be no more than common-sense, but the general principles are important. While this is true for educational settings, it is even more important in clinical settings, as we will see in the next chapter. Before ending this chapter, however, the reader is directed to a collection of papers by Skinner, entitled *The Technology of Teaching* (1968). This includes readable discussions of the use of teaching machines and the application of behavioural principles to curriculum development and to general disciplinary problems in schools.

CHAPTER 15
Operant conditioning and clinical psychology

In recent years there has been a remarkable surge of interest in the application of conditioning principles to the treatment of abnormal human behaviour. Such applications have been based on both classical and instrumental conditioning models. However, until recently it was the former, Pavlovian technique which had been explored the more fully in this context, being used most often in attempts to help patients who suffered from fairly specific difficulties, such as irrational and debilitating fears (phobias), mannerisms and tics, abnormal sexual behaviour, or addiction to alcohol or other drugs. The application of conditioning principles in general to clinical settings has become known as *behaviour therapy* and provides more than adequate scope for an entire book in itself. Fortunately, a readable review is readily available (Beech, 1969). This is a relatively eclectic account of the various forms of such therapy, and includes discussion of treatments overtly based on *operant* conditioning methods. The introduction of these techniques, together with the approach to psychology favoured by their advocates, has led to a sudden extension of the frames of reference for behaviourally-based treatments of 'mental disorder' in the widest context.

Bizarre and abnormal patterns of human behaviour were once taken to indicate that the unfortunate sufferer was inhabited by malignant spirits. According to this animistic view, the body of the person had fallen under the control of evil spirits, and it was therefore logical to attempt to help him by making his body too uncomfortable for these spirits, thereby encouraging them to leave. In this way, the 'madman' was subjected to various treatments which now appear little different from torture. This view of madness was eventually superseded by a medical model: if a person was behaving abnormally but there was no observable bodily ailment, it was assumed that he was 'mentally ill'. Behavioural abnormalities of a severe kind thus became a sign that the patient should be regarded as ill in a way substantially similar to any form of 'physical' illness, and this produced a change to far more humane therapies. Medical science also provided some support for the view that madness was an illness, by delineating certain patterns of physical abnormality which appeared to explain some forms of behavioural abnormality. These are sometimes to be located in damage to specific parts of the brain, in biochemical abnormalities which allow toxic by-products to circulate in the blood-stream, or in hereditary influences expressed through genetic abnormality in the chromosomes. Modern 'mental hospitals' contain, as a result, many patients whose illness is recognised to be physical in origin. However, they also still contain a greater proportion of patients in whom no physical abnormality has yet been established. These patients behave in abnormal ways, but, failing any sign of an explanatory organic illness, are described as 'mentally ill', or as suffering from 'functional disorders' which cannot be specified in physical terms. However, these functional mental illnesses may nevertheless take the form of extremely aberrant patterns of behaviour; most forms of schizophrenia, for example, fit into this category. Also, most of the circumscribed behavioural difficulties (such as the phobias mentioned above) are functional in this sense, for they too are rarely attributable to identifiable physical changes. Functional illnesses are therefore the major classification in mental illness.

The medical model, then, has led to an interpretation of abnormalities in *behaviour* as being the symptom of some underlying cause which, more often than not, cannot be identified in physical terms. Even where no physical abnormalities can be detected, behavioural abnormalities are still not regarded as the disorders themselves. For this reason, the diagnosis or categorisation of mental illnesses becomes crucial, for the treatment to be pursued will depend on this diagnosis, as with physical diseases. So if a person behaves in a peculiarly withdrawn and detached way, this may be taken as a sign of a certain sub-classification of schizophrenia, and the patient is given treatments designed to alleviate such schizophrenia. Unfortunately, psychiatrists often fail to agree on an appropriate diagnosis for a particular patient; and as a result, widely divergent treatments may be recommended for similar symptoms. On the other hand, any therapy which confines itself merely to a reduction of symptoms is usually regarded as inadequate because it does not strike at the root of the illness itself. Indeed, it is often suggested that such treatments result in no more than the substitution of a fresh set of symptoms to replace those treated, so that the illness exhibits itself in alternative ways. The evidence for this suggestion has, however been disputed by behaviour therapists (see Introduction to Ullman and Krasner, 1965).

Behavioural psychologists view this current medical model with some caution. The experiments discussed in this book, for example, have shown that a useful scientific description of complex patterns of behaviour may be achieved by relating these to identifiable events in the environment. Such patterns may be produced, maintained and manipulated (and also explained) without recourse to unobservable motivational concepts which may do no more than re-phrase the very events they are invoked to explain. Such an orientation inevitably leads to a suggestion that the concept of functional 'mental illness' may be no more than a similar explanatory scheme for unusual patterns of human behaviour. If the only criteria for classifying schizophrenia are behavioural (*how* the person behaves abnormally), what is to be gained by naming a patient's behaviour patterns as schizophrenic? This question becomes especially important if it is suggested that it is the schizophrenia which must be treated rather than the behaviour, and that changes in the behaviour can only be regarded as effective if they are brought about by therapies which alleviate the schizophrenia: this implies that a person is to be rated as schizophrenic only on the basis of behavioural observations, but that if his behaviour is changed by changing the environment, he remains schizophrenic.

Whatever the ultimate cause of abnormal behaviour it is undoubtedly true that the behavioural principles outlined throughout this book may be used in clinical settings. Mental hospitals can be dispiriting places to visit, and in saying this no criticism is intended of the staff, who usually show a remarkable degree of patience and forebearing. However, the more severely disturbed patients are usually left to their own devices throughout large parts of their day. Certain routines are established to ensure that each patient is regularly fed, washed, medicated and so on. The ultimate responsibility for the patient rests, in the usual way, with the medical doctors, who prescribe drugs or other treatments for the illness and see the patients regularly, but the staff who come into most contact with the patients are the nurses, since it is they who are usually responsible for maintaining the routines and for 'managing' the patients throughout the day and night. Inevitably, perhaps, the ratio of patients to nurses is such that it may be difficult to ensure that each patient receives as much personal attention as is desirable. Frequently the nurses are forced to lurch from one minor crisis to the next, being able to cope with only the most pressing demands from their group of patients, some of whom will need a great deal of attention while others who are quieter or more withdrawn may be safely left. The long periods of time spent in hospital wards by chronic patients may themselves result in behavioural difficulties, for it has been recognised for some time that patients may become 'institutionalised', developing new abnormalities or becoming more and more stereotyped in particular acts, such as shuffling up and down the ward, wringing their hands, hoarding useless objects, or just sitting in a chair for long periods.

In a comprehensive series of reports, Ayllon has drawn attention to the fact that it is the psychiatric nurse, not the doctor, who may be in the best position to modify some of the aberrant patterns of behaviour seen in the typical ward setting of a mental hospital. Indeed, in one of his earlier papers (Ayllon and Michael, 1959) this point was emphasised by the suggestion that the nurse might be considered as a 'behavioural engineer' who could be used to develop more normal patterns of behaviour in patients or to reduce the frequency of disruptive habits. The ward nurses were acquainted with some of the more basic principles of reinforcement; it was pointed out that certain events had the effect of increasing the frequency of any patterns of behaviour with which they were associated, so that desirable patterns could be developed by making reinforcers dependent on them while undesirable patterns might be decreased or extinguished by ensuring that no reinforcers were associated with them. It was suggested that in the ward setting, the attention of the nurses might be a reinforcer in this sense. The first step in the experimental programme was to measure the behaviour of individual patients in the ward as objectively as possible. This was achieved in terms of the frequency of specific acts, without recourse to any hypothetical reasons or motivations prompting these acts. A record was kept of what each patient was doing at the end of each 30 minute period – a technique known as a time-sampling analysis. Thus, it became possible to build up a picture of how each patient spent his time and of which patterns of behaviour occurred most frequently in the normal ward setting. Then an attempt was made to give attention (an assumed reinforcer) in such a way that beneficial changes in behaviour resulted. The time-sampling analysis provided an approximate measure against which the procedure could be evaluated.

One simple procedural change made by Ayllon and Michael was to withhold attention for certain patterns of behaviour by which some patients had previously gained the nurses' attention. One patient, Lucille, had for two years made repeated visits to the nurses' office, where she interrupted their work. She had been told that she should not do this and had been asked to stop, but nevertheless she continued to visit the office about sixteen times every day. Lucille had been classified as mentally defective, and the nurses had decided that it was useless to continue asking her to stop interrupting them; they reasoned that she was not able to understand, and so they had come to tolerate these visits. When she came, the nurses used to talk to Lucille and lead her back to the ward. However, they were now asked by Ayllon and Michael to ignore her if she entered the office. They were not to be nasty to her in any way, but on no account were they to talk to her or give her any attention. As a result of this change, Lucille's visits showed a progressive decrease in frequency, until after about 50 days she interrupted the nurses no more than twice per day.

A similar procedure was used with another patient, Helen, who caused difficulties in the ward by her persistent discussion about her illegitimate child and the men whom she claimed were constantly pursuing her. One of the doctors in the hospital described Helen as 'delusional', and as a patient who 'feels she must push her troubles onto somebody else'. Her behaviour had become so annoying to some of the other *patients* that they had on several occasions actually beaten her, presumably in an attempt to quieten her. Some of the nurses reported that when Helen spoke about these topics, they used to listen in an effort to get at the 'roots of her problem'; other nurses paid little attention to this talk, but simply nodded or said something innocuous such as 'Yes, I understand' in the hope of steering Helen's conversation onto another topic. Ayllon and Michael asked the nurses to ignore this patient if she was talking about her child or about her suitors, but to pay attention to any more sensible talk, reinforcing this by social interaction and discussion. It was thereby hoped to reduce the proportion of Helen's speech which centred on these two 'problems' and simultaneously to increase the frequency of more normal topics in her conversation. This simple procedure did result in a progressive decline in the proportion of Helen's speech which centred on the two 'problem' topics: instead of talking about nothing else, less than a quarter of her speech content was now about these topics. However, after this reduction had been achieved, the proportion of Helen's 'problem' speech suddenly rose again to about 50%; Ayllon and Michael later discovered that Helen had been visited by a social worker, who, unknown to the nurses, had been reacting to the 'problem' talk in the previous 'natural' way, and who had therefore reinforced it once more. Similar events occurred when volunteer ladies came to entertain the patients in the ward, and these difficulties show the problems of maintaining consistent schedules of reinforcement, even in the relatively confined environment of a ward. Nevertheless, the programme achieved considerable success, and, as a result, Helen was at least no longer attacked by her fellow patients.

Ayllon and Michael attempted to treat a number of other difficulties by procedures conceptualised in behaviouristic, operant-conditioning terms. A further example, is their approach to dealing with extreme hoarding, a common problem in mental hospitals. Three patients in Ayllon and Michael's study collected papers, rubbish and magazines, and carried these around with them inside their clothing next to their body. One of these three (Harry), did this so persistently that the nurses regularly 'de-junked' him several times throughout the day and before he went to bed, and yet he still hoarded so much next to his skin that rashes developed. The nurses were now instructed to provide no social reinforcement for hoarding, the reasoning being once again that the social interactions which such behaviour produced from the nurses were helping to maintain it. Ayllon and Michael also suggested that the hoarding might be due in part to the relative lack of papers and magazines in the ward; they ensured that there were always plenty, arguing that this satiation procedure would be like one in which the behaviour of animals is no longer maintained by food if they are provided with plenty of food before their test sessions. Some of the nurses were sceptical about this programme, for they thought that hoarding was to be explained in terms of the patient's deep-rooted need for security; since the programme did nothing to reassure the patients in this respect, it was felt that it would not only be ineffective, but would even be positively dangerous. However, such forebodings were not supported by the results of the procedure – the patients carried progressively less paper about with them. The most problematical hoarder (Harry), for example, no longer carried rubbish or magazines in his clothing. He did tend to keep a stack of magazines on his lap when he was sitting in the ward; this might be interpreted, perhaps, as a lingering manifestation of his 'problem', or of his 'lack of security', but it seems more likely that this much slighter eccentricity was of a form that was unaffected by the programme, for such behaviour was not regarded as abnormal hoarding, and so, presumably, social interactions were occasionally associated with it as with other patterns of normal behaviour. No general problems which might be attribu-table to a 'loss of security' resulted from the decrease in hoarding of the patients in this programme.

The paper by Ayllon and Michael (1959) from which these examples were taken, is of great importance. In particular, it directs attention to possible dynamics of reinforcement in any ward in a mental hospital. With the evidence of these early, and somewhat preliminary, demonstrations, one becomes aware of the ways in which nurses in unstructured ward schemes may in fact inadvertently contribute to the maintenance of the very patterns of behaviour which they regard as their biggest prob-lems. If a patient who sits quietly is ignored by staff, but is the subject of attention when he does something bizarre, there is a strong risk that this bizarre behaviour will increase and be maintained. However, Ayllon and Michael's work must not be taken simply as a recipe for ignoring undesirable patterns of behaviour, for this is only the beginning of a constructive policy. More exciting is the possibility that more normal patterns of behaviour may be developed and maintained by systematically relating available reinforcers with them, for if social attention is adequate to maintain *abnormal* behaviour, might it not also be sufficient to generate and maintain normal behaviour?

So the procedure which has developed from this approach to clinical psychology may be summarised as containing a number of general principles: first, describe how a patient is behaving, what he is doing, without attempting to explain this by motivational or other unobservable processes. Second, attempt to isolate events in the environment which may act as reinforcers in the simple, technical sense. Third, try to ensure whenever possible that such reinforcers are never associated with undesirable patterns of behaviour. Fourth, attempt to organise the situation in such a way that reinforcers *are* delivered when more normal or desirable patterns of behaviour are being exhibited. Of course, there can be no simple rule of thumb for modifying behaviour in this way, and separate programmes are necessary for each individual. Sometimes the effective reinforcers in a situation may be difficult to identify, and they may vary from one individual to the next. It may often be impossible simply to ignore certain patterns of undesirable behaviour, especially, of course, if they are acts which are dangerous to the patient or to others. But it may still be helpful to try to identify the environmental consequences of such behaviour, so that a deliberate attempt can be made to relate these events maximally to less destructive patterns of behaviour. Also, of course, the possible advantages of careful programmes of successive approximation should not be overlooked: reinforcers may be explicitly related at first to behaviour which is regarded as no more than a transitional stage on the way to a specifiable goal. Any programme should also pay careful attention to providing events which may act as discriminative stimuli, and so set the occasion for an appropriate pattern of behaviour. Also, gradually decreasing the frequency of reinforcement may maintain high frequencies of desirable behaviour without the need for continuous attention.

Social interaction may not necessarily be the most effective reinforcer in the clinical situation. Other things which may strengthen patterns of behaviour are sweets (especially for children) and cigarettes for adults. A number of programmes have attempted to use such reinforcers in addition to social interaction to shape patterns of behaviour which occur very infrequently, such as the verbal behaviour of mute schizophrenics (e.g. Isaacs et al., (1960), or to decrease the hyperactivity of some retarded children (e.g. Patterson, 1965). A very strong reinforcer indeed for most patients is food, especially if it is given after a period of mild deprivation as is the case in any society with relatively fixed meal times. For this reason, it is not surprising to discover that meal times are often difficult periods in managing mental patients. Ayllon (1965) has reported an attempt to modify one very frequent difficulty in this respect the behaviour of a patient who had been in the mental hospital for 20 years and who would not eat unless a nurse sought her out, led her to the dining-room, obtained her meal for her, sat her at a table, and urged her to eat, or even spoon-fed her. The organisational difficulties for nurses when many patients demand such attention need not be stressed. This patient's refusal to feed herself may have resulted from the attention she obtained from doing so which acted as a reinforcer, in addition to the food which was associated with it. As a first step, Ayllon asked the nurses *not* to take the patient to the dining-room, but to make sure that they helped her as much as usual once she entered of her own accord. This change resulted in the patient missing meals for four days, which was obviously a source of concern to the staff; she drank more frequently than usual during this period, but showed no signs of physical strain. However, she then started entering the dining-room unaided, where she was fed in the usual way. As a result, she quickly changed her behaviour, so that within a very short time she missed very few meals indeed. When this behaviour was entirely established, a minimal shaping procedure was used in the dining-room; the social encouragement was removed, and the patient was now given a highly preferred sweet only if she helped herself to a tray and to food. In the continued absence of special attention, the patient quickly began to eat her meals, the food alone eventually being an adequate reinforcer to keep her feeding herself. As a result of this simple change in procedure, the patient's behaviour was changed so that she continued to eat normally. One can see, also, that if these simple steps had not been adequate to induce a change, a more deliberate and gradual successive approximation procedure could have been used, in which attention was given only after she made some small improvement in feeding herself.

This particular experiment suggests that difficulties in feeding may also be maintained by the very procedures which are introduced to ensure that the patient is fed. In this case, it was decided that the patient could be allowed to go without food for a period of time at the beginning of the procedure. Certainly, this did result in a beneficial change which occurred suddenly and before any health problems could be observed. However, some people may feel that this was an unnecessarily severe decision. It may be possible to deal with similar behavioural problems without ever reaching a stage where meals are missed, if a sensitive technique of successive approximation is used, with the patients' specific difficulties being tackled separately and progressively. Ayllon's experiment is given here to show that environmental changes may be sufficient to reduce feeding difficulties: the procedures he used are not offered as necessarily the most appropriate technique for bringing about these changes.

An example of a more gradual approximation procedure using food reinforcement is to be found in a report by Wolf, Risley and Mees (1964). In this investigation, the behaviour of an autistic child, Dicky, was changed by methods of behaviour modification. Dicky was 3½ years old at the beginning of the study. He had developed in an apparently 'normal' way until he was nine months old, when it was discovered that the lenses of both his eyes were covered by cataract. Dicky began to behave in a difficult way, having severe temper tantrums. Eventually, a series of eye-operations was necessary, and the occluded lenses were removed. This made it essential that he wore glasses if his sight was not to be lost. However, his parents were unable to make Dicky wear his glasses, and his behaviour became more difficult to handle: he behaved oddly in social situations, and became very self-destructive in his tantrums — he would bang his head, slap his face, pull his hair, and make himself bruised and bleeding. He was variously diagnosed as mentally retarded, as suffering from physical damage to the brain, or as psychotic (i.e. suffering from a *functional* illness), and was admitted to hospital at the age of three. Eventually, Wolf and his associates were asked to try to train Dicky to wear his glasses, and thereby save his sight. In order to do this, they evolved a programme in which each of the undesirable ways of behaving was attacked separately by changing its environmental consequences. Of these procedures, only two will be discussed here — the way in which the temper tantrums were eliminated and the way the child was trained to wear his glasses.

The first of these was achieved by an extinction procedure. It was felt that personal attention (obviously the natural response of nurses or parents in this distressing situation) was helping to maintain the self-destructive behaviour. This was reduced by removing Dicky from a situation in which social reinforcers were available whenever he threw a tantrum. On such occasions, he was placed in another room, with the door shut, a procedure which Wolf and his associates also conceptualised as a slight punishment dependent on tantrums. In this way, appropriate behaviour could also be differentially reinforced by opening the door and bringing the child back into the ward. This procedure clearly involves a number of moral problems, for the idea of effectively ignoring the child when he may appear to need most help may seem entirely obnoxious. Yet, the result of this programme (which also incorporated shaping procedures) was the reduction of tantrums over a period of time, until they were eventually eliminated completely. We shall return to the general moral issue a little later. For the moment, it is sufficient to note that the distressing self-mutilation and temper tantrums were entirely eliminated in this way.

The problem of training Dicky to wear his glasses was also approached by means of a successive approximation procedure. In this case, the reinforcer was a small bite of fruit or candy; a conditioned reinforcer was established by initially following the click of a noisy toy with the delivery of the reinforcers to a container. In this way, reinforcement could be made immediately dependent on patterns of behaviour generated by a successive approximation procedure. At first, several spectacle-frames were left in the room and Dicky was reinforced simply for picking them up, for holding them or for carrying them about with him. Slowly the criterion for reinforcement was adjusted, bringing the frames closer and closer to his eyes. However, some difficulty was experienced in getting Dicky actually to put the frames on in the appropriate way, and it was at this stage that it was decided to use the greater reinforcing effectiveness of food rather than sweets. The training sessions were arranged to occur at breakfast time, and the reinforcers were now bites of breakfast. Even now, however, the vital transition to wearing the frames properly could not be accomplished. A number of modifications to the frames were therefore made to ensure that they sat more easily on the head, and Dicky was given a session of training at about 2 o'clock on a day when he had been given relatively little to eat before. In this session, the reinforcers were more effective, and it was easy to increase movements of the spectacles in an appro-priate direction, and before long Dicky put them on for the first time. The procedure was continued at meal times, and rapid progress was made, with Dicky wearing his glasses continuously during the meal sessions, and looking through the lenses which were subsequently incorporated. Thereafter, it became possible to keep him wearing his glasses by other reinforcers such as praise. Also, a deliberate attempt was made to ensure that Dicky wore his glasses whenever anything reinforcing occurred (during meals and snacks, when playing out-doors, when being taken for a ride or a walk, and so on), thereby making the glasses a generalised discriminative stimulus.

As mentioned above, the tantrums and the wearing of spec-tacles were only two of the behavioural repertoires modified by Wolf, Risley and Mees. Other problems were tackled in a similar way, and it is also important to note that these procedures were carried out increasingly at home rather than in the hospital. The conclusion of this report, indicates that Dicky (whom his parents had found impossible to manage earlier) was now able to return home, and six months later was still wearing his glasses, having no temper tantrums and, significantly, was reported as 'a new source of joy to the members of his family'.

A successful transition to a 'normal' home-life should, of course, be the goal of any programme whenever it is possible, and it is important to recognise that techniques such as those under discussion are particularly suited for this. An excellent example of this is to be found in a report by Bachrach, Erwin and Mohr (1965), in the context of a woman who would not eat. This report is therefore also of considerable theoretical interest since it deals with a syndrome in which the reinforcers which are normally very effective apparently had no effect on behaviour. At the age of eighteen, this woman had weighed about 8½ stone, but when this study began, she weighed only 47 lbs. Since no physical cause for her lack of eating could be located, she had been diagnosed as suffering from *anorexia nervosa*, a functional illness. Many explanations of this illness have incorporated the idea that the lack of eating reflects some internal symbolic conflict, often of a sexual nature. For example, Nemiah (1963) has suggested that anorexic patients are 'beset by sexual conflicts expressed in an *allied* disturbance of eating' (p. 237: italics added) and it has been suggested that patients have a fear of oral impregnation. Aggressive conflicts are also often imputed. Bachrach and his associates supply the medical history of their patient, and it is certainly true that a number of sexual problems might have been present for her. She had suffered from abnormally heavy and frequent menstrual periods, and had experienced some difficulties in her marriage as a result of being homesick for her parents when she accompanied her husband to California from Virginia. However, no attempt was made to employ traditional psychotherapy in the hope of identifying any conflicts of this nature. Instead, Bachrach and his colleagues suggested that she be regarded simply as eating insufficient amounts — in other words, that certain patterns of eating *behaviour* were absent and should therefore be re-established and maintained by manipulating environmental events.

At the beginning of this study, the patient had been admitted to hospital, where a number of physical treatments had been introduced without success; she was so debilitated that she was in danger of dying. She had an attractive room with pictures on the walls, flowers, and a pleasant view through the window. She also enjoyed free access to visitors, and had a radio, books, television, a record-player and magazines. Bachrach and his associates argued that any of these pleasant things might well act as a reinforcer in the technical sense if their availability were made dependent on a pattern of behaviour; they therefore instituted a programme in which they were made dependent on successive approximations to eating. The patient was moved to a rather dull room, which was furnished only with a bed, a night-stand, and a chair, and which overlooked a hospital courtyard. Free access to all the pleasant aspects of hospital life mentioned above was ended, and the patient was told that each of the three investigators would eat one meal per day with her in her room. No attempt was made to urge her to consume any of the food; instead, a procedure of successive approximation was introduced.

At first, conversations about something which interested her were made dependent on the patient's picking up a fork, and the criterion for this was slowly adjusted so that food had to be lifted toward her mouth, and then so that food had to be chewed. Also, the amount of food consumed provided a basis for some of the above reinforcers to be allowed after a meal. At first, if any part of the meal was eaten, she was allowed the radio or television. If the patient ate no food, none of these luxuries was allowed. Gradually increasing amounts of food were then to be consumed before these reinforcers were given. This led to the patient beginning to eat more and more, and she began to gain weight. At this stage other potential reinforcers were introduced dependent on eating; she was allowed to choose her own menu, could invite another patient to eat with her, was allowed visits, and taken for walks — but still only if she ate an appropriate amount of food. As a result of this treatment, the patient gained seventeen pounds in weight within eight weeks.

Perhaps the most important aspect of this work by Bachrach et al., however, is the great care which they took to ensure that the patient's progress was maintained when she was discharged from the hospital shortly after. Her family had been closely consulted from the outset, and their full agreement and cooperation had therefore been secured; their importance to the continued progress of the patient after she returned to them was consequently emphasised. Members of the family were asked to make sure that they never provided social attention if the patient failed to eat at home; they were requested to avoid making an issue out of such an event (the natural reaction of the family in the past, of course). On the other hand, copious social reinforcement was to be provided for appropriate behaviour at meal-times, namely eating; the patient was never to eat alone, and discussions at table were to be about topics which she found pleasant. In an effort to maximise the control of environmental events over eating (that is, to increase stimulus control by providing a discriminative stimulus to set the occasion for that behaviour), the table was always laid with a purple cloth, and meals were to occur at regular, fixed times. This detailed plan to maintain the woman's eating behaviour was successful. She was now able to lead an energetic and full life; she took a home study course in practical nursing, and subsequently worked as a general nurse in her previous hospital on a regular eight-hour shift. At this time, her weight was about 90 lbs. Five years after the therapy was begun, it was reported that the patient continued to eat satisfactorily and to lead a normal busy life (Reese, 1966).

Again, this treatment for *anorexia nervosa* used by Bachrach and his associates raises a number of moral issues. When discussing their report with a class of students, for example, I have been challenged by the view that the treatment was blatantly unethical. The objection is often made that it is unreasonable to subject a patient to procedures like these. Some people think that patients should never be coerced in this way: what right had the therapists to decide on the woman's behalf that she should eat food, when she appeared to have taken the decision for herself that she should not? I have even heard it argued that it would have been preferable to allow the woman to die, since she had effectively made it clear that this is what she wanted to do. Such an opinion opens up philosophical problems concerning free will and the nature of human actions, and emphasises how reluctant some of us are to consider that 'voluntary' patterns of behaviour are subject to the control of anything other than one's inner, rational self. In this case, the therapists consulted the patient's family, nurses and so on, and one might argue that the ends justified the means; however, this is not to suggest that any procedure which is effective in this sense is necessarily justifiable.

The general implications of operant conditioning for clinical psychology are further illustrated in a report by Haughton and Ayllon (1965). The authors first describe the behaviour of a long-term patient, a 54 year-old woman who had been in hospital for 23 years, diagnosed as a schizophrenic. She stayed in bed, or lounged on a couch for most of the time; she consistently refused to do any work or to join in recreational or occupational activities, and was regarded as 'idle'. However, she did smoke cigarettes. Haughton and Ayllon attempted to develop in this woman a novel pattern of behaviour, in order to assess in a preliminary way the power of operant conditioning principles with such a 'hopeless' case. As an arbitrary pattern of new behaviour they chose 'holding a broom in an upright position', and, since she smoked, they selected cigarettes as reinforcement for this behaviour. The details of the procedure need not be elaborated here, for they are similar to those described earlier. The woman was deprived of cigarettes, and these were then made available only by successive approximations to the designated final response. When this was achieved, the reinforcements were given for holding the broom, but only according to an inter-mittent (variable-interval) schedule. As a result, the patient quickly developed a stereotyped pattern of behaviour, pacing up and down in the ward while holding the broom. This behaviour was subsequently maintained by conditioned reinforcement, in the form of tokens which could be exchanged for cigarettes at particular times. Several other related patterns of behaviour were now observed in this patient; for example, if other patients attempted to take the broom from her, she resisted strenuously, and sometimes aggressively. She paced about with the broom to such an extent that this behaviour could easily be described as compulsive.

Having shown the power of the simple conditioning principles by changing an 'idle' schizophrenic into a 'compulsive' pacer, Haughton and Ayllon then invited two independent psychiatrists to observe and evaluate the patient. Their comments are interest-ing. The first suggested: 'The broom represents to this patient some essential perceptual element in her field of consciousness. How it should have become so is uncertain; on Freudian grounds it could be interpreted symbolically, on behavioural grounds it could perhaps be interpreted as a habit which has become essential to her peace of mind. Whatever may be the case, it is certainly a stereotyped form of behaviour such as is commonly seen in rather regressed schizophrenics and is rather analogous to the way small children or infants refuse to be parted from some favourite toy, piece of rag, etc.' The second psychiatrist suggested the following: 'Her constant and compulsive pacing holding a broom in the manner she does could be seen as a ritualistic procedure, a magical action. When regression conquers the associative process, primitive and archaic forms of thinking control the behaviour. Symbolism is a predominant mode of expression of deep seated unfulfilled desires and instinctual impulses. By magic, she controls others, cosmic powers are at her disposal and inanimate objects become living creatures. Her broom could be then: 1) a child that gives her love and she gives him in return her devotion; 2) a phallic symbol; 3) the sceptre of an omnipotent queen. Her rhythmic and prearranged pacing in a certain space are not similar to the compulsions of a neurotic, but because this is a far more irrational, far more controlled behaviour from a primitive thinking, this is a magical procedure in which the patient carries out her wishes, expressed in a way that is far beyond our solid, rational and conventional way of thinking and acting.' (Haughton and Ayllon, 1965).

This paper then illustrates the different orientations of traditional psychiatrists and psychologists with a background of operant conditioning. Of course, the 'compulsive' behaviour was generated deliberately and experimentally, but it again demonstrates the power over 'voluntary' behaviour which may be exerted by environmental events which occur only relatively infrequently. The psychiatrists' diagnoses illustrate well the dangers of interpreting unusual patterns of behaviour by reference to internal motivations rather than by reference to possible environmental determinants.

At this point it may be useful to draw once more the distinction made earlier between behavioural treatments based on classical, Pavlovian procedures and those using instrumental conditioning techniques. The former in particular often (though not always) use aversive stimuli, such as drugs which induce nausea, or painful electric shocks. In such cases, the rationale is to elicit reactions of the patient's autonomic nervous system which he might characterize as unpleasant, to condition these to stimuli associated with specifiable abnormal· behaviour, and thereby to reduce the likelihood of that behaviour. For example, apomorphine therapy is intended to condition feelings of nausea (or more specifically, responses of the autonomic nervous system which lead to the feelings of nausea) to the sight or taste of alcohol; shock treatments have been used to elicit 'fear' reactions to pictures of the same sex as the homosexual patient, and relaxation to pictures of the opposite sex, thereby leading, it is hoped, to more normal sexual preferences. Such behaviour therapies may or may not be useful and justifiable, but a book such as this on *operant* conditioning is not a suitable place in which to argue either case (but see Beech, 1969). It is undoubtedly true, however, that many laymen associate such therapies exclusively with aversive conditions like those mentioned here, and consequently express severe reservations about their desirability. Perhaps because of this, some writers have emphasised the distinction between the treatments based on instrumental conditioning and these more established behaviour therapies; the term 'behaviour modification' is now widely used to indicate the former (see Krasner and Ullmann, 1965), thereby leaving the more familiar term 'behaviour therapy' to the Pavlovian treatments. However, it should be recognised that these terms may therefore be misleading to a certain extent. On the face of it, behaviour therapies ought to include any behaviourally-oriented technique used in a recognised therapeutic situation to help patients to behave in more acceptable and usual ways; as such, the experiment discussed above on the anorexic woman might sensibly be described as behaviour *therapy*, although it is based on instrumental conditioning procedures. The term 'behaviour modification' tends to imply at first sight *any* procedure which changes behaviour even in non-therapeutic situations, such as child-rearing in the normal home. However, the phrases 'behaviour therapy' and 'behaviour modification' appear to reflect increasingly the different emphases of classical and instrumental conditioning procedures; the reader should recognise the inherent ambiguities of these phrases.

The behaviour modification movement, it may now be seen, provides a very general challenge to what have become the traditional analyses and interpretations of human voluntary behaviour. Operant conditioning principles have been employed already in many different contexts, the range of which may merely be noted here. Among specific patterns of behaviour which have been effectively reduced by operant techniques may be mentioned the thumb-sucking of a child (e.g. Baer, 1962), stuttering (e.g. Rickard and Mundy, 1965), tics (e.g. Barrett, 1962) and bed-time tantrums (e.g. Williams, 1959). Operant conditioning principles have also been employed to establish social co-operation in childhood schizophrenics (e.g. Hingtgen, Sanders and De Myer, 1965), verbal behaviour in mutes (e.g. Isaacs, Thomas and Goldiamond, 1960) and toilet training (e.g. Madsden, 1965). There even exists in the literature a report on the effective alleviation of constipation by operant conditioning techniques (Quarti and Renaud, 1964). Following Miller's recent experimental demonstrations of autonomic conditioning by instrumental, response-dependent procedures (1969 – mentioned in Chapter 4), one may perhaps expect greater application of such techniques to psychosomatic disorders generally, for such conditions may well be related to disturbances of autonomic functioning.

As has been shown in this chapter, however, the behaviour modification movement has proved particularly adventurous when applying itself to severely disturbed and abnormal behaviour. Its general principles have been tested with encouraging results, and are now being further developed by attempts to structure entire mental ward settings to supply diverse patterns of behaviour among the patients. A clear account of such techniques is given by Thompson and Grabowski (1972). They show how a programme based on operant principles changed a State Hospital for the mentally retarded from a custodial institution to one which emphasised the role of its staff as educators. Another example of this is to be found in a book by Ayllon and Azrin (1968) which reports how these patterns of behaviour are generated and maintained by the earning of response-dependent tokens which may be subsequently exchanged for various reinforcements; this book provides a clear account of the operant conditioner's appreciation and interpretation of clinical ward problems. An evaluative review by Kazdin and Bootzin (1972) shows how widely these programmes have been used in recent years. The principles and techniques of operant conditioning are also being applied in other less constrained settings. For example, Lindsley (1964) has discussed this approach to the understanding and modification of behaviour in geriatric settings, and Michael (1970) has discussed it in the context of the rehabilitation of the physically disabled.

One can see then, that the interpretation of behaviour prompted by operant conditioning experiments with animals is at present being tested with human behaviour in many different situations; the success it has achieved so far is promising. At the same time, these very successes underline a growing moral problem, for we are accustomed to viewing the behaviour of an individual as being the product uniquely of his own internal will. Success in modifying the 'voluntary' behaviour of the 'mentally ill' indicates the possibilities of behavioural technology to control the 'voluntary' behaviour of those whom we do *not* rate as abnormal in any sense — perhaps even ourselves. This general problem will be taken up briefly in the final chapter.

CHAPTER 16

'The Experimental Analysis of Behaviour'

A glance at the list of references reveals that many of the reports discussed in the preceding pages were first published in the *Journal of the Experimental Analysis of Behavior*. The last five words of this title form a phrase which has come to be widely used to characterise the approach to psychology of which the present book is a reflection. In this final chapter, we shall consider briefly the connotations of the phrase, and thereby try to provide a brief review of the preceding discussions.

'The experimental analysis of behaviour' incorporates three separate concepts, all of which have previously been explained in these pages. First, it implies experiments using free-operant techniques in which behaviour is usually measured in terms of the frequency with which an operant act occurs. So the proto-typical experiment (described in Chapter 4) involves the conditioning of an arbitrary but convenient skeletal act by its environmental consequences. The experimental subject is free to emit this pattern of behaviour at any time, and it is in this sense that operant conditioning experiments may be said to study voluntary behaviour. Yet we have seen that such behaviour nevertheless occurs lawfully, and its predictability in specified environmental circumstances is impressive. This leads on to the second important aspect of 'the experimental analysis of behaviour', namely the experimental strategy which has been described in Chapter 8 as steady-state methodology. Such an approach trys to develop scientific understanding of behaviour by bringing individual organisms under strong experimental control in various conditions, thereby making unnecessary the traditional statistical comparisons which are made between experimental and control groups of subjects. The third important aspect is the philosophical interpretation of behaviour which has been vigorously expressed by Skinner. He has developed the views of Watson (Chapter 1) and argued that psychology should attempt to relate observable behaviour to its consequences, and should refrain from using explanations of behaviour in terms of 'events taking place somewhere else, at some other level of observation, described in differerent terms and measured if at all in different dimensions' (Skinner, 1950). The suggestion is that such theories or explanations of behaviour, which usually emphasise the role of unobservable processes which are assumed to lie within the organism, may deflect attention away from important controlling variables which may be identified and directly manipulated. Skinner's approach has sometimes been described as an 'empty-organism' philosophy, and he is often accused of being anti-theoretical. This latter assertion appears to be an over-simplification, however, for his approach to behaviour and to psychology as a whole is itself a theoretical system; Skinner argues only against certain methods of theorising, as in the quotation above.

So, 'the experimental analysis of behaviour' may be said to be based on operant conditioning experiments which use steady-state methodology and whose results are interpreted in behaviouristic terms. However, it is crucial to recognise that there is no logical identity between these three concepts. There is, for example, no logical reason why one should not use a free-operant experimental situation, interpret one's data according to behaviouristic principles, yet use statistical experimental designs to isolate the effects of a variable. Indeed, some of the most important work on conditioned suppression or 'anxiety' (see Chapter 11) has employed standard statistical group designs in exactly this way (e.g. Kamin, 1965). Or again, conditioned suppression could be investigated as described earlier, but could be interpreted not in behaviouristic but in cognitive terms: one might suggest that the rat *knows* that he is about to *experience* a shock which he will not *like*. Such an interpretation will not change the observed facts, however, such as the fact that a rat's behaviour is less disturbed in some situations than in others. In more general terms, the findings of the experiments discussed earlier remain to be considered and evaluated whatever one's philosophical orientation (as mentioned in Chapter 1). In particular, it may be worth stressing that the work on behaviour modification outlined in Chapter 14 is important in clinical psychology even if one prefers to reinterpret the findings entirely in terms of the cognitive changes which one may feel underlie the overt behavioural changes, just as the findings of a behaviouristic science of animal behaviour may always be re-interpreted in more animistic forms of language (Chapter 1). Conversely, the behaviouristic outlook may be profitably explored outside the confines of the traditional experiment on operant conditioning: for example, Skinner (1957b) has developed an interpretation of verbal behaviour and of language (including meaning) in such non-cognitive terms.

This discussion emphasises, then, that 'the experimental analysis of behaviour' should be recognised as a combination of three separable aspects of psychological science. Of course, it will be apparent from the preceding discussions that many researchers feel the combination of the free-operant experimental techniques, the steady-state strategy for scientific research, and the behaviouristic philosophical orientation may offer a powerful analytical tool for the development of a science of behaviour. But it must be emphasised that there are respectable alternatives to each aspect of 'the experimental analysis of behaviour'. This phrase, with its definite article, may therefore be unfortunate. It may be taken to imply that other approaches to the problems of psychology are less valid from an experimental point of view. '*The* experimental analysis of behaviour' should not claim to be more (or less) scientifically respectable than other approaches. It remains to be seen whether it is more (or less) useful than these other approaches. The use of this biased phrase to characterise the approach to psychology indicated in this book may have contributed to a regrettable polarisation within psychology, a discipline which has a rich history of such discord. It seems quite likely, for example, that some psychologists dismiss data such as those discussed earlier merely because they may not themselves be of a behaviouristic persuasion, or merely because they feel that statistical designs are always desirable.

Scope for this polarisation in psychology may perhaps be found in attitudes to the ethical problems raised by the findings that human 'voluntary' behaviour may be manipulated and controlled by environmental events. The experiments reviewed throughout this book have provided increasing support for the view that 'voluntary' behaviour is nevertheless lawful in the scientific sense, and therefore a suitable subject for a deterministic science. As the systematic relationships between operant behaviour and environmental variables are clarified, we put ourselves increasingly in a position to manipulate them, and thereby to control the behaviour of others. It is clear from Chapter 15 that this may indeed be accomplished with people who might otherwise have been regarded as hopelessly unlawful in their behaviour, by reason of illness or abnormality. In these situations, the ethical problems associated with behaviour modification may be essentially similar in nature to those faced by a surgeon or medical practitioner: are we likely to be able to produce a beneficial change in the patient by our techniques? Would such an improvement justify the procedures which we would employ? In the case of specific behavioural abnormalities or deficits, there is often no great problem in reaching a consensus, for a change in this particular pattern of behaviour may lead to the discharge of the patient from hospital, and thus to general gains for him to enjoy (as with the anorexic whose treatment was discussed in the previous chapter). However, for many patients there may be no prospect of discharge from the hospital to the 'normal' world, and questions concerning the ethics of behaviour modification in such cases may be more difficult to resolve. Is it better to encourage in such people more varied behavioural repertoires, or should we leave them to their own disturbed and limited horizons? Opinions are clearly divided on this problem.

It is also abundantly clear, of course, that the principles of behaviour developed in this book may be used to manipulate and control the behaviour of people who would not be classified as abnormal in any substantive sense. In Chapter 14, we considered some of the ways in which this might be attempted in the educational field. Here again, moral problems would not appear to be too pressing, for most people would agree that effective educational techniques are to the ultimate benefit of the pupil. Another familiar situation in which behavioural control is clearly exerted is to be found, of course, in the context of parents' influence on their offspring. Most parents hope to inculcate certain values in their children, and thereby to influence their behaviour. Behavioural technology may open up nothing worse here than more effective (and often, probably, more humane) procedures for achieving such goals. Bijou and Baer (1961, 1965) have discussed child development within the tradition outlined in the present book, but their writings are unlikely to provoke strong hostile reactions in any of their readers.

It is in the less structured situations of everyday, normal human life that one may feel behavioural technology is to be treated with particular caution. We like to believe that we behave according to our own voluntary decisions, freely taken, and to some it is unpleasant to consider that we may not be as independent of others and of events as we might have imagined. Such a reaction may be a little over-dramatised, for Skinner (1955) has noted that 'we are all controlled by the world in which we live, and part of that world has been and will be constructed by men'. In fact, other people *do* control our behaviour now, for example by the way they react to us, and by things they say. In their turn, these very people are also controlled to a certain extent by *our* behaviour towards them. This power may be deliberately exerted (as by the insincere but effective salesman) or may often not be recognised (as in the case of the frequency with which we look at another person's eyes). Like it or not, our behaviour in crowded buses, in the street, in our personal interactions, and in our leisure activities — all this is clearly subject to causal influences which lie explicitly outside ourselves. In almost all these situations, we believe that we *could* choose to behave differently; if we did so, it often would have no aversive consequences, nor would it cause undue concern to others — but the truth is that our behaviour is nevertheless controlled and predictable, we *don't* choose to behave in different ways.

The undoubted anxiety which many feel at the prospect of more effective procedures to control behaviour may spring from a belief that such control would be unpleasant, and that it would induce a grey conformity which would be against the better interests of the individual. Such could be the case; however, an effective technology would surely incorporate neither of these outcomes. The power of differential *positive* reinforcement is the

most striking finding of operant conditioning: reinforcing consequences may, if exploited sensitively, develop capabilities which
might otherwise have remained dormant (as with the retarded or
the abnormal patient). Thus, an individual's behavioural repertoire might be effectively increased. It is the man with a limited
repertoire who may seem to lack most freedom, and whose
behaviour may be said to conform to a restricted life-style.
Skinner has written a novel, *Walden Two* (1948b), in which he
has speculated on the possibilities inherent in the application of
behavioural technology to the design of cultures or communities.
He envisages a community in which the members work for only a
few hours daily; they select for themselves the nature of this
work, according to their own interests and dispositions. Com-
pulsion forms no part of the community, yet it is engineered to
support itself by carefully regulating the consequences of the
various activities. Leisure activities flourish, and the inhabitants
have complete 'freedom' to 'decide for themselves' how to
behave. Skinner sees this as an indication of 'the good life' which
may be possible in a community based on principles of behaviour: other people, however, have attacked it as the opposite
of the good life (see Rogers and Skinner, 1956 and Skinner, 1969
for further elaboration of this controversy). Recently, Skinner
(1972a) has sparked off a lively controversy with his book
Beyond Freedom and Dignity, in which he develops his views
about a science of behaviour on a more general level.

The general implications of advances in behavioural technology have provided a subject for much discussion within 'the
experimental analysis of behaviour'. However, it is clear that
these ethical problems are not exclusive to this particular approach to psychology; they are the inevitable consequence of any
attempt to develop a science of behaviour (see Krasner, 1964). In
short, this is a further aspect of the more general problem of
ensuring that scientific advances are used to the benefit of
mankind rather than to its detriment, a subject which is rightly a
matter for lively public debate at present with respect to the
biological sciences. It is hoped that this book may help
the reader to appreciate these important problems in the context
of behaviour, and to formulate his own opinions concerning
them, for they are likely to become more pressing in the future.

Selected bibliography

Some books are listed below which provide convenient further reading on the topics introduced in the preceding pages. A brief description of the contents of each book is appended to its title; those marked with asterisks should prove particularly useful. This list is not intended to be comprehensive.

I Books written by B. F. Skinner

It is apparent that Skinner's writings have been largely responsible for formulating the approach to psychology represented in the present book. Skinner has a lively style, and many readers may wish to consult his original writings, among which are:—

The Behavior of Organisms. New York: Appleton-Century-Crofts (1938). The original theoretical exposition and experimental report on which current operant conditioning is largely based.

Walden Two. New York: Macmillan (1948). Skinner's novel about life in a community based on behavioural principles.

Science and Human Behavior. New York: Macmillan (1953). A non-technical account of 'the experimental analysis of behaviour' as it is applied to a wide range of human activities.

Verbal Behavior. New York: Appleton-Century-Crofts (1957). An extension of Skinner's approach to verbal behaviour in general. This book provoked a great deal of hostile comment when it appeared, but is currently enjoying something of a re-appraisal.

The Technology of Teaching. New York: Appleton-Century-Crofts (1968). Some of Skinner's more influential papers on psychology and education.

Contingencies of Reinforcement: a Theoretical Analysis. New York: Appleton-Century-Crofts (1969). A general and spirited advocacy of radical behaviourism in psychology.

****Cumulative Record.* (3rd Edition) New York: Appleton-Century-Crofts (1972b). A collection of Skinner's papers on a wide range of topics: experimental psychology, educational technology, abnormal behaviour, science and human behaviour, etc. Interesting and well worth dipping into.

Beyond Freedom and Dignity. London: Jonathan Cape Ltd (1972a). A general statement of Skinner's approach to psychology and to man.

II Operant conditioning: basic experiments and textbooks.

**Catania, A. C. (Ed) (1968). *Contemporary Research in Operant Behavior.* Glenview, Illinois: Scott, Foresman and Co. An excellent collection of experimental reports, which provides a good insight into operant conditioning. Many of the experiments discussed in the present book are to be found in this selection.

Honig, W. K. (Ed) (1966). *Operant Behavior: Areas of Research and Application.* New York: Appleton-Century-Crofts. When first published, this was the authoritative review of this area of research. Still essential reading for the serious student.

Millenson, J. R. (1967). *Principles of Behavioral Analysis.* New York: Macmillan. An introductory text in psychology, written from the point of view of an operant conditioner.

Rachlin, H. (1970). *Introduction to Modern Behaviorism.* San Francisco: W. H. Freeman and Co. A very clear and well-written introduction to operant conditioning.

Reynolds, G. S. (1968). *A Primer of Operant Conditioning.* Glenview, Illinois: Scott, Foresman and Co. A short, concise, but rather unexciting introduction to basic experimental findings.

Verhave, T. (Ed) (1966). *The Experimental Analysis of Behavior.* New York: Appleton-Century-Crofts. An alternative selection of original papers, but less comprehensive and useful than Catania's.

Whaley, D. L. and Malott, R. W. (1971). *Elementary Principles of Behavior.* New York: Appleton-Century-Crofts. A lively introduction to operant conditioning with most examples drawn from human rather than animal behaviour. The patronising style can be infuriating!

III Applications to human behavior.

**Ulrich, R., Stachnik, T. and Mabry, J. (Eds) (1966). *Control of Human Behavior.* Glenview, Illinois: Scott, Foresman and Co. An interesting and useful selection of papers: basic concepts, education, clinical, design of cultures, etc.

Ulrich, R., Stachnik, T. and Mabry, J. (Eds) (1970). *Control of Human Behavior II: From Cure to Prevention.* Glenview, Illinois: Scott, Foresman and Co. A further selection of readings on behaviour modification.

**Ullman, L. P. and Krasner, L. (1969). *A Psychological Approach to Abnormal Behavior.* Englewood Cliffs: Prentice-Hall, Inc. A particularly clear account of behaviour modification techniques and their relevance to clinical psychology as a whole.

Ullman, L. P. and Krasner, L. (Eds) (1965). *Case Studies in Behavior Modification.* New York: Holt, Rinehart and Winston. A selection of original reports on the application of operant principles to abnormal behaviour.

Thompson, T. and Grabowski, J. (1972). *Behavior Modification of the Mentally Retarded*. New York: Oxford University Press. Contains accounts of various aspects of the transition of a State Hospital from a custodial to an educational-therapeutic institution.

References

Some of the original papers in this list have been reprinted in books. This is indicated when appropriate, for such books are often more easily obtainable than scientific journals.

ANGER, D. (1956). The dependence of interresponse times upon the relative reinforcement of different interresponse times. *Journal of Experimental Psychology*, 52, 145–161. Reprinted in Catania (1968), pp. 101–112.

ANGER, D. (1963). The role of temporal discriminations in the reinforcement of Sidman avoidance behaviour. *Journal of the Experimental Analysis of Behavior*, 6, 477–506.

APPEL, J. B. (1961). Punishment in the squirrel monkey. *Science*, 133, 36.

APPEL, J. B. (1963a). Aversive aspects of a schedule of positive reinforcement. *Journal of the Experimental Analysis of Behavior*, 6, 423–428.

APPEL, J. B. (1963b). Drugs, shock intensity and the CER. *Psychopharmacologia*, 4, 148–153.

APPEL, J. B. (1963c). Punishment and shock intensity. *Science*, 141, 528–529.

ARDREY, R. (1970). *The Social Contract*. London: Collins.

ARGYLE, M. (1967). *The Psychology of Interpersonal Behaviour*. Harmondsworth: Penguin Books.

AUTOR, S. M. (1960). The strength of conditioned reinforcers as a function of frequency and probability of reinforcement. Doctoral dissertation, Harvard University. Edited version appears in Hendry (1969a), pp. 127–162.

AYLLON, T. (1965). Some behavioral problems associated with eating in schizophrenic patients. In Ullmann, L. P. and Krasner, L. (Eds.). *Case Studies in Behavior Modification*. New York: Holt, Rinehart and Winston, Inc. (pp. 73–77).

AYLLON, T. and MICHAEL, J. (1959). The psychiatric nurse as a behavioral engineer. *Journal of the Experimental Analysis of Behavior*, 2, 323—334 Reprinted in Ullmann and Krasner (1965), pp. 84—94.

AYLLON, T. and AZRIN, N. H. (1968). *The Token Economy*. New York: Appleton-Century-Crofts.

AZRIN, N. H. (1956). Some effects of two intermittent schedules of immediate and non-immediate punishment. *Journal of Psychology*, 42, 3—21. Reprinted in Catania (1968), pp. 227—235.

AZRIN, N. H. (1960). Effects of punishment intensity during variable-interval reinforcement. *Journal of the Experimental Analysis of Behavior*, 3, 123—142.

AZRIN, N. H. and HOLZ, W. C. (1966). Punishment. In Honig, W. K. (Ed.) *Operant Behavior: Areas of Research and Application*. New York: Appleton-Century-Crofts (pp. 380—447).

BACHRACH, A. J., ERWIN, W. J. and MOHR, J. P. (1965). The control of eating behavior in an anorexic by operant conditioning techniques. In Ullmann, L. P. and Krasner, L. (Eds.). *Case Studies in Behavior Modification*. New York: Holt, Rinehart and Winston, Inc. (pp. 153—163).

BAER, D. M. (1965). Laboratory control of thumbsucking by withdrawal and re-presentation of reinforcement. In Ullmann, L. P. and Krasner, L. (Eds.). *Case Studies in Behavior Modification*. New York: Holt, Rinehart and Winston, Inc. (pp. 285—289).

BARRETT, B. H. (1962). Reduction in rate of multiple tics by free operant conditioning methods. Reprinted in Ullmann and Krasner (1965), pp. 255—263.

BEECH, H. R. (1969). *Changing Man's Behaviour*. Harmondsworth, Middlesex: Penguin Books, Ltd.

BIJOU, S. W. and BAER, D. M. (1961). *Child Development, Vol 1: A Systematic and Empirical Theory*. New York: Appleton-Century-Crofts.

BIJOU, S. W. and BAER, D. M. (1965). *Child Development, Vol. 2: Universal Stage of Infancy*. New York: Appleton-Century-Crofts.

BLACKMAN, D. E. (1967). Effects of response pacing on conditioned suppression. *Quarterly Journal of Experimental Psychology*, 19, 170—174.

BLACKMAN, D. E. (1968a). Conditioned suppression or facilitation as a function of the behavioral baseline. *Journal of the Experimental Analysis of Behavior*, 11, 53—61.

BLACKMAN, D. E. (1968b). Reponse rate, reinforcement frequency and conditioned suppression. *Journal of the Experimental Analysis of Behavior*, 11, 503—516.

BLACKMAN, D. E. (1968c). Effects of drugs on conditioned 'anxiety'. *Nature*, 217, 769—770.

BLACKMAN, D. E. (1970a). Effects of a pre-shock stimulus on temporal control of behavior. *Journal of the Experimental Analysis of Behavior*, 14, 313—319.

BLACKMAN, D. E. (1970b). Conditioned suppression of avoidance behaviour in rats. *Quarterly Journal of Experimental Psychology*, 22, 547—553.

BLACKMAN, D. E. (1972). Conditioned 'anxiety' and operant behavior. In

Gilbert, R. M. and Keehn, J. D. (Eds.). *Schedule Effects: Drugs, Drinking and Aggression.* Toronto: University of Toronto Press (pp. 26–49).

BLOOMFIELD, T. M. (1967). A peak shift on a line tilt continuum. *Journal of the Experimental Analysis of Behavior*, 10, 361–366.

BLOOMFIELD, T. M. (1969). Behavioural contrast and the peak shift. In Gilbert, R. M. and Sutherland, N. S. (Eds.). *Animal Discrimination Learning.* London: Academic Press (pp. 215–241).

BLOUGH, D. S. (1957). Effect of lysergic acid diethylamide on absolute visual threshold of the pigeon. *Science*, 126, 304–305.

BLOUGH, D. S. (1958). A method for obtaining psychophysical thresholds from the pigeon. *Journal of the Experimental Analysis of Behavior*, 1, 34–43. Reprinted in Catania (1968), pp. 127–134.

BLOUGH, D. S. (1961). Animal psychophysics. *Scientific American*, 205, No. 1, 113–122.

BOE, E. E. and CHURCH, R. M. (1968). *Punishment: Issues and Experiments.* New York: Appleton-Century-Crofts.

BORGER, R. and CIOFFI, F. (Eds.) (1970). *Explanation in the Behavioural Sciences.* London: Cambridge University Press.

BRADY, J. V. (1956). Assessment of drug effects on emotional behavior. *Science*, 123, 1033. Reprinted in Thompson, Pickens and Meisch (1970), pp. 63–65.

BRADY, J. V. and HUNT, H. F. (1955). An experimental approach to the analysis of emotional behavior. *Journal of Psychology*, 40, 313–324.

BRADY, J. V., KELLY, D. and PLUMLEE, L. (1969). Autonomic and behavioral responses of the rhesus monkey to emotional conditioning. *Annals of the New York Academy of Sciences*, 159, 959–975.

BROWN, J. (1966). Information theory. In Foss, B. M. (Ed.) *New Horizons in Psychology.* Harmondsworth: Penguin Books (pp. 118–134).

BRUNER, A. and REVUSKY, S. H. (1961). Collateral behavior in humans. *Journal of the Experimental Analysis of Behavior*, 4, 349–350.

BUGELSKI, B. R. (1938). Extinction with and without sub-goal reinforcement. *Journal of Comparative Psychology*, 51, 109–117.

CAMPBELL, B. A. and CHURCH, R. M. *Punishment and Aversive Behavior.* New York: Appleton-Century-Crofts.

CATANIA, A. C. (1966). Concurrent Operants. In Honig, W. K. (Ed.) *Operant Behavior: Areas of Research and Application.* New York: Appleton-Century-Crofts (pp. 213-270).

CATANIA, A. C. (Ed.) (1968). *Contemporary Research in Operant Behavior.* Glenview, Illinois: Scott, Foresman & Co.

CHURCH, R. M. (1963). The varied effects of punishment on behavior. *Psychological Review*, 70, 369-402.

CLARK, F. C. (1958). The effect of deprivation and frequency of reinforcement on variable interval responding. *Journal of the Experimental Analysis of Behavior*, 1, 221-228.

CONRAD, D. G., SIDMAN, M. and HERRNSTEIN, R. J. (1958). The effects of deprivation upon temporally spaced responding. *Journal of the Experimental Analysis of Behavior*, 1, 59-65.

CUMMING, W. W. (1966). A bird's eye glimpse of men and machines. In Ulrich, R., Stachnik, T. and Mabry, J. (Eds.). *Control of Human Behavior.* Glenview, Illinois: Scott, Foresman and Company (pp. 246-256).

CUMMING, W. W. and SCHOENFELD, W. N. (1960). Behavior stability under extended exposure to a time-correlated reinforcement contingency. *Journal of the Experimental Analysis of Behavior*, 3, 71-82.

DARWIN, C. R. (1873). *On the Expression of the Emotions in Man and Animals*. London: Murray.

DESCARTES, R. (1637). *Discourse on Method*. Translated by Wollaston, A. Harmondsworth: Penguin Books, Ltd. (1960).

DEWS, P. B. (1955). Differential sensitivity to pentobarbital of pecking performance in pigeons depending on the schedule of reward. *Journal of Pharmacology and Experimental Therapeutics*, 113, 393-401. Reprinted in Thompson, Pickens and Meisch (1970), pp. 454-463.

DEWS, P. B. (1958). Stimulant actions of methamphetamine. *Journal of Pharmacology and Experimental Therapeutics*, 122, 137-147. Reprinted in Thompson, Peckens and Meisch (1970), pp. 464-475.

DEWS, P. B. (1970). The theory of fixed-interval responding. In Schoenfeld, W. N. (Ed.), *The Theory of Reinforcement Schedules*. New York: Appleton-Century-Crofts (pp. 43-61).

DINSMOOR, J. A. and WINOGRAD, E. (1958). Shock intensity in variable interval escape schedules. *Journal of the Experimental Analysis of Behavior*, 1, 145-148.

EGGER, M. D. and MILLER, N. E. (1962). Secondary reinforcement in rats as a function of information value and reliability of the stimulus. *Journal of Experimental Psychology*, 64, 97-104.

EGGER, M. D. MILLER, N. E. (1963). When is reward reinforcing?: an experimental study of the information hypothesis. *Journal of Comparative and Physiological Psychology*, 56, 132-137.

ESTES, W. K. (1944). An experimental study of punishment. *Psychological Monographs*, 57 (Whole No. 263). Reprinted in Boe and Church (1968), pp. 108-165.

ESTES, W. K. (1969). Outline of a theory of punishment. In Campbell, B. A. and Church, R. M. (Eds.). *Punishment and Aversive Behavior*. New York: Appleton-Century-Crofts (pp. 57-82).

ESTES, W. K. and SKINNER, B. F. (1941). Some quantitative properties of anxiety. *Journal of Experimental Psychology*, 29, 390-400. Reprinted in Skinner (1972b), pp. 512-523.

FANTINO, E. (1969). Conditioned reinforcement, choice, and the psychological distance to reward. In Hendry, D. P. (ED.). *Conditioned Reinforcement*. Homewood, Illinois: The Dorsey Press (pp. 163-191).

FELTON, M. and LYON, D. O. (1966). The post-reinforcement pause. *Journal of the Experimental Analysis of Behavior*, 9, 131-134. Reprinted in Catania (1968), pp. 72-74.

FERSTER, C. B. and PERROTT, M. C. (1968). *Behavior Principles*. New York: Appleton-Century-Crofts.

FERSTER, C. B. and SKINNER, B. F. (1957). *Schedules of Reinforcement*. New York: Appleton-Century-Crofts.

FOX, L. (1962). Effecting the use of efficient study habits. *Journal of Mathetics*, 1, 75-86. Reprinted in Ulrich, Stachnik and Mabry (1966), pp. 85-90.

GLASER, R. (Ed.) (1965). *Teaching Machines and Programmed Learning. II: Data and Directions*. Washington, D. C.: National Education Association.

GRUSEC, T. (1968). The peak shift in stimulus generalisation: equivalent effects of errors and non-contingent shocks. *Journal of the Experimental Analysis of Behavior*, 11, 239-249.

HARZEM, P. (1969). Temporal discrimination. In Gilbert, R. M. and Sutherland, N. S. (Eds.), *Animal Discrimination Learning*. London: Academic Press (pp. 299-334).

HAUGHTON, E. and AYLLON, T. (1965). Production and elimination of symptomatic behavior. In Ullmann, L. P. and Krasner, L. (Eds.). *Case Studies in Behavior Modification*. New York: Holt, Rinehart and Winston, Inc. (pp. 94-98).

HEARST, E., KORESKO, M. B. and POPPEN, R. (1964). Stimulus generalisation and the response-reinforcement contingency. *Journal of the Experimental Analysis of Behavior*, 7, 369-380.

HENDRY, D. P. (Ed.) (1969a). *Conditioned Reinforcement*. Homewood, Illinois: The Dorsey Press.

HENDRY, D. P. (1969b). Reinforcing value of information: Fixed-ratio schedules. In Hendry, D. P. (Ed.) *Conditioned Reinforcement*. Homewood, Illinois: The Dorsey Press (pp. 300-341).

HERRNSTEIN, R. J. (1964). Secondary reinforcement and the rate of primary reinforcement. *Journal of the Experimental Analysis of Behavior*, 7, 27-36.

HERRNSTEIN, R. J. (1966). Superstition. In Honig, W. K. (Ed.). *Operant Behavior: Areas of Research and Application*. New York: Appleton-Century-Crofts (pp. 33-51).

HERRNSTEIN, R. J. (1969). Method and theory in the study of avoidance. *Psychological Review*, 76, 49-69.

HERRNSTEIN, R. J. and HINELINE, P. N. (1966). Negative reinforcement as shock-frequency reduction. *Journal of the Experimental Analysis of Behavior*, 9, 421-430. Reprinted in Catania (1968), pp. 211-220.

HINGTGEN, J. N., SANDERS, B. J. and DE MYER, M. K. (1965). Shaping co-operative responses in early childhood schizophrenics. In Ullmann, L. P. and Krasner, L. (Eds.). *Case Studies in Behavior Modification*. New York: Holt, Rinehart and Winston, Inc. (pp. 130-138).

HOLLAND, J. G. (1957). Technique for behavioral analysis of human observing. *Science*, 125, 348-350.

HOLLAND, J. G. (1960). Teaching machines: an application of principles from the laboratory. *Journal of the Experimental Analysis of Behavior*, 3, 275-287. Reprinted in Ulrich, Stachnik and Mabry (1966), pp. 75-84.

HOLZ, W. C. and AZRIN, N. H. (1961). Discriminative properties of punishment. *Journal of the Experimental Analysis of Behavior*, 4, 225-232. Reprinted in Catania (1968), pp. 236-241.

HOLZ, W. C. and AZRIN, N. H. (1962). Interactions between the discriminative and aversive properties of punishment. *Journal of the Experimental Analysis of Behavior*, 5, 229-234.

HOLZ, W. C. and AZRIN, N. H. (1963). A comparison of several procedures for eliminating behavior. *Journal of the Experimental Analysis of Behavior*, 6, 399-406. Reprinted in Catania (1968), pp. 221-227.

HULL, C. L. (1943). *Principles of Behavior*. New York: Appleton-Century-Crofts.

HUNT, H. F. and BRADY, J. V. (1955). Some effects of punishment and intercurrent anxiety on a simple operant. *Journal of Comparative and Physiological Psychology*, 48, 305-310. Reprinted in Boe and Church (1968), pp. 188-198.

HURWITZ, H. M. B. (1957). Periodicity of responses in operant extinction. *Quarterly Journal of Experimental Psychology*, 9, 177-184.

ISAACS, W., THOMAS, J. and GOLDIAMOND, I. (1960). Application of operant conditioning to reinstate verbal behavior in psychotics. *Journal of Speech and Hearing Disorders*, 25, 8-12. Reprinted in Ullmann and Krasner (1965), pp. 69-73.

JAHODA, G. (1970). *The Psychology of Superstition*. Harmondsworth: Penguin Books.

JENKINS, H. M. and HARRISON, R. H. (1960). Effects of discrimination training on auditory generalisation. *Journal of Experimental Psychology*, 59, 246-253. Reprinted in Catania (1968), pp. 140-145.

JOHNSTON, J. M. and PENNYPACKER, H. S. (1971). A behavioral approach to college teaching. *American Psychologist*, 26, 219-244

KAMIN, L. J. (1965). Temporal and intensity characteristics of the conditioned stimulus. In Prokasy, W. F. (Ed.). *Classical Conditioning: A Symposium*. New York: Appleton-Century-Crofts (pp. 118-147).

KAY, H., DODD, D. and SIME, M. (1968). *Teaching Machines and Programmed Instruction*. Harmondsworth: Penguin Books, Ltd.

KAZDIN, A. E. and BOOTZIN, R. R. (1972). The token ecomony: an evaluative review. *Journal of Applied Behavior Analysis*, 5, 343-372.

KELLEHER, R. T. (1966). Chaining and conditioned reinforcement. In Honig, W. K. (Ed.). *Operant Behavior: Areas of research and application*. New York: Appleton-Century-Crofts (pp. 160-212).

KELLEHER, R. T. and FRY, W. T. (1962). Stimulus functions in chained fixed-interval schedules. *Journal of the Experimental Analysis of Behavior*, 5, 167-173. Reprinted in Catania (1968), pp. 178-185.

KELLEHER, R. T., FRY, W. and COOK, L. (1959). Interresponse time distribution as a function of differential reinforcement of temporally spaced responses. *Journal of the Experimental Analysis of Behavior*, 2, 91-106.

KELLEHER, R. T. and MORSE, W. H. (1964). Escape behavior and punished behavior. *Federation Proceedings*, 23, 808-817. Reprinted in Thompson, Pickens and Meisch (1970), pp. 613-631.

KELLEHER, R. T. and MORSE, W. H. (1968). Determinants of the specificity of behavioral effects of drugs. *Ergebnisse der Physiologie*, 60, 1-56.

KELLER, F. S. (1968). 'Good-bye teacher.....'. *Journal of Applied Behavior Analysis*, 1, 79-89.

KELLER, F. S. and SCHOENFELD, W. N. (1950). *Principles of Psychology*. New York: Appleton-Century-Crofts.

KENDALL, S. B. (1969). Discriminative and reinforcing properties of differential trace stimuli. In Hendry, D. P. (Ed.). *Conditioned Reinforcement*. Homewood, Illinois: The Dorsey Press (pp. 261-280).

KINNARD, W. J., ACETO, M. D. G. and BUCKLEY, J. P. (1962). The effects of certain psychotropic agents on the conditioned emotional response behavior pattern of the rat. *Psychopharmacologia*, 3, 227-230.

KRASNER, L. (1964). Behavior control and social responsibility. *American Psychologist*, 17, 199-204. Reprinted in Ulrich Stachnik and Mabry (1966), pp. 317-321.

KRASNER, L. and ULLMANN, L. P. (1965). *Research in Behavior Modification*. New York: Holt, Rinehart and Winston.

LACK, D. (1943). *The Life of the Robin*. Harmondsworth: Penguin Books Ltd.

LATIES, V. G., WEISS, B., CLARK, R. L. and REYNOLDS, M. D. (1965). Overt 'mediating' behaviour during temporally spaced responding. *Journal of the Experimental Analysis of Behavior*, 8, 107-115. Reprinted in Catania (1968), pp. 82-89.

LINDSLEY, O. R. (1964). Geriatric behavioral prosthetics. In Kastenbaum, R. (Ed.). *New Thoughts on Old Age*. New York: Springer. Reprinted in Ulrich, Stachnik and Mabry (1966), pp. 156-168.

LUMSDAINE, A. A. and GLASER, R. (Eds.) (1960). *Teaching Machines and Programmed Learning: A Source Book*. Washington, D. C.: National Education Association.

MCKEARNEY, J. W. (1969). Fixed-interval schedules of electric shock presentation: extinction and recovery of performance under different shock intensities and fixed-interval durations. *Journal of the Experimental Analysis of Behavior*, 12, 301-313.

MCKEARNEY, J. W. (1972). Maintenance of responding under schedules of response-produced electric shock. In Gilbert, R. M. and Keehn, J. D. (Eds). *Schedule Effects: Drugs, Drinking and Aggression*. Toronto: University of Toronto Press (pp. 3-25).

MADSDEN, C. H. (1965). Positive reinforcement in the toilet training of a normal child: a case report. In Ullmann, L. P. and Krasner, L. (Eds.). *Case Studies in Behavior Modification*. New York: Holt, Rinehart and Winston, Inc. (pp. 305-307).

MICHAEL, J. L. (1970). Rehabilitation. In Neuringer, C. and Michael, J. L. (Eds.). *Behavior Modification in Clinical Psychology*. New York: Appleton-Century-Crofts. pp. 52-85.

MICHOTTE, A. (1954). *La Perception de la Causalité*. 2nd Ed. Louvain: Publications Universitaires de Louvain.

MILLENSON, J. R. and DE VILLIERS, P. (1972). Motivational properties of conditioned anxiety. In Gilbert, R. M. and Millenson, J. R. (Eds). *Reinforcement: Behavioral Analysis*. New York: Academic Press (pp. 97-127).

MILLER, N. E. (1969). Learning of visceral and glandular responses. *Science*, 163, 434-445.

MILLER, N. E. and CARMONA, A. (1967). Modification of a visceral response, salivation in thirsty dogs, by instrumental training with water reward. *Journal of Comparative and Physiological Psychology*, 63, 1-6.

MORGAN, C. L. (1894). *An Introduction to Comparative Psychology*. London: Scott.

MORGAN, M. J. (1968). Negative reinforcement. In Weiskrantz, L. (Ed.). *Analysis of Behavioral Change*. New York: Harper and Row (pp. 19-49).

MORRIS, D. (1967). *The Naked Ape*. London: Jonathan Cape.
MORSE, W. H. and KELLEHER, R. T. (1970). Schedules as fundamental determinants of behavior. In Schoenfeld, W. N. (Ed.). *The Theory of Reinforcement Schedules*. New York: Appleton-Century-Crofts (pp. 139-185).
MOWRER, O. H. (1947). On the dual nature of learning as a reinterpretation of 'conditioning' and 'problem-solving'. *Harvard Educational Review*, 17, 102-148.
MUENZINGER, K. F. (1934). Motivation in learning: I. Electric shock for correct response in the visual discrimination habit. *Journal of Comparative and Physiological Psychology*, 17, 267-277. Reprinted in Boe and Church (1968), pp. 14-26.

NEMIAH, J. C. (1963). Emotions and gastrointestinal disease. In Lief, H., Lief, V. F. and Lief, N. R. (Eds.). *The Psychological Basis of Medical Practice*. New York: Hoeber. pp. 233-244.
NEURINGER, A. J. (1970). Superstitious key-pecking after three peck-produced reinforcements. *Journal of the Experimental Analysis of Behavior*, 13, 127-134.
NEURINGER, A. J. and CHUNG, S. (1967). Quasi-reinforcement: Control of responding by a percentage reinforcement schedule. *Journal of the Experimental Analysis of Behavior*, 10, 417-424.

OLDS, J. (1956). Pleasure centers in the brain. *Scientific American*, 195, 105-116.

PATTERSON, G. R. (1965). An application of conditioning techniques to the control of a hyperactive child. In Ullmann, L. P. and Krasner, L. (Eds.). *Case Studies in Behavior Modification*. New York: Holt, Rinehart and Winston, Inc (pp. 370-375).
PAVLOV, I. P. (1927). *Conditioned Reflexes*. G. V. Anrep, Trans. London: Oxford University Press, (Reprinted, New York: Dover Publications, 1960).
PICKENS, R. and THOMPSON, T. (1968). Cocaine-reinforced behavior in rats: Effects of reinforcement magnitude and fixed-ratio size. *Journal of Pharmacology and Experimental Therapeutics*, 161, 122-129. Reprinted in Thompson, Pickens and Meisch (1970), pp. 298-309.
PIERREL, R. and SHERMAN, J. G. (1963). Barnabus, the rat with college training. *Brown Alumni Monthly* (Feb.). (Reported in Ferster, C. B. and Perrott, M. C. *Behavior Principles*. New York: Appleton-Century-Crofts, 1968).

QUARTI, C. and RENAUD, J. (1964). A new treatment of constipation by conditioning: a preliminary report. In Franks, C. M. (Ed.). *Conditioning Techniques in Clinical Practice and Research*. New York: Springer. Reprinted in Ulrich, Stachnik and Mabry (1966), pp. 138-143.

RAY, O. S. (1964). Tranquilizer effects as a function of experimental anxiety procedures. *Archives Internationales de Pharmacodynamie et de Therapie*, 153, 49-68.
REESE, E. P. (1966). *The Analysis of Human Operant Behavior*. Dubuque, Iowa: Wm. C. Brown Co.

REYNOLDS, G. S. (1961a). Behavioral contrast. *Journal of the Experimental Analysis of Behavior*, 4, 57-71.

REYNOLDS, G. S. (1961b). Relativity of response rate and reinforcement frequency in a multiple schedule. *Journal of the Experimental Analysis of Behavior*, 4, 179-184.

REYNOLDS, G. S. (1968). *A Primer of Operant Conditioning*. Glenview, Illinois: Scott, Foresman and Co.

REYNOLDS, G. S. and CATANIA, A. C. (1961). Temporal discrimination in pigeons. *Science*, 135, 314-315.

RICKARD, H. C. and MUNDY, M. B. (1965). Direct manipulation of stuttering behavior: an experimental-clinical approach. In Ullmann, L. P. and Krasner, L. (Eds.). *Case Studies in Behavior Modification*. New York: Holt, Rinehart and Winston, Inc. (pp. 268-274).

ROGERS, C. R. and SKINNER, B. F. (1965). Some issues concerning the control of human behavior. *Science*, 124, 1057-1066. Reprinted in Ulrich, Stachnik and Mabry (1966), pp. 301-316.

ROMANES, G. J. (1882). *Animal Intelligence*. London: Kegan Paul.

RYLE, G. (1949). *The Concept of Mind*. London: Hutchinson.

SCHNEIDER, B. A. (1969). A two-state analysis of fixed-interval responding in the pigeon. *Journal of the Experimental Analysis of Behavior*, 12, 677-687.

SCHOENFELD, W. N. (1950). An experimental approach to anxiety, escape and avoidance behavior. In Hoch, P. H. and Zubin, J. (Eds.). *Anxiety*. New York: Grune and Stratton (pp. 70-90).

SCHOENFELD, W. N. (1957). (Discussion of four research papers). In Hoch, P.H. and Zubin, J. (Eds.). *Experimental Psychopathology*. New York: Grune and Stratton (pp. 55-65).

SCHOENFELD, W. N. (1970) (Ed.). *The Theory of Reinforcement Schedules*. New York: Appleton-Century-Crofts.

SCHOENFELD, W. N., CUMMING, W. W. and HEARST, E. (1956). On the classification of reinforcement schedules. *Proceedings of the National Academy of Science*, 42, 563-570.

SCHUSTER, C. R., DOCKENS, W. S. and WOODS, J. H. (1966). Behavioral variables affecting the development of amphetamine tolerance. *Psychopharmacologia*, 9, 170-182. Reprinted in Thompson, Pickens and Meisch (1970), pp. 539-551.

SCHUSTER, R. H. (1969). A functional analysis of conditioned reinforcement. In Hendry, D. P. (Ed.). *Conditioned Reinforcement*. Homewood, Illinois: The Dorsey Press (pp. 192-234).

SCHUSTER, R. H. and GROSS, C. G. (1969). Maintained generalisation gradients in the monkey. *Psychonomic Science*, 14, 215 and 217.

SIDMAN, M. (1953). Two temporal parameters of the maintenance of avoidance behavior by the white rat. *Journal of Comparative and Physiological Psychology*, 46, 253-261. Reprinted in Cantana (1968), pp. 196-203.

SIDMAN, M. (1955). Technique for assessing the effects of drugs on timing behavior. *Science*, 122, 925. Reprinted in Thompson, Pickens and Meisch (1970), pp. 511-513.

SIDMAN, M. (1960). *Tactics of Scientific Research*. New York: Basic Books.

SIDMAN, M. (1964). Anxiety. *Proceedings of the American Philosophical Society*, 108, 478-481.

SIDMAN, M. (1966). Avoidance behavior. In Honig, W. K. (Ed.). *Operant Behavior: Areas of Research and Application*. New York: Appleton-Century-Crofts (pp. 448-498).

SIDMAN, M., HERRNSTEIN, R. J. and CONRAD, D. G. (1957). Maintenance of avoidance behavior by unavoidable shocks. *Journal of Comparative and Physiological Psychology*, 50, 558-562.

SIDMAN, M. and STEBBINS, W. C. (1954). Satiation effects under fixed-ratio schedules of reinforcement. *Journal of Comparative and Physiological Psychology*, 47, 114-116.

SIDMAN, M. and STODDARD, L. T. (1967). The effectiveness of fading in programming a simultaneous form discrimination for retarded children. *Journal of the Experimental Analysis of Behavior*, 10, 3-15.

SKINNER, B. F. (1938). *The Behavior of Organisms*. New York: Appleton-Century-Crofts.

SKINNER, B. F. (1948a). Superstition in the pigeon. *Journal of Experimental Psychology*, 38, 168-172. Reprinted in Skinner (1972b), pp. 524-528.

SKINNER, B. F. (1948b). *Walden Two*. New York: MacMillan.

SKINNER, B. F. (1950). Are theories of learning necessary? *Psychological Review*, 57, 193-216. Reprinted in Catania (1968), pp. 4-21, and in Skinner (1972b), pp. 69-100.

SKINNER, B. F. (1951). How to teach animals. *Scientific American*, 185, 26-29. Reprinted in Skinner (1972b), pp. 559-566.

SKINNER, B. F. (1953). *Science and Human Behavior*. London: Collier-MacMillan Ltd.

SKINNER, B. F. (1955). Freedom and the control of men. *American Scholar*, 25, 47-65. Reprinted in Ulrich, Stachnik and Mabry (1966), pp. 11-20.

SKINNER, B. F. (1957a). The experimental analysis of behavior. *American Scientist*, 45, 343-371. Reprinted in Skinner (1972b), pp. 125-157.

SKINNER, B. F. (1957b). *Verbal Behavior*. New York: Appleton-Century-Crofts.

SKINNER, B. F. (1961). Teaching machines. *Scientific American*, 205, No. 5, 91-106.

SKINNER, B. F. (1968). *The Technology of Teaching*. New York: Appleton-Century-Crofts.

SKINNER, B. F. (1969a). *Contingencies of Reinforcement*. New York: Appleton-Century-Crofts.

SKINNER, B. F. (1969b). Contingencies of reinforcement and the design of cultures. In Skinner, B. F. *Contingencies of Reinforcement*. New York: Appleton-Century-Crofts (pp. 3-71).

SKINNER, B. F. (1972a). *Beyond Freedom and Dignity*. London: Jonathan Cape Ltd.

SKINNER, B. F. (1972b). *Cumulative Record*. (3rd Ed) New York: Appleton-Century-Crofts.

STEIN, L., SIDMAN, M. and BRADY, J. V. (1958). Some effects of two temporal variables on conditioned suppression. *Journal of the Experimental Analysis of Behavior*, 1, 153-162.

STEINER, J. (1967). Observing responses and uncertainty reduction. *Quarterly Journal of Experimental Psychology*, 19, 18-29.

STEINER, J. (1970). Observing responses and uncertainty reduction. II. The effect of varying the probability of reinforcement. *Quarterly Journal of Experimental Psychology*, 22, 592-599.

STRETCH, R. (1972). Development and maintenance of responding under schedules of electric-shock presentation. In Gilbert, R. M. and Millenson, J. R. (Eds.). *Reinforcement: Behavioral Analysis.* New York: Academic Press (pp. 67-95).

STRETCH, R. and GERBER, G. J. (1970). A method for chronic intra-venous drug administration in squirrel monkeys. *Canadian Journal of Physiology and Pharmacology*, 48, 575-581.

STUBBS, D. A. (1971). Second-order schedules and the problem of conditioned reinforcement. *Journal of the Experimental Analysis of Behavior*, 16, 289-314.

TERRACE, H. S. (1963a). Discrimination learning with and without 'errors'. *Journal of the Experimental Analysis of Behavior*, 6, 1-27.

TERRACE, H. S. (1963b). Errorless transfer of a discrimination across two continua. *Journal of the Experimental Analysis of Behavior*, 6, 223-232. Reprinted in Catania (1968), pp. 155-161.

TERRACE, H. S. (1963c). Errorless discrimination learning in the pigeon: effects of chlorpromazine and imipramine. *Science*, 140, 318-319.

TERRACE, H. S. (1964). Wavelength generalisation after discrimination learning with and without errors. *Science*, 144, 78-80.

TERRACE, H. S. (1966). Stimulus control. In Honig, W. K. (Ed.). *Operant Behavior: Areas of Research and Application.* New York: Appleton-Century-Crofts (pp. 271-344).

THOMPSON, T. and GRABOWSKI, J. (1972). *Behavior Modification of the Mentally Retarded.* New York: Oxford University Press.

THOMPSON, T., PICKENS, R. and MEISCH, R. A. (Eds.) (1970). *Readings in Behavioral Pharmacology.* New York: Appleton-Century-Crofts.

THOMPSON, T. and SCHUSTER, C. R. (1964). Morphine self-administra-tion, food-reinforced, and avoidance behaviors in rhesus monkeys. *Psychopharmacologia*, 5, 87-94. Reprinted in Thompson, Pickens and Meisch (1970), pp. 319-326.

THOMPSON, T. and SCHUSTER, C. R. (1968). *Behavior Pharmacology.* Englewood Cliffs, New Jersey: Prentice-Hall, Inc.

THORNDIKE, E. L. (1913). *Educational Psychology. Vol.2: The Psychol-ogy of Learning.* New York: Teacher's College, Columbia University.

THORNDIKE, E. L. (1932). *The Fundamentals of Learning.* New York: Teacher's College, Columbia University.

ULLMANN, L. P. and KRASNER, L. (Eds.) (1965). *Case Studies in Behavior Modification.* New York: Holt, Rinehart and Winston, Inc.

ULRICH, R. E., HUTCHINSON, R. R. and AZRIN, N. H. (1965). Pain-elicited aggression. *The Psychological Record*, 15, 111-126.

ULRICH, R., STACHNIK, T. and MABRY, J. (Eds.) (1966). *Control of Human Behavior.* Glenview, Illinois: Scott, Foresman & Co.

ULRICH, R., STACHNIK, T. and MABRY, J. (Eds.) (1970). *Control of Human Behavior II: From Cure to Prevention.* Glenview, Illinois: Scott, Foresman & Co.

VERHAVE, T. (1966). The pigeon as a quality-control inspector. In Ulrich, R., Stachnik, T. and Mabry, J. (Eds.). *Control of Human Behavior.* Glenview, Illinois: Scott, Foresman & Co. (pp. 242-246).

WATSON, J. B. (1924). *Behaviorism*. Chicago: University of Chicago Press.

WEISS, B. (1970). The fine structure of operant behavior during transition states. In Schoenfeld, W. N. (Ed.), *The Theory of Reinforcement Schedules*. New York: Appleton-Century-Crofts (pp. 277-311).

WEISS, B. and LATIES, V. G. (1961). Changes in pain tolerance and other behavior produced by salicylates. *Journal of Pharmacology and Experimental Therapeutics*, 131, 120-129. Reprinted in Thompson, Pickens and Meisch (1970), pp. 368-382.

WIKE, W. L. (1966). *Secondary Reinforcement: Selected Experiments*. New York: Harper and Row.

WILLIAMS, C. D. (1959). The elimination of tantrum behaviour by extinction procedures. *Journal of Abnormal and Social Psychology*, 59, 269. Reprinted in Ullmann and Krasner (1965), pp. 295-296.

WOLF, M. M., RISLEY, T. and MEES, H. (1964). Application of operant conditioning procedures to the behavior problems of an autistic child. *Behaviour Research and Therapy*, 1, 305-312. Reprinted in Ulrich, Stachnik and Mabry (1966), pp. 187-198.

WYCKOFF, L. B., JR. (1950). The role of observing responses in discrimination learning. Doctoral dissertation, Indiana University. (Edited version appears in Hendry (1969a), pp. 237-260).

ZIMMERMAN, E. H. and ZIMMERMAN, J. (1972). The alteration of behavior in a special classroom situation. *Journal of the Experimental Analysis of Behavior*, 5, 59-60. Reprinted in Ulrich, Stachnik and Mabry (1966), pp. 94-96.

Subject Index

Name Index

The SAGES Manual